D0066090

THE ULTIMATE SEDUCTION

Also by Charlotte Chandler

HELLO, I MUST BE GOING

Charlotte Chandler

❧ ❧ ❧

The Ultimate Seduction

Doubleday & Company, Inc., Garden City, New York
1984

DESIGNED BY LAURENCE ALEXANDER

Library of Congress Cataloging in Publication Data
Chandler, Charlotte.
The ultimate seduction.

Includes index.
1. Success. I. Title.
BJ1611.2.C47   1984   158'.1
ISBN 0-385-18953-2
Library of Congress Catalog Card Number 83–14149
Copyright © 1984 by Charlotte Chandler

*For King Vidor, George Cukor, "Jack"
Tati, Arnold Weissberger, and Groucho—to
all of whom I wish I could show this book.*

With appreciation: Camilo Jose Cela, S. M. Estridge, Federico Fellini, Avery Fisher, Brendan Gill, Milton Goldman, Johnny Goyen, Theodore Kheel, Robert Knittel, Goddard Lieberson, Ken McCormick, James Moser, Le-Roy Neiman, Tom Paynter, Joe Reece, Martin E. Segal, Sidney and Jorja Sheldon, John Springer, Sam Vaughan, and Herman G. Weinberg.

Contents

THE ULTIMATE SEDUCTION

Part I

❦

THE DRIVE
TO GET
THERE

"It is your work in life that is the ultimate seduction"

PABLO PICASSO

THE ULTIMATE SEDUCTION is not about sex, but about passion. It is the thrill that cannot be surpassed. For the people in this book, that passion was for their work. Sex was the ultimate distraction, work the ultimate satisfaction.

They all followed strong drives toward goals not always known, and found—themselves. All were able to work at what they wanted to do and to do it successfully. All were willing to risk everything when the chances for success seemed small. All gave everything to their work and received everything from it. All had luck, but none was just a lottery winner. All began by defining their work, and then were defined by *it*.

"What is always there is your work," Pablo Picasso told me during my visit with him at his home, Notre Dame de Vie, in Mougins. "It is the extension of you—not your child, but *you*. When you are very young, you start out thinking that success will open up the doors to sex for you. The pretty girls will want you, and that is always the great drive in a man. You believe that success can bring you friends, that it can keep you from being lonely, and that it can make you rich. Thus, people believe that all problems will be solved and happiness guaranteed.

"So, you do your work for these reasons and for any others that can be imagined. The reasons do not matter. Always, you put more of yourself into your work, until one day, you never know exactly which day, it happens—you *are* your work. The passions that motivate you may change, but it is your work in life that is the ultimate seduction."

In my many conversations with people of outstanding achievement, what always emerged was the concept that their work had become a vital passion in their lives, often *the* vital passion. This work had grown out of their realization of a dream, a vision that they felt compelled to share with the world. They were the ones who put on the ruby slippers, followed the yellow brick road, and found Oz.

Marc Chagall began my visit to La Colline, his home in the South of France, by apologizing in advance for what he explained would be my disappointment in him as a man talking about his work. "It is the art, not the artist," he said, instinctively expressing a concept that I call *the extended self*—the personality of the person as projected by his work and achievements. "It is my painting, not my talking. My pictures are my words. They say everything I have ever had to say. You should really talk with my paintings."

My visit with Chagall occurred just after I had seen Groucho Marx in Los Angeles. In his entire life, Groucho had painted only one painting. Though he had always believed that he *could* paint, he never tried until he was in his late seventies. When he did, he was so proud of his whimsical creation that, feeling he could never do better, he retired as an artist. Visitors to his home were always commenting on how like Chagall the picture was. When I left for France to see Chagall, I took with me a color transparency of Groucho's only painting.

Scrutinizing it, Chagall said, *"Très* Chagall." Then he gave me a book of his work to take back to Groucho; but first, as I watched, he drew a little picture in the book. It was a sketch of a lady with long wavy hair floating over a house by the light of a crescent moon. "She is an angel searching for a vision, an ideal," he explained. "That search is what gives meaning to art, and to life."

On my return to Beverly Hills, Groucho, whose private self was far more sentimental than the legendary extended self of his film and television character, was tremendously pleased.

"You oughta write a book about all those famous people you meet," he said, adding quite pointedly, *"but only after you write one about me."*

It is difficult now for me to believe that I hesitated, but I did— for a few seconds.

When I was finishing *Hello, I Must Be Going,* which was indeed about Groucho, he asked about my next book. I told him that it was going to be based on conversations with many famous people, as he had originally suggested. I had found delight and revelation in the company of so many stimulating presences, and I hoped to share it.

"Good," he said. "I'm glad you're not replacing me with just one person."

Of the many people I met while writing this book, the most unusual encounter was with Eva Perón—twenty years after her death. I had tea with her, or rather with her carefully preserved body, at the home of Juan and Isabel Perón near Madrid. I was able to speak with Perón and his third wife, but not, of course, with Evita, who was lifelike only in appearance. All during our tea, Eva's embalmer, Dr. Pedro Ara, who was also present, meticulously combed her hair, which kept falling out in small blond clumps onto the highly polished parquet floor.

Perón characterized Evita as a person "seduced" by her work:

"They said she was seductive," he told me, "but *she* was the one who was seduced. No one could have put more of her life, and even her death, into her work. Poor Eva Perón! Even as she was dying, she was so transported by her obsession with her work that she was not greatly affected by dying until the very last moments."

I received some advice from Federico Fellini, who cautioned me against deciding in advance what the title of this book would be. "A title is a limitation," he told me. "If you limit yourself too early with a title, you will find what you look for instead of what is really interesting; so you have to go into it with an open mind. A title does not help you, it leads you." Playfully, he added, "Perhaps you should write a book without a title. That would solve the problem and be original."

Jean-Paul Sartre advised me against entering into what I was doing with preconceptions. "If you arrive expecting something of the people you see based on the way you think they will be because you know their work and their public image, you have destined yourself for disappointment."

My first meeting with Jacques Tati, however, was surprising

because I hadn't expected that knowing him would be so much like living in a Mr. Hulot movie. He came to the hotel in Paris where I was staying, and we met at the appointed hour in the lobby. I asked him if he would like to go into the tea salon or the restaurant, but he said he preferred privacy. "Let's go up to your room," he suggested. I hesitated.

"Are you afraid to be alone with me?" he asked, in a hopeful tone.

"It's not that," I said. "It's just that I don't have much to offer." I had a room I loved, but it was only a bedroom in the attic and not very big. I explained that a brass bed took up most of the space and we would have to sit on the bed.

"That sounds perfect," he said.

In my room I rang for room service. Then we sat and talked. When he heard the sound of a table being wheeled through the hall, Tati jumped to his feet. Almost simultaneously, he pulled off his shoes and socks. Before I could say anything, he had taken off his jacket, shirt, and tie. Then he pulled back the pink coverlet on the bed and dove under the sheets.

There was a knock at the door. "Come in," Tati called out. As the waiter entered, wheeling in the table, Tati pulled the down comforter up to his chin. Now all that showed of him was a head at the top of the bed and bare feet sticking out at the bottom. He was wiggling his toes. His face wore a blasé, man-of-the-world expression. Stealing one look, the waiter quickly averted his glance, never taking his eyes off the dishes and table until he had finished serving. Then he rushed out, leaving behind someone else's order, for which he never returned.

In Tati's presence, one could live briefly in a world of foolishness. Tati was childlike, but never childish. In childhood one has the luxury of foolishness and the even greater luxury of not knowing it is a luxury. He had an innate sense of the inane, a perfect sense of nonsense.

Eating with Tati was always an experience, whether at the handsome Grand Véfour or at any local bistro. Whenever a stiffly formal maître d'hôtel would approach, Tati would suddenly look at me with piercing intensity and lean forward, lowering his voice to indicate unspeakable intimacy while the maître d' pretended he saw nothing out of the ordinary. As the bistro waiter served the food, Tati would pantomime an exaggerated argument with me. It shocked everyone—unless it was a restaurant where Tati ate frequently.

This could have been a very fattening book, since so many of the meetings involved meals—breakfast, lunch, tea, dinner, and snacks. I believe that food actually played a very real part because food is one of the pleasures of life, and meals are a shared pleasure. Fortunately, I encountered many who shared my enthusiasm. Prominent among them was Alfred Hitchcock, who enjoyed talking about food as well as eating it.

It was in Paris that I first met Alfred Hitchcock, who was there to receive the Legion of Honor. We were sitting at the Plaza Athenée, and the several-course dinner was completed with a Grand Marnier soufflé surrounded by small macaroons and topped with a hot apricot sauce. I felt Alfred Hitchcock's eyes upon me, following my spoon from the plate as I cut into the soufflé and lifted it to my lips.

"Happiness is being thin," he said. "I envy you, being able to eat so much without getting fat. In fact, I hate you for it. I have decided to give up the soufflé tonight. I am just going to finish my drink. Do you realize that I have lost thousands of pounds in my life?" He went on drinking the mimosa in front of him, sighing as the waiter passed the table carrying the last quivering soufflé. "I suppose it's my destiny to be fat," he said in resignation. Snapping his fingers to summon the waiter, he motioned for him to serve the last soufflé—a soufflé for two, which Alfred Hitchcock consumed for one.

A common feeling among the successful people who spoke with me was a sense, early perceived, of their own destiny, though not in the facetious sense employed by Alfred Hitchcock. They felt not only the need to achieve something, but that life held something special in store for them. From Woody Allen to Vladimir Zworykin, this feeling was common. I noticed that they seemed to do their best even in what might seem low priority situations. Once committed, they could only try their hardest. The expenditure of energy and enthusiasm was impressive.

While some felt the need to do something specific—to write, to paint, to sing—others felt a vague but no less intense desire: the desire to succeed. Those who did not totally visualize the road ahead felt the need to do something even before they knew what it was. If what they did was difficult, *not* to have done it would have been more difficult.

Henry Moore told me that the greatest difference between those who succeed and those who do not is the intensity of what he called "the longing." He spoke of an energy or force within the person that is separate from talent, a determination to accomplish something.

"For them, as for me," he said, "working is the important thing. The creative habit is like a drug. The particular obsession changes, but the excitement, the thrill of your creation lasts." He added that those who achieve the most may not all begin with the greatest talent, but they have the greatest wish and need. They have to make that longing come true.

Those who possessed this kind of drive did not do what they did solely to achieve success. No matter how immense their need to excel or how intense their desire for the acclaim that came with the attainment of the goal, they could not have sustained the unrelenting discipline if they had not also loved their work; but, however great the success, the longing remained and was never completely satisfied.

At Chagall's home, we were surrounded by his paintings. The walls were white to show them off, and high ceilings provided the necessary unbroken expanse to display the larger canvases. Windows were located where they would admit the best light, but not directly onto the paintings. It was a house for paintings to reside in, and incidentally a house for people. Chagall told me that it was the first home he had ever owned that was exactly what he wanted it to be. The house had been built expressly *for* as well as *by* his art.

"I have always felt a pressing need to work," Chagall said. "It was like a great emptiness inside. Only by painting could I satisfy that emptiness. If anything kept me from painting for very long, I felt in pain."

"One must be hungry," Martha Graham told me at the party

given in her honor after her 1980 New York Met opening—and she was not referring to the dinner being served that night. "We must be hungry to live life and more life. It's all in the *need*. If you feel that need, you find the energy and drive to do something about it. If you ever get satisfied, it's the end. For me, the dance is life, and I'm always hungry for more."

Rudolf Nureyev was standing with us. Speaking for himself, he added, "It is obsession."

On her last birthday, Marilyn Monroe wrote a letter to Lee Strasberg from California. In his New York apartment, which was filled with the souvenirs of their friendship, he read to me from that last letter:

" 'This is the time I wanted to tell you straight out that the most important thing in my life is my work with you. I wonder if you realize what the work has meant to me, aside from the work as an actress—what you, Lee, call my parts—what it's meant to me as a human being. When I think of home, it is New York and the Actors Studio. That is where I can exist in the human race.' "

Sidney Sheldon had the drive for success before he knew exactly what form it would take:

"I remember being an usher and barker in New York. I was seventeen and I'd gone there to become a songwriter. To support myself, I got this job working mornings at the RKO Jefferson. You probably don't know what a barker did. He wore a big funny hat, and walked up and down in front of the theater saying, 'No waiting for seats. Immediate seating. No waiting for seats.' The manager of the theater had me watch the other barker so I'd get the idea.

"As soon as I was in front of the theater working, I called out, 'No waiting for seats! Immediate seating! You've gotta see these two wonderful pictures with Tarzan,' and then I gave the Tarzan yell. I had people for blocks coming over to see what was happening. We hadn't been doing so well, but now we sold out all the time.

"I created so much of a stir that a couple of weeks later, I was on one morning, and this man came up to me. He said, 'Where's the son of a bitch from Chicago?' I said, 'I don't know. Why?' And he said, 'Because the manager of the chain said all of us from all the theaters have to come here and watch him and start doing what he's doing.' He was really angry.

"He figured I'd done it to show the other barkers up, to get a raise or something. But that had never occurred to me. I just wanted to add more to the job, to make it more interesting for myself. I couldn't do anything unless I was trying my hardest and doing the best I could."

Sidney Sheldon found out that drive and individuality are not automatically rewarded and can even antagonize people. Mae West understood that resistance. "They think you're doing it just to show them," she told me, "which is pretty foolish, because you don't even know they're there."

Although Mervyn LeRoy realized early that he had the drive to be in show business, he could not know precisely what his role would be:

"When I was ten years old I sold newspapers in front of the Alcazar Theater in my home town, San Francisco. I had to sell more newspapers than anyone else or I wasn't happy. My best customers were the ladies of the night from the wild Barbary Coast. They were really very nice, and they seemed to like me. I know they sure read a lot of newspapers, or at least they bought a lot.

"Where I really wanted to be was inside the theater, instead of outside in the cold, although to tell you the truth, it wasn't really very cold in San Francisco. I wanted to be right there on that stage, and one night I got the chance. It was just a bit at three dollars a week, but I saw it as my big chance. I was supposed to climb a tree onstage. The first night I did it, I fell out of the tree. Well, the audience loved it—my falling, that is—so it became a permanent part of the act. I was raised to five dollars a week to fall every night and twice on a day with a matinee. I was black and blue through the whole run of the play, and I could've broken something, but I didn't think that way. I was careful not to let my father and mother know what I was doing. All I knew was that I was started on the first rung of show business, and that I was going to make it even if I had to break my neck because it was something I *had* to do."

From the time she was a little girl, Bette Davis felt that life had something exceptional waiting for her, and that it would find her or she would find *it*. She wanted the lioness' share.

"I had to be the best," she told me. "I'm an overachiever. I always had the will to win. I felt it baking cookies. They had to be the best cookies anyone ever baked."

When drive exists in those who lack the ability to achieve success, the effect can be negative and even destructive. Father Gilbert V. Hartke, head of Catholic University's drama department, suggested as a title for this book "The Undeniable Urge." He pointed out that this was a prime element of success as he had observed it in his students—essential, but no guarantee against failure. He described a heartrending world of those who have the requisite drive which is the undeniable urge, but who cannot find where or how to convert that energy into success. Too often when that happens, they turn that frustrated energy against themselves.

Sometimes these people did have drive, confidence, and talent, but they could not find their moment of opportunity. Chagall told me, "The greatest tragedy is for those who do not find what it is they are meant to do in life, and have to work at something they do not want to do."

Drive can be just as strong in those without ability as in those with it. The dream has nothing to do with talent or the lack of it. The wish alone, unsupported by ability, can have frustrating, even tragic consequences. One may, of course, give up without encouragement, but failure is an unhappy alternative.

When Groucho admired his performance as Archie Rice in *The Entertainer,* Laurence Olivier gave him a copy of the book, writing on the flyleaf, "To Groucho, The Entertainer—Larry." In the last year of his life, Groucho wrote in that same book, "To Marvin, The Entertainer—Groucho," and gave the book to Marvin Hamlisch, who was then expected to assume the responsibility for one day passing it on.

I told Laurence Olivier the fate of his gift to Groucho, and he commented, "Just like Excalibur." He went on to explain the feeling he had for the role of the wholly committed but mediocre music-hall performer:

"I loved that part. It was my favorite for various reasons. Of course, it's simply a wonderful part. It was something different. But the real reason is I can identify totally with Archie Rice. I might have wished for what I did, but had neither the talent nor the opportunity."

Billy Wilder, himself intensely frustrated as he waited for the end of the 1981 strike that had caused the Hollywood studios to close, told me that what really hurt was not being able to find a constructive outlet for one's creative energies:

"There is nothing more terrible than to want to ride and not to have a horse. This gives a man a terrible sense of impotence, because a man *is* his achievements. To be able to work twenty-five hours a day, eight days a week is a privilege. To have this desire, these hopes and dreams, and the creative energy without any-where to put it—that is what is hard. Those are the people who are unlucky."

I asked Picasso if he could have gone on as an artist without any hope of success, or whether he would have tried something more certain. In other words, what did he want most, to be an artist or to be successful? He replied that he could not have gone on indefinitely without some acceptance and tangible recognition because, as he expressed it, "Failure is too unhappy." After a few minutes of conversation he was still apparently considering this response. Then he amended it: "No, it is not true. I could not have done anything else."

Laurence Olivier told me that he could not have imagined doing anything in life but what he did, although he was glad he did not have to spend all those years "as an unappreciated work-man." He had survived enough serious illnesses to incapacitate several people while remaining as active as ever. Already seated at the table when I arrived at Le Chantilly Restaurant in New York City, he said:

"You'll forgive me if I don't rise. It's only because I can't."

"The table does have you rather pinned in," I observed.

"That's not the reason," he said. "It's because I'm an invalid."

It certainly didn't show. I had never seen anyone apparently in more glowing health. I told him that he probably never got any sympathy at all.

He replied that he was glad he didn't look the way he felt. He preferred to feel terrible and look good rather than feel good and look terrible. "If there is anything a man doesn't want, especially from a woman, it's sympathy. But I'm still working; that's the important thing."

Though we were just beginning lunch, his eyes lit up when an elaborate dessert cart was wheeled by our table. "I suppose it's a little early to think about dessert," he said a bit wistfully. Then, in a more serious tone, he continued:

"I *have* to work. I must. I could never retire. Work is the most important thing in a man's life. It *is* the man. It's what keeps me going. Without it, I know I'd drop. Perhaps it's that I feel I'll go on living as long as I go on working.

"It wasn't always this way, you know. I always wanted only to work, but I do miss the old energy. It's strange to have to give thought to something like energy, something you always took for granted. Now I'm happy so many people still want me, because working is all I want to do.

"I'll play a part in a wheelchair if that's what I have to do. It's not my first choice, but I'd even be willing to play the part lying on my back in a bed, if it's all I can do."

"The trap" is how Laurence Olivier described his total commitment to whatever it was he was doing.

"I've just made a picture for 'shame money,' " he told me. "I call it that because the money is to console me in my shame and compensate me for when I take a part in a film I'm not certain is going to be good. I take the part, and I say to myself, 'Well, I'll just do it, and then I'll be able to pay my bills, and I'll be free to direct or act in something I really want to do that doesn't pay much.' But for me, life is enthusiasm, zest. I can't do anything halfheartedly. That's how I get myself into the trap.

"I have to be careful what I accept because once I'm doing it, even though I'm only doing it for the money and it isn't what I want to do and I'm not getting *enough* money, I still can't just say to myself, 'I'll only put half as much of myself into it. I won't try as hard.' I've got to do everything my very best, as if it were the greatest part of my life and as if I owned the film. The poorer the picture, the more exhausting the effort I have to make."

Agatha Christie told me that the love of your work has its greatest advantages in old age. She said it was always important to her, "but what else is there to do at my age? [She was in her eighties at the time.] When you are young, there are competing interests. You have the choice of using your life for your work or of living it. Having wide interests makes you more interesting as a person and perhaps as a writer, but the interests compete with your work.

"If you want to be a writer, you must choose. Choosing, making the decision, is a great strain. That is an advantage of growing old—you don't have to make choices anymore, because you don't *have* any choices.

"I am very lucky. I still have one thing that chooses me—my work."

The fantasy world he created became the real world for Ray Bradbury. In the world of reality, the author of *The Martian Chronicles* not only refused to fly but lived in southern California without knowing how to drive. In his life at the typewriter, however, there were no limitations. He could pilot the spaceships of his imagination to anywhere in the universe.

"It's interesting about my writing," Ray Bradbury told me. "The more I did it, the more I wanted to do it. Finally, I just didn't want to do anything else, because there wasn't anything in real life that was more exciting. I was living in my dreams and fantasies, and the ideas drove me to write them.

"In the beginning, I was more concerned about pleasing a lot of people, but then I realized that the most important person to please was myself. Then, if nobody liked what I did, I could just pack up my dinosaurs and go away."

Fashion designer Edith Head was one of the fortunate ones who was able to convert her play into her life's work. Whenever I saw her, she would encourage me to play "dress-up" with her costume collection. I didn't need much encouragement. I regretted not being able to try on Veronica Lake's dresses, so evocative of 1940s glamour, but they were not much larger than dolls' clothes.

Never having lost her enthusiasm for clothes, Edith Head asked me during lunch at the Beverly Hills Hotel if she could have a closer look at the dress I had worn to the Oscars. I went upstairs to my room to get the Sybil Connolly Irish linen dress and carried it back down to the lobby where Edith Head was waiting. Touching it respectfully, she shook its hem, as if being formally introduced to the dress, and said, "I'm pleased to meet you."

LeRoy Neiman was fortunate in knowing very early what he wanted to do and in being able to do it—to draw. In almost any circumstance, all he needed to be complete was a pencil and paper.

During World War II, he was on a troopship that sank in the middle of the North Sea. It was an icy winter Sunday evening and the ship's public-address system was turned up full-blast with a broadcast of the Army-Navy afternoon game in Philadelphia, where it was five hours earlier. The sportscaster was describing what a beautiful day it was for football when a sudden mysterious impact almost split the ship in half.

Fires broke out, water started seeping into the hull, and there was pandemonium. Not enough lifeboats could be lowered, but instead of announcing instructions for abandoning ship, the public-address system continued to broadcast the big game. In his sanguine style, the sportscaster informed everyone aboard the foundering vessel just how exciting it was to be there in Philadelphia watching the game.

Meanwhile, LeRoy was drawing. As he explained, "There was no use joining in the panic, and, besides, there didn't seem to be enough lifeboats." The announcer continued in excited tones his suspenseful play-by-play account of the game and its colorful half-time festivities as the crippled vessel slowly sank into the sea. The hysteria of the football game was in dramatic contrast to the silence of those waiting to abandon ship.

In the last minutes of the game, another lifeboat was located, and LeRoy, carrying only his drawing pad and pencil, was lowered into the ocean. The conversation in the lifeboat centered around whether or not they would be pulled down by the undertow when the ship finally sank. LeRoy heard the mellifluous voice of the sportscaster booming out over what seemed an endless expanse of water, "Wherever you are, we're glad you could be with us on this beautiful Sunday afternoon . . . it certainly has been an exciting [blub-blub-blub] . . ." The ship went under with a gurgle like bath water going down the drain, but gigantically amplified, as LeRoy continued to draw.

"I was so busy drawing," LeRoy said, "I didn't really feel any panic. The observer always has that advantage, even when your own life is on the line. The only thing I cared about was my sketches."

Martha Graham related a similar experience:

"Once I saved my reason by dancing in my head. I was on a plane in Iran, and suddenly we were caught in a terrifying snowstorm. The plane was tossed about, and the pilot was totally lost. Everyone on board was in a terrible panic. It seemed there was no hope—we were going to crash.

"For me, the escape has always been the dance. So I began dancing—in my head, that is. As I took my first steps, I was still conscious of the nightmare situation in which I was trapped, but I was somewhat distracted. As I took my next steps, my concentration shifted to the dance I was performing while I sat perfectly still. I created *Errand into the Maze* step by step.

"Just as I completed it, we came safely out of the snowstorm. Though they were relieved to be safe, most of the people had had a terrifying and traumatic experience. I felt wonderfully elated because there is nothing more elating and intimate than creating something out of yourself."

The word "workaholic" may have negative connotations, but fortunate indeed are those who find work they passionately want to do and then are able to do it successfully. "Workaholic" for them has positive, not negative, connotations. Garson Kanin was pleased to be their spokesman:

"You know what I object to? People are always saying to me, 'You're a workaholic, aren't you?' It's like, 'You're an alcoholic, aren't you?' Well, I *am* one—a workaholic, that is.

"Someone invited me to go to the races, and I happened to mention that I'd never been, and everyone was so shocked. It isn't that I have anything against horses. I just never had time. I never made time for it because I'd rather be writing than doing anything else. So, I don't need a hobby. But if I had one, it would be writing."

Dr. Denton Cooley, who termed himself "a work addict," told me, "Heart surgery is fun. It's more fun than anything else I could do with my clothes on.

"Sometimes I meet my wife at a party at ten at night after I've been working since six in the morning. I don't have time to change to black tie even if that's what everybody else is wearing, but I'm always welcome in a business suit.

"I stand there and look around. I see women who've spent all day at the beauty parlor. Some of the men I see went home after work and took a two-hour nap so they'd be fresh for the party. It might have been a day with thirty operations, and I'm standing there completely exhausted, but I don't envy anyone. I think about what I did with my day, and I feel proud."

Hubert Humphrey, talking with me about the drive for accomplishment, mentioned the concept of a guilt many successful people feel about "wasting" time.

"I was never able to spend a week that I didn't think to myself, 'What have I done with this week? What did I accomplish?' Even each day, I'd think at the end of the day, 'What did I do today that was worth something?' And when I did something for pleasure, the only way I could really enjoy it was to feel I'd earned that time."

King Vidor called it "earned pleasure":

"Directing films was the ideal life. You worked hard, and then in between, you'd have a vacation you could really enjoy because you knew you'd earned it. Otherwise I couldn't just waste time without feeling guilty."

Even Picasso, who loved his work more than anything else in life, said, "I always liked to get a lot of painting done before I went to the beach because then when I got there, I could enjoy it."

Drive for success can grow out of dissatisfaction with the status quo, in which instance the success is achieved in the manner of an oyster that involuntarily creates a pearl to relieve the irritation caused by a grain of sand. Picasso believed that an artist remains young only as long as he experiments. "At whatever age he is content with what he has already done, happy only to repeat himself, he is in old age."

By this standard, the risk of failure is an integral part of success. Henry Moore concurred with Picasso's need for change. He thought that it was not failure as much as success that stops the artist because "success tends to stop growth and change, and one is encouraged to repeat oneself. An artist must take the line of most resistance to keep growing and changing after success. It's conflict within the person that makes things happen. If you are very happy and satisfied, you will do less. In my student days I enjoyed more and did less. I realized as a young man that the price of contentment is less accomplishment."

Chagall said that he was actually grateful for having endured poverty as a boy, explaining to me that an artist is better off for being poor in his youth. During his early years in Paris, he knew actual physical hunger, and while he did not believe it was essential for an artist to feel hunger, it was not so terrible, either.

"The very worst thing for an artist to have too early is a little success, a little money, a little wife, a little house, a little car, little children, a little satisfaction. The last is the most formidable to overcome. The little satisfactions dull his expectations and hold him back from the big dedication."

Noticing that as he spoke I was looking around at his beautiful home, Chagall added with a smile, "In my youth, poverty enriched me, but now I can afford wealth."

Lee Strasberg believed that he was changed by confrontation with tragedy—the childhood death of his older brother. He had been only faintly aware of his family's poverty, but the loss of his brother was the end of childhood and frivolity. It was terrible losing the person with whom he shared his memories. "The price you pay for life is death," he told me. From that time on, he felt a drive, as though his brother had become a part of him—as though he had to accomplish for both of them.

From Sophocles to soaps, revenge has always been a preeminent theme in drama, as it is in life itself. This negative drive can have positive and constructive aspects. The desire to "show" those who did not deem one worthy, to prove how wrong they were, is a feeling most people have experienced. Some have actually been prodded to outstanding achievement—pushed toward success by those who said they could not succeed, by those who wronged or thwarted them, or by those who rejected them.

Of course, the person inspired by such a negative drive to show the world or someone in particular always runs the risk of being personally changed by it. While Electra was rewarded by the gods, Orestes was pursued by furies. For Frank Sinatra, the desire to "show" Hollywood saved his career and brought him even greater success. Sidney Sheldon, who in _The Other Side of Midnight_ created the character of Noelle, a woman whose life was dedicated to revenge, told me:

"If someone says, 'You're wonderful, of course you can do that, you can do anything,' and someone else says, 'You can't do that,' I think the stronger motivation is, 'You can't do that.' The feeling that's missing in the praise is your own anger over being mistreated. You want to prove that those who underrated you were wrong, to show them. Sometimes anger can be very constructive.

"Frank Sinatra once told me a story about himself and his drive for success, and about the role of the negative in success, the desire to show someone who wronged you. It's all a very real motivation, especially for a man.

"Frank read the book _From Here to Eternity_ and felt that he _had_ to play the part of Maggio. He felt he was born to play that part. And he knew Harry Cohn.

"Frank was then married to Ava Gardner, who was going off to do a picture for Goldwyn in Africa. Yet Frank was out of work. In the parlance of the business, he was 'cold.' No one wanted him. He was through as a singer. His records weren't selling. No one wanted him for personal appearances or for movies. His career was dead. And usually when that happens in this town, that's it. It's very hard to rise like the phoenix from those ashes. Once in a while it happens, but chances are it's never going to happen.

"He was determined to get the part of Maggio in spite of the fact that he was cold. He called Harry Cohn and told him he wanted to play the part. Cohn said no. Sinatra offered to make a test. Cohn wasn't interested. Cohn signed another actor, and

Sinatra read about it. He knew he'd lost the part, so he went to Africa to join Ava.

"While there, he heard that the person who'd been signed was accused of being a Communist and had been fired from the picture. The role was open again. Sinatra called his agent and said, 'Get me that part. I'll fly back and test for it.'

"Harry Cohn was now desperate, because the picture was starting to shoot. They had no Maggio, and it was an important part. Cohn was so desperate he agreed to test Sinatra even though he told the agent it was a waste of everybody's time.

"The agent called Sinatra and offered it, but said, 'He offered you twenty thousand dollars for the movie.' Frank Sinatra's last salary had been a hundred and fifty thousand. 'I'll try to get you thirty,' and Sinatra said, 'No, I'd rather have the part. Don't risk it. Set it at twenty.'

"He called Sinatra back the next day and said, 'I've got bad news. There's no way you can do this. Cohn won't give you any billing.' Which meant that Cohn could put Sinatra's name anywhere—at the bottom of the credits, in the middle of the credits. Billing is as important to an actor as money, and Sinatra had always had star billing.

"Sinatra said, 'Take it.' The agent said, 'Okay, but you have to pay all your expenses to fly back and make the test.' Sinatra said, 'I'll do it.' He flew back, made the test.

"Now—when he went back to make that test, he had an appointment with Harry Cohn just before the picture. Cohn kept him waiting in his outer office for three hours, just to teach him a lesson for being a pest. Sinatra, who has a very short temper, sat there and waited till Cohn was ready to see him. Then he went in, and he was very polite. He got the part, made the picture, and of course the rest is history. The picture was a smash; Sinatra was the hit of the picture. He got the Academy Award.

"But Harry Cohn had forgotten one thing: He was so sure Sinatra would be no good that he hadn't bothered to get an option on him for another picture. Columbia had a project called *Pal Joey,* and suddenly the only person in the world who could do it was Frank Sinatra. They went to his agent and said, 'Hey, we want Frank for this part.' He went to Sinatra, and Sinatra said, 'Do it. I'd like the part. But show 'em!' The agent went in and got a deal that murdered the studio.

"Now, they wanted Sinatra for another picture, and the locale was Hawaii. They built the sets here, and the picture's ready to shoot. Sinatra said, 'I'd like to shoot it in Hawaii.' They said, 'Frank, we have the sets here. We'd have to build all new sets over there.' He said, 'Build them.' And production shut down till they built the whole village and everything they needed for the movie in Hawaii. They had to take the whole company over, and this cost about half a million dollars extra.

"They started shooting, and in the middle of the shooting, Sinatra said, 'There's a presidential election going on. I'm going back to help my candidate.' They said, 'But we're in the middle of the picture! We're shooting over here.' He said, 'Shoot it in Hollywood.' And back everybody had to fly. They had to rebuild the sets and shoot it in Hollywood.

"All this comes under the heading of vengeance. Sinatra made Hollywood pay for all the ignominy that they had heaped upon him, all the crow you have to eat.

"That's only one example. This town is full of stars who are sons of bitches, and the reason they are is because of what they had to take fighting their way up that ladder. All the terrible things that the producers and directors and other people did to them on the way up. They don't forget. And when they get there, this town pays for it.

"I like the story because Sinatra did that himself. I mean, no one *gave* Sinatra anything. He fought for that part. When he got it, he was great. Then they didn't like him because he was a tough man. And because of the way they made him earn it, he made it tougher on them than he had to, and I'm sure he took enormous satisfaction in doing it."

I was at lunch with King Vidor and Ray Bradbury, and their conversation was entirely about their work. Ray Bradbury said he couldn't write something he felt "casually" about. "If you're not madly in love with your idea, you just have to keep searching."

King agreed. "You have to fall in love with what you do, or you can't stay with it. It's not easy to fall in love, and it's harder as you get older. You get more critical, and you have different standards. I haven't been able to fall in love with a script for years. It's like trying to find a person to fall in love with."

What is involved is commitment. Creating something that will hold an audience's interest is difficult. Holding one's own interest is even more difficult because no one will ever have to be so intimately involved with the project as its creator. The audience only has to like it one time.

"It's hard to live in the same world of imagination for a year or more," Fellini told me, "and it's hard to get started because you know once you begin you will be possessed. Yet, one *must* be possessed."

"This ultimate seduction you're writing about—I'll tell you what it is for me," Marvin Hamlisch said. "It's something that happens between my piano and me. It's when I've been working and struggling for a long time, and I just can't get what I want. Then, maybe about three in the morning, suddenly it happens.

"There it is, and I don't know why it took so long and didn't come to me right away. But I've got it, and I know it. That moment—it's like sex."

All the while Eubie Blake talked with me in his Brooklyn home, he played piano on the arm of his chair. The house, which was more than one hundred years old, had belonged to his second wife when he married her. "I got the coop with the chicken," he said, laughing.

"The keyboard, which was my work," he went on, "that was always the most important thing in my life. Girls came next. When I was very young, I had this beautiful girl I was in love with, and someone came along who played the piano better than I did and took her away from me, so I decided that nobody was gonna play the piano better than me.

"Girls and show business. It's like livin' in a flower garden— you might pluck one, but it would wilt. You could have a girl and still feel lonesome. But I could never feel lonesome as long as I have my piano. I just sit down and touch those keys and say, 'Talk to me.'

"You know, I got my start in hookshops, and hookshops always had pianos. The piano was the most important piece of furniture, even more important than the beds. Thirty minutes to an hour with a girl cost five dollars. That included time in the salon before, plus drinks.

"People say to me, 'You been a lot of places, you been every-where.' I don't say nothin' when they say that, but the truth is, I've never really been anywhere, because all I ever seen are pi-anos and keyboards and theaters and hotel rooms. I never wanted anything else."

Anita Loos told me, "Passion is passion, and the people who have a passion for life put that into everything they do."

We had been talking about the idea I had for this book and its title. "It's not just work these people have a passion for," she continued, "it's life. Passionate people like everything more. They have to put it all somewhere. It's more convenient to put it into writing than into sex because you can write alone. It gets you into less trouble than an exciting man!"

"Was there one man in your life," I asked, "who was more exciting than the others?"

She smiled. "There was only one—so far out ahead of the others, there was no number two. He was a scoundrel. He was really a rat."

"In what ways?" I asked.

"All of them," she said. "For example, he cheated at cards. But he was *so* handsome. So handsome. And he was so witty, wittier than H. L. Mencken. But maybe what he said wouldn't sound so bright now. Who knows? Memory plays tricks."

"I know the kind of man you were looking for," I said. "You were looking for Mr. Wrong."

She reflected for a moment, then smiled. "I never thought about it that way, but it's true. I've always thought it was just my luck. But actually I was looking for Mr. Wrong. And I found him —more than once. I should have met you sooner, so you could have explained it to me."

"Why?" I said. "Wouldn't you have done the same thing? You just would have known what you were doing."

"Yes, that's true," she agreed. "We can't change what we are."

"Especially if we don't want to," I added.

"The trouble with Mr. Wrong in real life is he won't behave the way he should," Anita Loos went on. "You can pretty much make the characters in your books do it your way, though not exactly, because they, too, have a will of their own. But Mr. Wrong won't do it the way you think he should in the plot you make up. Work never got me into trouble the way men did."

"Are diamonds *really* a girl's best friend?" I asked.

"No," Anita Loos admitted. "Your work is."

During tea at the Paris Ritz, Coco Chanel told me, "I have lived more successfully the life of a man than that of a woman. In my working life, my professional life, I would not let anything stop me, while in my private life I was totally vulnerable, and everything wounded me.

"When I was still very young, I would spend a great deal of time thinking about what I had missed and what I was missing. You know—marriage, children—what we are taught we must have if we are to enjoy a full life. I think my problem was that I was too romantic for marriage.

"I have always liked men for their faults. I do not know if this is true of women generally or only of me.

"When you are young, it is easier to find a man you can love. That is because the element of surprise exists. The man's mystery and glamour are not threatened by your own experience and sophistication. After you have known many men, it is easy to become bored by their repetition. It is so terrible to feel one day that you understand men.

"It is difficult for a woman to be alone, but it seems even more difficult to find a life with a man who will give you help and encouragement in your work, particularly when you start to be very successful. There seem to be more men prepared to comfort you in your failure than to applaud your success."

I suggested that perhaps she had always chosen one kind of man—a highly competitive man. She smiled and shrugged, saying it didn't matter anymore.

"When I was young I was afraid. It was a terrible thing always to feel that way—not to know if you can take care of yourself. I believe that every little girl should be taught as early as possible something she can do to take her through her whole life. I shall always be grateful to my work because it gave me not only the means to express myself, but also independence. Even more important, it saved me from boredom. Boredom is a terrible thing."

"Is there anything else you would like to have been in life?" I asked.

She smiled almost shyly. "Yes. I would like to have been a mannequin—a very tall and thin model."

"But this would have been the very opposite of what you advise," I pointed out, "because it's the last thing that could take you through your whole life. It's the worst possible choice."

"Yes," she said wistfully, "I know. But it might have been worth everything to be truly beautiful for a while."

"If a man is dedicated to his work," Bette Davis told me, "he's more of a man. If a woman feels that way, she's *less* of a woman. Those same qualities that women find so absolutely wonderful in a man, men don't find so wonderful in a woman."

Bette said that in her drive to reach the top she had "murdered" Ruth Elizabeth Davis. "Do you know who Ruth Elizabeth Davis was?" she asked me.

"Yes," I answered. "You."

"I had to kill her, you see," she proclaimed as dramatically as she would have in one of her Warner Brothers films. Her eyes flashed as she stood there in a draped, clinging red dress, exactly what Edith Head would have created for that moment. "I had to do it or she would have gotten in my way. But I'll tell you the funniest thing. When I killed her off, I just marched past the body and didn't even notice it until years later.

"Ruth Elizabeth wanted all kinds of things, a gold wedding band and a silver thimble, a good man and an ivy-covered cottage filled with babies. But I had always heard the sound of the music I was going to march to. I knew that life held something for me, some kind of destiny, and I wasn't going to let anyone or anything stop me. Poor Ruth Elizabeth! She didn't stand a chance. She thought she only wanted to be happy. As if that weren't the hardest thing to get. I knew I had to achieve something, make something of myself, to be someone. But, you know, sometimes I wonder about Ruth Elizabeth. I wonder if she had lived, would she have been happy?"

At the opening of New York City's Lincoln Center Film Festival, a mutual friend introduced me to Shelley Winters, saying I was a writer.

"I guess a career is all right for a woman as long as she knows what she's choosing *not* to have," Shelley Winters told me. "I always acted for the moment.

"I'm a person who always wanted two things that didn't go together. Whenever there was a choice, I wanted everything. I wanted a career, a great one. I didn't just want an ordinary marriage, but the supreme passion, and I didn't want just one child. I never could make up my mind between the things I wanted, so I went in both opposite directions at once, and I went hard. It made for a full life, but I got a lot of grief. Men don't have to make the choice. They can have it all."

Just then a woman went by who was wearing a ruby and diamond flower pendant. Shelley Winters gasped audibly, and with innocent glee she rushed up to her.

"It's beautiful! So beautiful! You must have a wonderful husband," she said. "And he must love you a lot."

As a young girl Maureen Stapleton was an avid film fan, and she was madly in love with a leading man, a star she knew only on the screen. It was her ambition to become a successful actress so she could display her accomplishment for this famous actor. She achieved the professional part of this goal many years before she met her idol, and when she did finally meet him, he had been happily married for over forty years.

They actually met for the first time in 1982 shortly before she received her Oscar for best supporting actress. In her Oscar acceptance speech, she thanked "everyone I have ever met—and Joel McCrea." She had never made a film with Joel McCrea, and she did not explain to the audience why she thanked him. Perhaps no one was more surprised than Joel McCrea, who had lived his life blithely unaware of what he had inspired. In her desire to win his approval and perhaps a part in a film with him, Maureen Stapleton had fulfilled not that girlhood dream, but a different dream—one that had taken her on her own road to stardom.

"I always wanted to be in a film with him," she told me. "I really wanted to play the romantic lead opposite him, but I would have taken anything. I heard he was doing a picture called *Mustang Country*, and I told Milton [Goldman], 'Get me a part in that picture, any part.'

"Milton came back and said, 'There aren't any parts for women. They're all men, and it's been cast except for the part of a ten-year-old Mexican boy.' I said, 'I'll take it!'

"I finally met him at 'The Night of One Hundred Stars' in Radio City Music Hall. They asked me to appear, and of course I would have done it anyway, but when I heard Joel McCrea was going to be one of the hundred stars . . . Well, I really had butterflies in my stomach. I've never been so nervous."

I asked her if he lived up to her dreams. It seemed to me difficult, perhaps impossible, for any real person to compete not only with his younger self, but with the man in her imagination.

"Oh, no," she said, stopping me before I could finish. "He was perfect," she sighed, "just as handsome as ever."

When Milton Goldman asked her how she could possibly have been in love all those years with a man she had never met, she just looked at him and said, "Are you kidding?"

After "The Night of One Hundred Stars" Joel McCrea had called her. "He said it had been very nice meeting me. He was so gracious. He was perfect. I was so tongue-tied, I didn't know what to say. Then I probably said too much. Afterwards, I didn't know *what* I'd said. I was sorry for everything."

It didn't all end there, however. There was more. Maureen went on:

"Elizabeth Taylor is the most generous person in the world and the last of the big spenders. When we did *The Little Foxes*, she had this wonderful party and gave me a diamond chain. Of course, with my wonderful luck, it was stolen. I gave her a little garnet pin of my mother's. But, I mean, what do you give someone who has everything? And Elizabeth really has everything.

"Someone told me about this woman who made the most

beautiful portrait puppets. I thought Elizabeth would like that, so I had this puppet made. I figured she would enjoy it.

"Well, it was finally delivered, and I never saw anything so ugly. It was huge and deformed and . . . ugh! I wasn't going to show it to Elizabeth, but some friends said I should. 'She'll laugh,' they said. So I called Elizabeth when she was in New York and said I would come by.

"She was at the Helmsley Palace on the fifty-third floor. I said, 'You know how I feel about high floors. Couldn't you meet me in the lobby?' She said, 'Oh, you know it's a zoo. You must come up.' So I drank a whole bottle of champagne, fast, to get up my courage. Then Elizabeth had someone meet me to bring me up. We made it, and she had a bottle of Dom Perignon waiting for me.

"Drinking it, I got up my courage to show her the puppet. I took it out and explained about this woman who made the portrait puppets. And Elizabeth said, 'Who is it?' I said, 'It's you.'

"It was really ugly. I'd forgotten how ugly it was. Well, you know those people who said Elizabeth would laugh? They were wrong. She wasn't laughing. She said, 'We'll burn it.' But first she looked at my dress and said, 'What's that you're wearing? You can't wear that thing,' and she brought out this great jeweled brown caftan, and made me take off my dress and put it on. I didn't understand why what I was wearing wasn't good enough for burning a puppet.

"She said some other people were coming. Just then the phone rang announcing them, and they arrived at the door. It was a little surprise for me—Joel McCrea. Elizabeth had invited him and his wife, Frances Dee.

"We had some more of the champagne, then Elizabeth tried to burn the puppet, but it wouldn't burn. So she called and asked the hotel to send someone up to help us burn the puppet. Well, they sent a lot of people and a special fireman and fire extinguishers. We all went up on the roof, and Elizabeth burned this ugly puppet of herself. It was really big.

"Then we went downstairs, and Joel McCrea and his wife said they had to leave. I guess they really did after all that. I'm sure he thought I was crazy."

A gladiator in pantyhose, Lina Wertmüller always viewed the inhibition barrier the way a bull supposedly sees the waving red flag. In the days when she was still Arcangela Felice Assunta Wertmüller von Elgg, little Lina had already developed her indomitable, defiant, nonconformist personality in the Fascist-controlled Italian schoolroom. In the living room of her Rome apartment, she recalled not only this event, but exactly how she had felt at the moment as clearly as if it had happened only the day before:

"I raised my hand for permission to leave the classroom. But the Fascist supervisor said, 'No,' so I lifted my skirt, dropped my panties, and did it right there. I have never forgotten the look on her face, and whenever I need the fortitude, I see that face before me, and I am able to go on.

"Life is simpler for a man," Lina Wertmüller told me. "For a woman it's different. There are two Lina Wertmüllers. One of them must have her work. Without it, she cannot live. That one is like a man. Then there is the other. She needs the personal happiness of a woman, and a lover, who in my case is my husband. Alone in paradise would not be paradise for me. It would be hell. For me, happiness is my husband, a home, friends. Happiness is Eros, logos, and spaghetti—love, which is romance and sex, both the spiritual and physical; logos, which is your work; and eating. To eat all the spaghetti you want and not get fat—and not know the price of anything. Children are the only thing I would have liked in life that I missed."

She patted the head of one of the stone sphinxes which she called "my pets" and added, "Women are the earth, and men are the seeds, so it's a different kind of energy."

For Lina Wertmüller, the most difficult kind of relationship would be the two-career marriage in which both partners have irreconcilable similarities. She asked me if I had ever thought of marriage, and I answered that of course I had. "Never marry another writer," she advised me. "Not because a writer would be a worse husband than anyone else, but because the marriage with the least chance of success is the one in which both people want to do the same thing. Both have similar personalities and both are under pressure. The only thing more terrible would be if the woman's career is the more successful."

She believed that she had been truly fortunate in having as her husband a man who had his own career as an artist and who was also a person of calmer temperament. Though he valued acclaim, especially peer-group acclaim, he did not need it as she needed the applause of an audience.

Lina's own parents' marriage was only a limited success. Her mother celebrated her golden wedding anniversary by divorcing Lina's father. After half a century of apparent domestic docility and resignation in "a man's world," the Italian divorce law was passed, and Lina's mother had the last word. That word was *basta* —"enough." One evening she greeted Lina's shocked father with a neatly packed suitcase, and they were happily divorced.

Lina Wertmüller paused momentarily, looking out over Rome from her Piazza del Popolo apartment where we were having lunch. Then she turned back to me and raised her glass in a toast: "To work—it's the only thing."

Picasso told me that he loved working even better than making love. "At least that is the way I remember it now," he quickly added.

"Of course, there were times when if you had asked me precisely at a certain moment, I would not have said at that exact moment work was more urgent than making love. It is a matter of perspective."

Picasso was one of many of the creative people with whom I spoke who told me that through their work they could express emotions that they were unable to express in real life. He said that for him words were the most limited way to express feelings. "Painting and making love were very much the same for me. At the greatest moments for each, painting and sex were the same. But painting you can do alone.

"I have revealed my intimate self in my paintings as I could never have done in words. It is difficult for a man ever to communicate his most intimate feelings to another person. There is so much I could never say to a male friend, but I could not hold it

back in my paintings. I could not say to a woman in bed what my paintings speak. In art there is a sexual release."

The sex drive and the success drive were often linked by the famous people who spoke with me. Picasso stated it unequivocally:

"Sex drive and success drive are the same thing. It is about men I speak. I know that those who have the strongest drive for one thing have it for all things. It is male energy. In men who have the strongest drive for success, there is also the strongest drive for sex."

"Do you think the same is true for women?" I asked.

He answered that perhaps I could tell *him* because he had never understood women at all. "You know, the bullfighter always abstains from sex before the *corrida*. The juices are the same." He laughed. "But, of course, it is easier for the bullfighter and the painter than for the novelist."

"What is the first thought or impression you can remember?" I asked Picasso.

"Sex," he answered without hesitation.

"What was your second thought?"

"The same."

As a little boy, he noticed that when he drew pictures, little girls liked what he was doing. They came and watched, and they stood close. He enjoyed that. As he grew older, girls continued to gather about admiringly, still standing close to watch him work, and he enjoyed it even more. He found that his work got him girls, more girls, "better" girls, and that they said yes instead of no.

This made being an artist appear an even more attractive career for the young Picasso. "In the beginning," he said, "I believed the girls were enraptured by my artistic proficiency. But later, when I had grown up and they had grown up, they were more fascinated by the success of my achievement than by the achievement itself. Women like to fuck success."

"Did thinking that diminish your pleasure?" I asked.

"No," he answered. "But as I worked, my work became more and more important in my life—everything—and the only woman who could be part of my life was the one who could accept its priority and fit her life around it. There were not really many women who were prepared to accept that, and then not for long. Jacqueline [his wife] is the only one who is the perfect companion and who regards the work as I do."

Virgil Thomson remembered Marcel Duchamp, who was "somewhat jealous of Picasso's success," commenting, "Picasso got sexually excited by the smell of turpentine, so he *had* to work every day."

Laurence Olivier suggested that the sex drive spills over into other things. "It cannot be contained. It is energy. You don't feel a cold when you're on stage. When you're working at your best, you forget you're sick. At that moment nothing else exists. Being on stage is like good sex."

Arthur Rubinstein told me that musicmaking and lovemaking are really the same thing. "Ideally, both are a combination of inspiration and magic. In each, the act is always the same, yet it is always different." While he spoke, his fingers moved as if they were playing an invisible keyboard on the restaurant tablecloth. Watching those celebrated fingers in motion was a magical experience for me. When he stopped, I asked him what he had played.

"A passage from Brahms' second piano concerto," he responded as if I should have known. "Couldn't you hear it?"

"No, I'm sorry to say."

He smiled. "I could."

Fellini said that the important place for a creative artist to have an active sex life is in the mind. There, one can create the most exaggerated fantasies, which can then be lived out risk-free by the artist and his audience.

"The frustration of it being contained in your head leads to a more fanciful release on paper, on canvas, or on the screen," he explained. "Total satisfaction would remove the necessity of fulfilling yourself in your work—besides leaving you too tired!"

Alfred Hitchcock told me, "I was very innocent and sexually repressed in my youth. I was a virgin when I married, you know." He hesitated momentarily, having noted the frown on his wife's face, and then continued. "I think that repressed sex is more constructive for the creative person. It must get out, and so it goes into the work. I think it helped create a sense of sex in my work."

Luise Rainer, who had a tumultuous marriage to Clifford Odets during her Hollywood career, said, "If you have a great lover and a great part in a film or a play, during the time you are working it is better that your lover be about three thousand miles away."

Fritz Lang said that as a young man he was always thinking about girls, and it was to impress them that he became a film director. "I thought I was very romantic. I did not understand then that the sex urge and the love urge are very different things."

He said he would have liked to make a film called *Blue Martini.* Then he asked me if I had ever had a blue martini. I admitted that I had not only never had a blue one, but I'd never even had a regular one.

Savoring his recollection, he explained that it had been his infallible seduction technique. He would invite a girl he was "in love with at the moment" to his place and mix blue martinis. "She would be mystified, intrigued, enchanted, and fall into my arms. Do you know what made the blue martini blue?"

I didn't.

"Blue food coloring," he said. "I never told a girl that before. If you write a book about me, I want you to call it 'Blue Martini.' It always worked, every single time, so that proves it was the greatest seduction technique. They never could resist my blue martini."

I suggested to Fritz that maybe the reason the blue martini was so effective was that it offered women an excuse for doing what they really wanted to do anyway—that *he* was the blue martini.

"There is something I want to ask you," he said, ignoring my comment. "Would you like a blue martini?"

Tennessee Williams, who didn't do anything casually, believed that the sex and success drives were matters of life-and-death intensity, so inextricably linked that they were the same:

"I am always drawn to the passionate person. The person who is passionate about one thing is passionate about all things. It is a

matter of energy. I have never felt that a person's sexual preferences—or perhaps his aberrations, depending on the perspective
of those judging—were at all pertinent to his creative artistry.
However, those who are more sensitive in art may well be more
sensitive in their sexual pursuits, and those with the greatest
appetites for one thing, I believe, have the greater capacity and
drive for other things.

"Early sexual repression may have been an important factor in
my work. It forced the immense drive and frustration and guilt
that I felt into my writing. I didn't even masturbate. I had sexual
feelings very early, and I was always thinking about it, but I didn't
have the experience, not even counting gropings, the usual fum-
bling and stumbling, until my middle twenties. From then on, you
might say I made up for lost time. But before that, I was the shyest
person in the world. I could have expired from embarrassment.
Also, I was never physically an attractive person. Sexuality was
very dominant in my works because I wasn't getting any.

"I didn't masturbate till I was twenty-six. I consummated my
first love affair with a girl when I was twenty-seven. My first
homosexual encounter was at twenty-eight, even though I realized in my teens that I had homosexual tendencies.

"I have never been a passive person. I live an intense life, both
professionally and personally. Impotence in either is terrible.
You must be able to have a mental erection. The sad thing is that
when you become sexually impotent, you have more time to
work, but you are impotent in that, too.

"The drive for sex and success are the same. When a man dies
sexually, he is as good as dead. When he dies creatively, he *is*
dead. One can only go on with the hope of regaining one's
powers."

Dudley Moore told Groucho and me that he did it all for the
"birds." Girls, in fact, were all he thought about; but all they
thought about, or so it seemed to him, were tall men. He couldn't
add inches, so he resolved to add stature by adding success once
he realized that girls like men who excel nearly as much as they
like men who are tall.

"Better," Groucho added. "Girls were why the Marx Brothers
wanted to be successful. Being in show business got us girls,

especially Chico." Even his name, pronounced *chick-o,* indicated a predisposition for the "chickens" who later became known in England as "birds." Groucho's favorite photograph of Chico was the cast picture of *The Cocoanuts* road company. The whole cast was there except for one empty chair in the front row—Chico's.

"Chico was out getting laid," Groucho explained.

No one felt more strongly than did Mae West about the relationship between the success drive and the sex drive. She expressed the belief that those with the strongest sex drive also had the strongest passion for their careers and for everything else in life. She stressed the importance of saving one's sexual energies for creative endeavor. "Sex energy is in everything you do," she would tell me. "The greater your sexual energy, the greater your creative energy. That's why I always abstained when I was working, to save it all for my work." The last time I saw her, she added, "You know, honey, you want to be sure and do that, too."

"I ached for it, the spotlight, which was like the strongest man's arms around me"

MAE WEST

MAE WEST HELD OUT her hand to me. As I took it, I scratched my palm on one of her diamond rings. Noticing what had happened, she commented in a matter-of-fact tone, "They're old-cut, very sharp. That's the best kind."

All of her fingers were covered with diamonds. She wore a diamond necklace, diamond bracelets, and a diamond anklet. These, she explained, were just her "daytime diamonds." Holding out her hands so I could examine them, she said, "Look, they're all real. They were given to me by admirers." Her gaze settled on my own unadorned hands. "Oh, my, you poor kid! You don't have any!"

For a moment she regarded me silently with amazement and pity. Then she brightened. "But you have some at home?"

I shook my head.

Her look of deep sympathy returned. She studied me for a moment, then said encouragingly, "You *could*, honey. But you've gotta try, and you've gotta know *how* to try. There's nothing better in life than diamonds."

"Maybe that's what one has to believe in order to get them," I said.

"You're right," she said. "You put your finger on it. Everything's in the mind. That's where it all starts. Knowing what you want is the first step toward getting it." She held out her hands for both of us to admire. "These diamonds here—they're my friends. Aren't they beautiful? The only thing more important is health."

I found myself aware of a distracting sound—something like the fluttering of the wings of little birds. Trying not to appear inattentive to what she was saying, I could not resist glancing around the room. But I saw no birdcages. The sound continued at frequent intervals. Only after Mae had been speaking for a while did I realize that it was the sound of her heavily mascaraed, multilayered false eyelashes brushing her cheeks whenever she blinked.

Mae West had been giving no interviews at all. Whenever she answered her telephone, which was rarely, she would pretend to be the maid. Mae already knew all the people she ever wanted to know, especially in light of the many hours she felt compelled to spend on her hair, makeup, and dress before she could see anyone. Her face was nearly hidden by its mask of makeup, but her throat and décolletage revealed strikingly fair, soft, and youthful skin. I had cost her three hours, as I was told more than once, but it would have been double that if I had been a man. If she were going to see anyone at all, a man would have been preferable any day, and especially any night.

"They always sent a man," she told me, not specifying who "they" were. "I considered spending my time with girls a waste of time, so I didn't mingle with any." The only exceptions were her beloved mother and her sister, Beverly. Men were the ones doing the interesting things, and they were the ones who had the power to enable her to do them.

For Mae West, Hollywood had real unreality, and that was the way she liked it. To that end, she nobly resisted any assault on her fairy-tale castle. The apartment in Hollywood's Ravenswood was truly an extension of Mae West, not only reflecting her, but also enhancing her and probably inspiring her. She had put a great deal of herself into it, and in return got a great deal back. The furniture was upholstered in eggshell-white silk and satin, and appeared virginal, as if it had just been moved in for my visit. Actually, the white and gold furnishings had been there since the early thirties when Mae first arrived, with time out only for reupholstering or cleaning.

There were none of the ubiquitous house plants. "Plants use up too much oxygen," Mae explained erroneously, but with certainty. The apartment was cool because, as she said, "It's good for the furniture and the complexion. I like the air filtered and moving."

I wondered how her apartment was maintained in such pristine condition, wishing that the answer would be something I could apply to my own, but knowing instinctively that the sorcery could not be transferred. It seemed somehow natural that Mae West's furniture would not get dirty. Magic has a certain fragility; any answer would only spoil the illusion.

Once Mae had achieved perfection by her own standards, she hated any change. She had never forgotten the life of the stock company and vaudeville when she had no control over her environment. "I did enough traveling when I was very young, so I didn't need to do that anymore. I got it out of my system. I have everything I want right here." She said she never wanted to have to move.

Mae West's apartment was a home for her and by her which reflected not some noted interior decorator but Mae herself. The accumulation of memorabilia, gifts from fans, and treasured family souvenirs indicated that the private Mae West was a more sentimental person than her public character pretended to be. The celebrations of herself on display throughout the apartment —the nude marble statues and oil paintings in "classical" style of Mae West at the moment of her greatest success—evinced no false modesty. They also signified that in her mid-eighties she was not afraid to be in competition with her younger self. She was still optimistic and had future plans and ambitions.

Whenever Mae interjected one of her celebrated epigrams or aphorisms to make a point, she would change from a serious tone to the sultry flippancy of Diamond Lil. Sometimes she would break up long words into several syllables, pausing between the syllables to create an exaggerated sensual effect. As she spoke, her sculpted platinum hair would swing as in a shampoo commercial, but without a wind machine to blow it. She frequently tossed her head and the movement of her hair would punctuate her comments.

Always the mistress of illusion, Mae wore long dresses or flared-bottom pants designed to cover her stiltlike shoes. Her shoes had the highest heels I had ever seen, and the heels seemed higher than the shoes were long. Just looking at them made my feet hurt. They reminded me of the heels on Carmen Miranda's platform shoes I had seen exhibited at the museum in Rio de Janeiro. Edith Head speculated that it was the height of those heels that had caused Mae West's famous suggestive walk. In those shoes it was the only way she *could* walk! They were so heavy it was actually difficult for her to rise from a chair. I asked Mae how she thought men would do if they had to live their lives in high heels.

"They wouldn't make it," she answered. "They'd be wiped out."

Perhaps she didn't like to give interviews to women because she couldn't act her part. With a woman she had to reveal a lot more of the private person. Mae West had to be there herself; she couldn't just send Diamond Lil. She pointed out that although she was Diamond Lil, Lil was not Mae because there was more to Mae West. Public and personal success are two different things. It was easier for Lil to be happy than it was for Mae. For Lil, happiness was sex. For Mae, it was work.

Mae gave me a hard look and said there was something she had to tell me before we really "got into it."

"If you want to smoke," she said, "you'll have to leave the room and go out into the hall. We don't keep any ashtrays here. I don't let anyone smoke in my presence. I don't breathe it, and I don't want it getting into the furniture. Let me know when you want to go out into the hall."

I assured her that this wouldn't be necessary because I didn't smoke and never had. Her approving look indicated that I had passed an important test.

MAE WEST

Then you'll keep your soft skin. That's how I kept mine. I always use baby oil. Baby oil's good for the whole body. But the secret is it has to be warm, and you have to have a man put it on you—all over.

I can smell you're telling the truth about smoking, because if you smoked, your clothes and hair would smell from it, especially your hair. You know, I never liked being touched by a man who smoked.

Her next query had the same tone of entrapment as the smoking suggestion. She asked me if I wanted to have a drink. I declined. She said it was a good thing because she didn't have any liquor.

MAE WEST
My mother was a health nut and my father an athlete. I never understood drinking. It isn't good for your health or your looks, and it cuts down on what you are. I never wanted to cut down on what I am.

I was indefatigable. I never knew exactly why. I always had this extraordinary energy that I had to do something with. They only just found out that I had a double thyroid. Always had it, but I didn't know it. Maybe that's always been the source of my energy, especially my sex energy. When they told me I had a double thyroid, they wanted to take one away, but I wasn't doing that. I don't believe in tampering.

I
Differences the world considers odd or eccentric may actually be a person's good fortune, but there are always those who value conformity over individuality.

MAE WEST
Individuality is everything—individuality and enthusiasm.

I
I think enthusiasm is a big factor in energy. There's nothing more tiring than things going wrong—discouragement and disappointment.

MAE WEST
I could hardly wait for life. I wanted to run toward it with open arms.

Is that scarf because you're cold, or do you have something to hide? *[I take it off]* That's better. Now, if you'd unbutton a few buttons. . . . Men like it if you show them a thing or two. I dress for women and undress for men.

Mae loved clothes and was a collector of them. Her perfectly kept gowns were not just stored but seemed to have a life of their own, rather like a row of headless ladies standing there waiting for a party to rescue them from their boredom. The feathered boas and lacy peignoirs looked as though they had stories to tell if I could have interviewed them, but they were forever keeping all confidences. Mae's final fashion show was for her best and favorite audience—herself, alone.

When she encouraged me to try on some of the clothes, I was hesitant, but she persuaded me to model a black peignoir. "Doesn't it make you feel sexy?" she asked. Her words were barely spoken when she looked at me in disgust. I had put it on over my blouse and skirt. "You can't get the feeling like *that,*" she explained. "You have to be naked underneath."

MAE WEST
When I was making a film, I would stand during the whole shooting—five, six, seven hours a day—so I wouldn't wrinkle my dress. I even stood to eat. They'd say to me, "Mae, aren't you tired?" But I didn't let myself get tired. I'd say to myself, "Do I want to look my best for my public that expects it of me? Or would I rather sit down?" That ain't no choice.

First impressions are what count. I was always careful about the first dress I wore onstage or in a picture. It's like when you arrive at a party. That's the important moment. That's when people take a real look at you, size you up, and if they're impressed, that's how they think of you and remember you. If your makeup fades a little and you get a few creases in your dress later and you look a little tired, that isn't what they remember.

I
What would you do if you didn't make the best first impression on a man?

MAE WEST
Get a different man. I'd figure there was something wrong with him.

See that gold lion under my piano? A fan sent it to me. They send me gifts all the time. I have some women fans, too. I added the costumes to my shows to get the women. The women came to see my clothes, and the men came to see *me.* Clothes are important to a woman because a woman feels sexier in a black nightgown with lace.

I

It seems to me that elegant nightgowns are of more interest to women than to men.

MAE WEST

Well, I never needed clothes to make *me* feel sexy. I felt that way all the time, and that's the kind of thing men can tell. The nearness of an attractive man kept me in a constant state of sensual unrest.

I

You summed it up at the end of *I'm No Angel* when Cary Grant asked you, "What are you thinking about?" and you answered, "The same thing you are."

MAE WEST

That's very exciting for a man. When men sense a woman is ready for sex, they're ready right away. Men are simpler than women that way. It's the way they're made—very uncomplicated. When men came to see me, I had to try to calm them down a little first.

I

It was probably the scenario in their minds on the way over here that did that.

MAE WEST

Yeah, calming them down wasn't easy. *[Sighing]* I had a lot of great love affairs.

I

I almost had dinner with you the last time you were at Groucho's house. Elliott Gould was there, and he told me about that evening.

MAE WEST

Elliott's a bear of a man. I've always loved bears. Say, you know what I just thought of? I remember my first sex dream. It was with a bear. I guess I was about ten, maybe younger. He came through the door standing up—a giant male bear. I never had the dream again. It worried me for a long time. I really haven't thought about this for years. I never told anyone. I learned later that the bear is a symbol of sex.

I

Maybe it has something to do with "bare."

MAE WEST

Sex and work have been the only two things in my life.

I

But in reverse order of importance . . .

MAE WEST

Yeah. If I ever had to choose between sex and my work, it was always my work I'd choose. I'm glad I didn't ever have to choose between them for more than a week at a time, though. Since I was grown up, I've never been without either for more than a week.

I

What's "grown up"?

MAE WEST

Thirteen. I was active before that, but it wasn't on a regular basis. Before that, I was finding my way.

I

Didn't you ever have any trouble finding a man?

MAE WEST

[Puzzled] What do you mean?

I

I mean one you really liked.

MAE WEST

I never had any trouble. They always found me. I could always find something to like about every man. Well, *almost* every man.

Paul Novak, Mae's friend who lived with her and who had opened the door for me, came in from the kitchen carrying a tray with glasses and bottles of mineral water. Each glass had on it a different illustration of a glamorously costumed Mae.

MAE WEST

Would you like some mineral water? It's all we drink here. I even take my bath in mineral water. You know, I never had a cold.

I
To what do you attribute that?

MAE WEST
My mind. I made up my mind. People don't understand its power. *[Touching her forehead]* Everything's right here. Everybody's busy thinking about what's in other people's heads. It's your own you've gotta live with.

I
So much of what seems to be happening to us, I suppose, is only happening in our minds, and it's really our perception of it that makes us happy or unhappy.

MAE WEST
Imagination can make you happier. People don't have to use their minds to torture themselves. I think you've gotta take as good care of your mind as you do of your body. Just like you put oil on your body and take bubble baths to keep it soft and in good shape, you don't want to clutter up your mind with negative thoughts and bad news.

Paul asked me how I had managed to get through the Ravenswood's protective lobby and up in the elevator without even being announced. I said that I had asked for him, assuming that strangers gave Mae West's name but knowing his name would be the password.

Mae kept looking at the gift-wrapped box from Krön I had set down on the table. "What's that?" she asked with childlike enthusiasm.

"George Cukor told me you have a passion for chocolates," I explained.

"I do have a passion," she said. "What kind of chocolates are they?"

"One is made very healthy, with hardly any sugar. It has prunes and dried apricots inside because I was told you like healthy things. The other is a cream truffle."

Opening the first box, Mae almost destroyed the contents in her haste to get inside. Then she voraciously attacked the second box, nearly mashing a few creams. It was only after she had both boxes open that she made her choice. As if fearing someone might take the box away from her, she snatched two chocolate truffles.

"I like my pleasure," she said, composing herself and holding out the box to me. "You can have one, too, honey." She never let go of the box. Not wishing to deprive her, I selected one chocolate-covered apricot and began to eat it.

"You have nice manners," Mae said. "You eat like a lady. When I was a little girl, I watched myself in the mirror while I ate so I'd do it right. Some people chew like cows chewing their cud." Then she took the box away, as if she thought I was going to be too much of a lady and eat another piece. Mae indulged in one more and was reaching for a fourth when Paul firmly took the box away from her. She looked petulant, but not displeased.

MAE WEST

I like my men to be men. You know, my mother never let me have any chocolate when I was a child. She said it was bad for my teeth. I have every one of them.

PAUL NOVAK

[To Mae] Do you want anything else?

MAE WEST

[Suggestively] Maybe later . . . *[To me, as Paul leaves the room]* That's a nice pair of shoulders, isn't it? Did you see those biceps? *[Crashing sound of glass from the kitchen]* I hope he didn't hurt anything . . . important. Paul's handsome, and he's a wonderful man. He never tries to change me. Men always liked me because I wasn't like any other woman they'd ever known. They'd all say to me, "I never knew a woman like you, Mae," because I was unique. But you know what was funny—when a man was courting me, he'd want to put a diamond on my finger, and as soon as he thought he had me, he wanted to put an apron around my waist. I didn't want any diamond handcuffs. I had my career to think about, and any man who wanted me to be less than I was, I didn't need.

You're sure you don't smoke?

I

I never have.

MAE WEST
The next time you come, I'm gonna give *you* some chocolate.
Have you ever eaten Ragtime chocolate?

I
I don't even know what it is.

MAE WEST
Hardly anyone does anymore. I know the last place in America
that still makes it, and it's not far from here.

I want to show you my mother's picture. Isn't she beautiful?

I
She's lovely.

MAE WEST
She was soft and feminine, completely the opposite from my
father. My father was called "Battling Jack." He was a real man.
He'd fought in the ring and on the streets. He had a stable, but
later he was a detective. I remember sitting outside his office,
playing with my doll and watching the people. Then, when they
left, I'd go in and give him my opinion of them. I was always
right. He'd say, "How could Mae know so much about people?" I judged people that way all my life. If I didn't like you
when you came in, I would've told you to go.

My mother lost a baby girl just before me. My sister only
lived a few months, so I was her whole world. She treated me
like a jewel. She never even used a bad tone with me. She did
everything I wanted. If I saw a doll, she got me the doll I
wanted. Once we went to a store, and there were a hundred
dolls. Everyone thought all the dolls looked alike. The one I
wanted was on the highest shelf no one could reach. They had
to go and get a ladder and someone to climb the ladder. It drew
a crowd. Everyone in the store thought I just wanted that one
because I was difficult. But I wanted her because she had a
mauve dress, a beautiful mauve dress. I don't know where that
color went. It used to be real big. I was four years old, but I
knew I only wanted that one. They didn't see the difference. If
you see the difference and other people don't, they think
you're just being difficult. I always knew what I wanted. My
mother never questioned it. She made them get a ladder and
get me the one I wanted.

I
Do you know where that doll is now?
MAE WEST
No. I wish I did. Maybe the doll's with my mother.

I was an only child for a long time. I was lucky that way. I had a sister and a brother, but they came along later, and it wasn't the same for them. I had my mother alone for the first five years. My sister and brother had to share her with each other and with me. By the time they came, I didn't need so much from her anymore. I was never jealous of my sister and brother. In my whole life, I've never envied anyone. I was too busy thinking about myself.

My mother wanted to be an actress. She finally got that through me. She always came to see me. She had a box seat. I took her out on the stage with me for a curtain call before she died. That really made me happy, that I could give her that. On a New Year's night, I was playing with Harry Richman. Everyone came onstage, and I brought her out. She loved it. She lit up. I threw the audience a kiss, and she did, too.

The hardest thing that happened to me in my life was when my mother died. I cried. I never got over it.

On the white piano Mae had pictures in old silver frames of her parents. "I lost a lot of pictures when the basement flooded," she told me. "It was terrible. I lost a part of me."

MAE WEST
The success I had on the stage was worth it for my mother to come out and take that bow with me. And all the money I made, it was worth everything, because it paid for the most important thing I ever bought. My mother loved hats, and I saw this hat which was the most wonderful hat in the world. She had a black dress with lace sleeves, long tight-fitted lace sleeves, and black lace up around the neck. One day in New York I saw this hat, and right away I knew it was made for my mother, and that she could wear it with her favorite black lace dress. It was mauve.

I can see that hat in my mind just as clear today as I did the day I was holding it in my hand in the store. It was turned up on one side so you'd be able to see her blond hair. The crowning touch was the feather, the greatest ostrich feather you ever saw. The hat cost eighty-five dollars, which was really a lot then. I'd never seen a hat that expensive before. But I knew I had to have it for my mother. I didn't hesitate a second. I would have bought it whatever it cost.

I took it home, and I couldn't wait for any special occasion. I just rushed in the door and gave it to her. She couldn't wait either. She put it right on and kept it on for a long time. She just didn't want to take it off at all, she loved it so much, just the way I knew she would. It was worth everything—that look of pleasure on her face. That's what money's for, when it's really worth something—to buy someone you love so much happiness. That meant more than any diamonds.

I always loved hats just the way my mother loved hats. I loved buying them. I still have just about all of them I ever bought. I can go into the bedroom and try them on by myself all afternoon and be happy. I own more than anyone could wear, but show me a great hat and I can always make room. The funny thing is I live in California where nobody wears them, and many of my hats have never been out of my bedroom. Some people thought I ought to see a psychiatrist, but why spoil a good thing?

I

I believe the more things we have in life that give us pleasure and make our lives richer, the better off we are.

MAE WEST

My mother used to massage me with baby oil after my bath as a child. It's my earliest memory. Nothing ever felt more wonderful than that. I was always more like my father than like my mother, more like a man. My mother took wonderful care of me, but as I grew up, it was like I became her mother and she was my child. I wanted to take care of her and spoil her the way she had done for me.

My mother always started out talking to me with, "Dear, would you please do this," or she'd say, "Would you do this for mother." She had beautiful manners. Mother knew I could never be forced. Even a wrong tone of voice upset me terribly. I've never liked arguments. They ruin making love.

I always knew when I came offstage my mother would be there waiting for me, holding my favorite little fur muff. My mother is so much a part of my life, I didn't know how I could go on without her. Later, I realized that as long as I live, she lives.

When I was a little girl, my father built me a small stage in the basement of our Brooklyn brownstone. It was all white with a beautiful white curtain. White was always my color. My father wasn't as sure as my mother about me going on the stage so young. He thought maybe I could wait till I was eight. But I couldn't. He said, "Let her have a chance, and we'll see how she does. But if she gets stage fright, she'll have to wait till she's older." Can you imagine? Sometimes even one of your own parents doesn't know you. Stage fright! I didn't know the meaning of the word. Still don't.

My mother didn't listen to my father. She knew I could do anything I wanted. As a child I had perfect confidence. Maybe that's why I wasn't ever afraid of anything. Earthquakes don't bother me. I was always happy on boats. It never bothered me that I couldn't swim.

Once when I was a little girl at the beach, I heard someone screaming. There was this little girl drowning. There wasn't anyone else around, so I just jumped in and pulled her out, and got her back to shore. I didn't think about it before I did it because there wasn't any time. Afterwards my father was really angry. "How could that child have done it when she couldn't swim?" he asked my mother. "You gotta watch Mae. You never know what she's gonna do." It was the only time I ever heard him raise his voice to her.

I'd always admired lions. Lions are so beautiful. When I'd go to a new city, I'd go to the zoo just to see the lions. I'd stand outside their cages and have this fantasy:

I'd be in there with them, and they'd be doing just what I wanted them to do, surrendering to me. I would totally command them. I had this tremendous passion for it and no fear. I knew the lions would recognize me and wouldn't hurt me. I'd always wanted to be a lion tamer. It was a kind of dream of mine. *I'm No Angel* was a circus picture, and through being an actress I really got to do it. I didn't use a double.

They weren't gonna let me do it. The professional lion tamer couldn't be there because, just before, a lion had attacked him, and he had to be taken to the hospital. I told them I wasn't gonna wear the fur cape they had for me. I just didn't like it. But it was a good thing. Maybe the lions wouldn't have liked the fur. There had been some dogs near the fur, and they might have smelled them. The lions were wonderful. They were nervous, though, probably because of what had happened just before, but I wasn't. I was thrilled. I was able to stand my ground and dominate those big male lions.

When I came out of the cage, everyone applauded. I didn't ever have to go back because I'd done it.

I

Very few of us have the opportunity to live out our fantasies. An actress may have that opportunity.

MAE WEST

Being an actress and a writer both—that's the best thing you could be in life because you can be anyone you want to be. You just write yourself the part, and then you play it. That way you can skip the dull stuff. And when you get tired, you can be somebody else.

Say, do you want to know about my first love affair? It was when I was five. I made my debut in Brooklyn at the Royal Theater. I fell in love on that stage. It was my first love affair with my audience, and it's lasted all my life. That was the only one that ever really counted. No man could equal that. I could hardly wait to be on the stage—in the warm glow of the lights. Even then I knew that's when I'd really be alive. I heard the applause, applause just for me, and I knew they really liked me, and I knew then there wasn't any other place I ever wanted to be. I've never been more secure than when I'm onstage. I had to have the spotlight more than anything else, shining full on me. I ached for it, the spotlight, which was like the strongest man's arms around me, like an ermine coat.

As a child I was always imagining my name up in lights. I

would fall asleep at night seeing my name up there in lights. I used to sit and practice my autograph for hours. I'd try one way and then another until I got it just right. I'm the one who changed my name from May to Mae. It looked better to me that way when I was a little girl signing the autographs. Besides, I didn't like that 'y' hanging down below the line. I don't like anything downbeat.

I always changed things in my parts. When I was eight years old, I would see a piece of business that could be added. Sometimes I'd add lines of my own. I always got my way. I was always putting fresh things in my act to keep my own interest. If you don't keep your own interest, it shows. I used to write myself extra material so I could do fresh stuff for my encores. You gotta believe in yourself. I knew the theater was my destiny, and I always worked hard. That's all I wanted, to work. I didn't want a life of dull routine.

I

Who were the performers who influenced you when you were beginning your career?

MAE WEST

Nobody influenced me. I've always just been myself.

I

And you got to be more yourself as you went along.

MAE WEST

Maybe so. I created Diamond Lil. She was one of the great characters of all times. I respected Groucho and the Marx Brothers because they were funny, but what I admired most was they created their own characters. Chaplin was a really great artist who also created his own character.

My education was the theater. I saw Billie Burke and Tyrone Power, the father. Bert Williams was my favorite when I was a child, and I wanted to meet him. One night my father came home and said, "Mae, I have a big surprise for you. Bert Williams is here. I've brought him home to have dinner with you." I rushed in, looked at this man, and screamed, "It's not! It's not!" I went up to my room and cried. I was terribly upset. My mother told me my father wanted to go up to me, but Bert Williams stopped him. He said, "I'll do it." He stood outside my door and started to sing. Then I knew and came right out of my room, and we all had dinner.

Do you know why I didn't recognize him? He was too light. He was a black man, but he was too light, so onstage he wore blackface. He was a great star, but they used to make him use a separate entrance. He died a long time ago, before I came to Hollywood.

I cried because I couldn't bear the thought that my father had lied to me. I never cried again except when my mother died. I had no other reason to cry. I got everything I wanted.

I

Was there ever something you wanted a lot and didn't get?

MAE WEST

No. Some women know how to get what they want. Others don't. I've always known how.

I

How what?

MAE WEST

If you gotta ask, that's bad. You know, honey, you're one who *doesn't* know how. You're missing something. You haven't got wiles, woman's wiles. Am I right?

I

Probably. I've always believed that pretending only gets you what you *don't* want. As a woman who *does* know how to get what she wants, what advice would you give to the ones who don't?

MAE WEST

I couldn't give advice to a woman unless I knew her, and I don't know any.

This room makes me feel rich. I always liked nice things around me. Money does that. People judge you by the value you put on yourself—in show business, in sex, in life. But in my first show I didn't even sign a contract. The show was a tremendous success, and people said to me, "Now you can hold 'em up and get plenty." I didn't care. I just wanted to be the star of a hit show.

I

Did you prefer being on the stage or making films?

MAE WEST

I liked both. It was nice to have the live audience, but the films are so important. We can look at them now. All those people who weren't even born when the films were being made are my fans now. My pictures are on television just about every night. I hope you've been watching. I haven't changed, have I? *[She doesn't wait for my answer]* Men were always most of my audience. They got to the box office first! *[Laughs]* But seriously, I used to wonder about it. We put a lot of beautiful clothes into the shows so we'd have the fashion to attract the women. Even when I was doing the nightclub act, there were still a lot more men in the audience. But some of the men brought wives, so I decided to ask the women why they were there. "It's for our husbands." So there it was.

I've stayed in demand because I never gave 'em too much. I've always left 'em wanting more. Today television is the fastest way to finish yourself off. Now you don't see great people like there used to be in the world.

I

Giants are in short supply.

MAE WEST

Too many people see you for nothing. They're always wanting me to be on those talk shows, but I don't go. Television's okay for people who've got something to sell. I don't need to.

I

Of what in your career are you proudest?

MAE WEST

I saved Paramount Pictures. They were selling out. The Paramount theaters would've been finished. But my pictures made so much money for them, they were able to stay in business during the thirties. They oughta have a statue of me. At least a bust. Miss Bette Davis didn't save Warner Brothers. Miss Joan Crawford didn't save any studios. Paramount oughta have put up a statue of me.

I

[Indicating a nude statue of Mae West in her living room] Like that?

MAE WEST

No. One of Diamond Lil in a beautiful dress. After my picture about Diamond Lil, sex was more out in the open. I'm proud of that because I always believed that sex was nothing to be ashamed of. I didn't see love as a sin. Overwhelming desire is wonderful.

I

Do you think sex is better with love?

MAE WEST

Honey, sex with love is the greatest thing in life. But sex without love—that's not so bad either. Sex is the best exercise for developing everything. It's very good for the complexion and the circulation. Keeps it all moving along. I've always had the skin of a little girl. Go ahead, touch it. *[I touch her skin]* That's all real. I didn't ever have to lift *anything*. Never go out in the sun. I never did. It'll ruin your complexion. You have nice skin, too.

I

Thank you.

MAE WEST

Don't thank me. I didn't do it. You're just lucky.

I

Lucky is the best thing to be.

MAE WEST

Timing is very important in life. And in sex. Life and sex are a lot alike, don't you think?

I

Life is discovery of the unknown, and I suppose sex is the discovery of the unknown in another person.

MAE WEST

We oughta know everything about ourselves, but it's better not to know everything about each other. Each of us oughta draw up a private, a very private, accounting of our sexual needs. Sex isn't common, to be handed around like a box of chocolates. First sex meetings are very special. The first time with each man is important. I remember one who did it the first time for fifteen hours.

I

Do you remember when you first thought about sex?

MAE WEST

I can't remember when I didn't. I was curious about the boys and what they had that I didn't. I always played with boys. They used to gather 'round me. They called me "Peaches." I liked to see how each one kissed. A man's kiss is his signature.

At twelve I'd kiss all the boys at parties. I liked comparing their techniques. But kissing and all that stuff, that's all we did. I liked to feel their muscles.

I always liked having a lot of men around. On a rainy night it's like having more than one book to choose from, only better. Men's thoughts and ambitions were like mine. If you were out in the world doing interesting things, it would be men you'd meet. It was a man's world, and you'd be with men because men were the ones doing things.

I found one man who had beautiful hair, another had great muscles, and another one . . . umm. I didn't see why I should deprive myself of anything, so a lot of men was better for me than just one man. That way I could enjoy what was great about each one, but I wasn't tied to him. I didn't have to waste any time worrying about what he didn't have and trying to change him.

All of my ideas about women are what men's ideas are about women because all I know is what men told me. I never mingled with too many women. Men were so surprised by me, I knew there must be a lot of women out there doing it badly. Or maybe not doing it bad enough. Women spend too much of their lives saying no. Most women are so used to practicing no, they get to stay home and wash their hair on Saturday night. They expect a man to answer all their problems for them. There's nothing better than a man's shoulder to lean on, but you don't want to lean too hard.

I

It always seemed to me it's difficult being a man. So much is expected from a man. With women, the problem is often just the opposite—not enough is expected.

MAE WEST

You've gotta help your man, to put him at his ease. He's gotta be relaxed to get excited.

I

It's like trust and lust. Trust has to precede lust.

MAE WEST

Yeah. I made my man feel like a hero as long as it lasted. Then I was always the one who said good-bye. A few times I was drawn to falling in love, but I didn't let myself fall. I made an effort, and I cut it off. I know why they call it "falling." I never let that happen to me.

When I was very young, there'd be all these boys hanging around, and I'd start to think I liked one of them better than the others. Well, my mother wouldn't say anything much against him, but if she saw me liking one too much for my own good, she would point out some little flaw he had, like big ears that stuck out or something. Then I'd see it right away. So I'd like another one, and she'd just mention lightly some little fault he had. That gave me the idea early, which was very important —there wasn't just one.

I never could understand women who would almost die over one man. It wasn't what he had but what qualities they gave him in their own minds. I never wanted anyone to have power like that over me. All the wrong man is, is a bad habit. When you get rid of one, you don't want to waste any time getting another, so you don't sit around moping. When you mope, your mouth turns down; it puts lines in your face. There isn't any man in the world worth getting lines over. I felt it could mean the loss of my identity. That kind of all-consuming love threatened me. And you can't tell who's going to give you the most fun. You never know in advance what any man's physical capacities are going to be. He doesn't even know himself what he might be capable of. Until he finds the right inspiration—the right woman. Too many women wait around depending on men to bring them happiness. I didn't depend on men for mine. I knew how to handle men: Handle them a lot. I have a code though: No drinking, no smoking, and no married men. There are enough men to go around. I never needed to take away another woman's man. Women sell themselves that there's only one man in the world they want. Men are really all alike.

I

Men are all alike except the one who's different.

MAE WEST

But you gotta watch out for men who are heels. A heel is a completely selfish man. He can be clever. He knows how to say just enough of what you want to hear, and to do just enough of what you want, to give you hope. Then when he wants to disappear, he just does. But he comes back after a while just to test his power. He only likes conquest because he's really only making love to himself. The heel likes to keep you waiting for his phone call. You know, a lot of women think, "I'll be the one it'll be different with. I'm the one he'll change for." But they're always wrong. While they last, heels can be a lot of fun. I prefer a forty-ripened man, a man who's been around. Of course, there's fun in teaching a young man. He's so thrilled when he learns what he's capable of.

I've heard men say that they were afraid of the responsibility with a girl who was a virgin. But I always thought that initiating a virgin man was a privilege. A certain lack of expertise can have its own kind of charm, and they learn fast. Women don't like a man with *too* much experience. If he's too experienced, too good at what he does, they know how he arrived at his well-practiced techniques. It's fun to be able to teach a man something. Don't you think so?

I

I find it more interesting to play tennis with a better player.

MAE WEST

My best lover was a Frenchman who would pick me up in his car after *Diamond Lil* and take me over to the other theater to rehearse *Pleasure Man*. One Saturday night we were at it till four the next afternoon. A dozen rubber things. Twenty-two times. I was sorta tired. Like I always said, "It's not the men in my life, it's the life in my men."

I

What kind of "life" do you look for in a man?

MAE WEST

Fire. A man can be short and dumpy and getting bald, but if he has fire, women will like him.

I

What if he's tall and slim with plenty of hair?

MAE WEST

That's no problem. But even if he hasn't got fire, maybe you can be the one to light it. A man who could only do it once or twice a night suddenly finds he's got more talent than he knew, and he could do it twelve times. But after that, the same man couldn't ever do it like that with anybody else.

I

Do you think it might be in the head rather than the bed?

MAE WEST

I don't think about it. Thinking spoils the fun, like talking.

I

Don't you think talking can actually enhance making love, if it's the right conversation? It seems that conversation between two people and making love are really quite similar.

MAE WEST

You can talk it all away. The talk of love shouldn't ever be put down on paper, either. It looks silly.

I

I suppose that's because other people's sex seems funny, but not one's own.

MAE WEST

Sex can be funny, but men take it pretty seriously. The most terrible thing you can do to a man is to laugh at him.

I

Who were some of the men you've known who had that fire you mentioned?

MAE WEST

John Barrymore wasn't so bad. I wouldn't have minded playing with him. In a movie, that is.

I

You mean you'd rather have had him as a leading man in a film than as a lover in real life?

MAE WEST

If I'd had to make the choice, yeah. Because movies are forever, and sex doesn't last.

I

You don't think sex and passion *can* last a long time?

MAE WEST

No. Not for the same two people together. What happens is,

you might get to be friends, and you could keep that. But being good friends isn't good for sex.

I

If excitement and security don't go together, that could be a problem in marriage.

MAE WEST

Well, I'm not married. I could've married a lot of people, but I was busy.

I

Besides John Barrymore, what other men had that fire?

MAE WEST

Cary Grant. I heard him before I saw him, talking in the alley outside my dressing room at Paramount. Then I went out to take a look, and I liked what I saw. I liked his voice first, but I saw right away that the rest of him measured up. They didn't want him for my second picture, but I insisted. In my second picture he got to dress up, and he got noticed.

I

I gather that most of the men with whom you've had affairs were not performers.

MAE WEST

You weren't in the bedroom with us, honey. With me, they were *all* good performers. But actors don't make good lovers. A man who's just thinking about himself can't be much of a lover.

I

Jean Renoir told me that he always felt a woman who was an actress was more of a woman, while a man who was an actor was less of a man.

MAE WEST

I always liked a strong man, and not many actors seemed that way to me. I liked boxers, wrestlers, body builders. My father was a weight lifter, and he taught me how to use the weights. I taught myself how to use the lifters. Feeling biceps always excited me. Have you felt any good biceps lately?

I

Not today.

MAE WEST

Maybe tonight.

I

Is there a kind of atmosphere or situation that you found conducive to good sex?

MAE WEST

There's something about love under pressure—stolen moments. There's something about knowing you can't get all you want that makes for greater passion.

I

You were married once . . .

MAE WEST

It was a secret marriage. I wish it had been a secret from me. I didn't know it then, but I wasn't the marrying kind. I was asked why did I get married at seventeen. I certainly can't remember now. I guess it was just this physical thing. I always took marriage very seriously. It just wasn't for me. I don't believe in being married and not keeping the contract. And I never fooled around with a married man if I knew he was married. Once one fooled me, and as soon as I found out, I told him to get out. I've never taken a man away from a woman—even in a play.

I

You once said, "Men are easy to get but hard to keep." What do you think women should do to keep their men?

MAE WEST

You have to keep your eye on the balls. If you don't take good care of your man, someone else will.

I

Do you ever feel you missed something by not having children?

MAE WEST

Maybe, but I knew I didn't want children. When I was a little girl, I wanted a doll. But I knew that a doll wasn't a baby. You can just put your dolly away when you don't feel like playing that game anymore. Maybe if I missed something, that was it— having a baby. But I don't think I was meant to be a mother. I respect those who make the sacrifice. Motherhood's a full-time career. I already had a career. I didn't think I could do both things right. And they never persuaded me that men don't have the more fun part of having babies. The pill made women feel freer. I didn't need anything to make me feel free. The kind of guy a woman oughta like is one who wouldn't let her take the pill and take a chance on hurting her health.

I

How do you find these times different for women?

MAE WEST

These are vulgar times. I wouldn't discuss my sex life even with my sister. It wouldn't be proper.

I

What do you find vulgar?

MAE WEST

Four-letter words. I'm no puritan, but I don't like bad language. You know, I was always a lady.

I

What's a "lady"?

MAE WEST

I never said anything vulgar or used rough language, and I never made a beeline for anyone else's man. I never did anything that hurt other people.

I

Do you think that being a lady means something different now from what it did?

MAE WEST

You'd know better about what it is now than I would.

I

One thing that's changed is talking about it as a value. You were a lady or you weren't anything. You were a good girl or a bad girl.

MAE WEST

I was a bad girl with a good heart.

I

You defined lady for yourself. Now, I think, one of the differences is that more girls are defining it for themselves. It used to be that a lady did what other people *said* a lady did. She dressed according to a certain style. Her demeanor was in keeping with a more formalized code of behavior, and she was supposed to want only certain things. The rules were totally prescribed and not open to question. Now there seems to be a less objective definition and a more subjective one, with more women defining it for themselves.

MAE WEST

It used to be a woman was a lady because of what she held back. She was a lady because she didn't give it away unless she had the right contract and everybody said, "I do," first.

I

That presupposed that she was only giving and not getting, with marriage being all she had to gain.

MAE WEST

I don't think things have changed so much. The rules used to be made by men for men. The rules are a little different, but it's still a man's world, with men making the rules that suit them best.

I

Which time do you think was better for women?

MAE WEST

I think it was better then. The way it is now is really a lot better for men. Now a woman's *expected* to do it, and the man doesn't even have to court her. The woman used to be a bigger prize. She could do what she wanted, but she didn't advertise. I never understood the kind of woman who could write a book and tell who was in her bed. That's selling it. Why would a woman do that?

I

Notches on her garter belt, I guess, though it's pantyhose now.

MAE WEST

I didn't see why marriage and divorce, and marriage again and divorce again was better than two unmarried people making love. I never believed some things were all right for a man and not for a woman. It didn't seem right to me that in a marriage the woman is married all the time and the man only some of the time—when he chooses. I was about six when I noticed that. You've gotta have plenty of self-esteem, nerve, and be bold in life. I've been liberated all my life. I always did what I wanted to do.

I

That's quite a definition of Women's Lib! That would be a lot of liberty for a man.

MAE WEST

Men and women aren't the same. Men worry about what they haven't got, and women *know* what they haven't got.

I

Do you see advantages to being a woman?

MAE WEST

In lovemaking, men run down, but a woman can just go on. Men are a lot better off in life, but not better off than me. No man ever had a better life than I did.

I

[Indicating a picture of a monkey on the wall] Who is he?

MAE WEST

One of my best friends, Boogie. But that monkey isn't really my Boogie. He doesn't even look like him. Boogie never ate a grape without peeling it first, and he ate a lot of grapes. He was fastidious. That's where I got my line in *I'm No Angel.* You know, when I say to my maid, "Peel me a grape." I loved him. When I was at Paramount I had a dog. My dog loved me so much that when I left him at home, he followed me all the way to Paramount. Of course, I never had any trouble finding men to love me.

I

Perhaps it's more important and even more difficult to find someone *to* love.

MAE WEST

I miss George [Raft]. There was a thing between me and him after *Night After Night.* We stayed friends. That's a real man. I never liked sissies.

I

Who were the directors with whom you liked working?

MAE WEST

Leo McCarey was good, but I was really always the director. Nobody could tell me how to be me. George [Cukor] was the only director I ever wanted to work with. I never worked with him. He's the biggest and the greatest. There's still time.

I
He told me he went to see *The Drag* in New Jersey.
MAE WEST
The Drag was a landmark in treating homosexuality. I did a drag
ball in it that caused a sensation. People came from all over the
country. They paid scalpers as much as a hundred dollars for a
ticket.

The difference between the greatest directors and the ordinary director is that the greatest makes *you* create. It isn't that
he tells you exactly what you should do. That would cramp my
style. I wouldn't let them hurt my films. They're good pictures.
I'd rather watch myself than anyone else. I feel sorry for people
who aren't proud of what they do.
I
What do you think about as you're watching?
MAE WEST
It's just like I'm there in them, and then is now. I relive it every
time. There was never anyone like me. You know, the female
impersonators really like to do me. Some of them are pretty
good, but they never fool me.
I
They don't fool me either.
MAE WEST
I'm glad to hear you say that. I used to worry people would be
fooled and think it was me.
I
Only striking originality lends itself to imitation.
MAE WEST
They could only do that because I was an original. I didn't
understand then what films meant, every new generation redis-
covering you. When I first came out here, I didn't understand
how important Hollywood was going to be. I always held
Hollywood at arm's length—like a would-be lover you can't
exactly trust.
I
Do you find Hollywood greatly changed now?
MAE WEST
The star system's gone. I was a real star. The star is someone

who has a love affair with her audience. They want to know everything about you, but they can't because you have mystery and romance.

I

There is a delicate balance between access and magic.

MAE WEST

I didn't go out to restaurants and places as much as I might have liked to because who wants to pay money to see someone who's always there for free? These days they're telling every detail of the sex act. Well, I don't think people want to know everything about other people's love lives. I think the two-dimensional figure is more lovable. I think two-dimensional with illusion beats three-dimensional. Valentino had great star quality. When he died, thousands of women wept at his funeral. That's star quality. Now me, I fill a need. If everybody had the most stimulating sex life and the greatest romance, maybe they'd have been less interested in Mae West, and they wouldn't care so much about stars in films.

Garbo was a star, too. Garbo always conducted herself right. She was a real professional. I admired her. She didn't let other people make her live her life the way they wanted her to live it. She had style; she was her own person. She was the only star I wanted to meet I hadn't met, so George [Cukor] arranged for us to meet. He gave a dinner for me and invited her, and she wanted to meet me, too. I kissed her on the cheek. I felt like we knew each other because we were the biggest stars in the world. She didn't say much. She had a wonderful voice and was just the way I thought she would be.

I

Being a celebrity opens up a relatively closed world of famous and, one hopes, interesting people. Was there someone you wanted to meet whom you didn't meet?

MAE WEST

Amelia Earhart. I thought it would be fun to fly, and the sky was a man's world. She was never afraid and she was smart. Brains are an asset—if you hide them. Men think a gal with good lines is better than one with a good line. But if you've got some brains in reserve, people can't use you.

I

Did you feel that people used you?

MAE WEST

I did the using. Like we were talking about, a lot of women thought they were giving something away every time a man had some pleasure. I did it for my own pleasure. So why should I begrudge the man having some fun, too?

I

Are there any ways you feel you're different from the public image of Mae West?

MAE WEST

I'm glad you asked that. When people think you're funny, they start to laugh at everything you say. There was a lot of serious reflection in what I said. I hope you're going to show me that way. You know, my head was always working. And I was always writing.

I

I know you're especially proud of your writing.

MAE WEST

The secret of it is to keep everything moving. Don't let the audience think of the dishes. Once you lose an audience for a moment, it's so hard to get them back. You've gotta milk an audience. You need to have some lines they can take away and remember, like songs they go away humming. I'd have everything in my mind before I'd start to write, so I wouldn't have to stop. I'd imagine it all first, then I'd just write it down. I'd be living it while I was writing it. I never read much because I was too busy living.

Do you type or write longhand?

I

I write longhand.

MAE WEST

That's the only way I could do it. They offered to teach me to type when I was in prison. Did you know I was in prison?

I

Yes. But you weren't an ordinary prisoner.

MAE WEST

I was never an ordinary anything. I had to stand trial because of my show, *Sex.* They said I could pay the fine, but I decided it would be more interesting to go to prison. I was always fascinated by prisons and mental institutions. They told me I had to wear the prison clothes, but I said I was bringing my own underwear. I wore my silk underwear the whole time. It was ten days.

I wanted to help the girls there, but I couldn't do much. A lot of them had made just one mistake. They all wanted to meet me. They admired me, and they weren't jealous. What I wrote was ahead of its time, and I took other chances of going to jail with what I put on stage.

I

How do you feel about censorship?

MAE WEST

I *believe* in censorship! If a picture of mine didn't get an "X" rating, I'd be insulted. Don't forget, dear—I *invented* censorship. Imagine censors that wouldn't let you sit in a man's lap. I've been in more laps than a napkin! They'd get all bothered by a harmless little line like "Is that a gun in your pocket or are you just glad to see me?"

I had my tricks for handling the censors. I'd write some lines I knew they would take out so the others could stay in. You had to let them earn their money. You might say I created the Hays Office. They had to do it because of me. I'm a kind of godmother to the Motion Picture Code. Now they use nudity and talking dirty to take the place of a good story and good characters. I didn't have to take off my clothes. Men imagined what was under them.

I

A man's imagination is a woman's best friend.

MAE WEST

Do you know what question I'm asked the most? About the mirrors on my bedroom ceiling. I say, "I like to see how I'm doin'." I've never been able to sleep with anyone. I like to have my own bed. I need a lot of room. I don't know if the bed's made, but you can go look at my bedroom.

As in the living room, everything in the bedroom was white. The perfectly made bed was covered with a white satin spread. The mirrored vanity wore a white ruffled skirt and held a queen's ransom of crystal and silver perfume bottles, porcelain powder boxes, and pots of makeup. The white rug looked as if it had known only bare feet. The white drapes were drawn in secrecy. The room and its occupant of half a century were clearly symbiotic as well as sybaritic.

I returned to the living room.

MAE WEST
Did you like what you saw?

I
I did. I appreciate your inviting me to see it. It's one of the most famous bedrooms in the world.

MAE WEST
The most famous.

Are you gonna get a mirror on *your* ceiling? *[Not waiting for my answer]* But it isn't any good when you see your reflection alone. What did you think of my bed?

I
I thought what an interview *it* might give!

MAE WEST
I wish I could've shown you my beach house. But I sold it. I miss it. I had murals of naked men on the walls. Great art. Nudity in art isn't sex, it's art. I never lost any money in art or real estate. Real estate and diamonds, those are the best investments. I always put my money into my own projects, something I was doing or something I could see. Money is sexy for men, but people don't find it feminine for a woman to talk about it. So, you don't have to talk about it, just have it. The real security is yourself. You know you can do it, and they can't ever take that away from you.

I
Do you think money buys happiness?

MAE WEST
No, but money is a great love potion for an affair. It buys a good bed in a nice bedroom with clean linens and time to enjoy

it all. If you have money, you don't have to worry about it, and worrying spoils your looks.

Are you doing this whole book about me?

I

No, there are other people in it, too.

MAE WEST

I don't usually like to share. What are you calling your book?

I

Do you have a suggestion?

MAE WEST

[After thinking for a moment] You could call the book "Mae West and others." That's "others" with a small "o," and I want to be the first. Being first is important in life.

I

For you, what's the most important thing in life?

MAE WEST

Getting what you want. My career is everything. Always was. I never changed. Inside, I feel like the same little girl I was. But it was the way I grew up outside that men liked.

I

What else do you think men like in a woman besides physical beauty?

MAE WEST

That's what men care about, except in their wives. Men admire devotion in their wives, beauty in other women. What do you think?

I

It seems to me that for the world a woman is the way she looks, and a man is what he does.

MAE WEST

A man should take as good care of his body as a woman does. I liked physically strong men who could fight over me. I didn't incite them. They just did it and I couldn't stop them.

I

These men seem to be quite a lot like your father, as you've described him.

MAE WEST

I never thought about it, but it's true. I remember once a man looked the wrong way at my mother, and my father took care of him. My mother said, "You shouldn't have done that," but she was really pleased.

When my mother died, just living was hard, but going on-stage, that was terrible. Then when I was able to do it, working made it easier. *[Indicating the photo of her mother on the piano]* I didn't want her buried underground. I bought a family place above ground for her. I cried for days and couldn't stop crying. It was the only time I cried. They thought my heart was going to give out. It's the only time I was ever depressed. I always have too much to do to be depressed. I don't believe in depression. Wipe it out! You've got to replace a bad thought with a good one. Happiness is a habit, a good habit. People get depressed because they are bored. I don't get bored because I know how to go into the unknown. I can just sit here and go off into the world of my own thoughts. I could always make up a story. If I wanted to be anyone besides Mae West, I just wrote a story and played the part. I always liked Catherine the Great. She was great. Maybe I was her in another life. After my mother, I never needed another person.

I

Do you feel you deliberately tried not to need another person so you wouldn't feel such pain again?

MAE WEST

Yeah. I knew I couldn't go through that again. When I was a child, I could always talk things over with my mother. Even after she died, in my thoughts I'd be talking with her. I knew her so well that I knew what she'd tell me.

What have you got there?

I

A camera. I was hoping . . .

MAE WEST

I don't have my picture taken with other women. I never like to see myself in a picture, except surrounded by men. I only keep the best pictures of myself, you know. You should always keep the best picture of yourself in your own head. You should have beautiful pictures of yourself all around to look at. Throw away the bad ones. When you don't look your best, you shouldn't even look at yourself in the mirror. You should put on your most beautiful wrapper and all your makeup, and you should wear a wig if your hair doesn't look right. If you don't think you're wonderful, why should anyone else? You should look your best for yourself when you're alone.

I

Especially when you're alone.

MAE WEST

Yeah, you can't afford not to look good alone or you'll stay alone. I don't usually go on talking so much.

I

"Too much of a good thing can be wonderful."

Now that you aren't working as much, how is your life different?

MAE WEST

I'm lazier. I was always scribbling. Whenever I got an idea, in bed or in a restaurant, I'd write it down on a napkin or a little piece of paper. I saw you scribbling on that little bit of paper, and it reminded me of me.

You know, honey, I see something men must like about you: You're a brilliant listener!

I

It's easy. I've had a wonderful time.

MAE WEST

Do you know my idea of a wonderful time? Sex and chop suey.

I

Together?

MAE WEST

No, not at the same time. The chop suey tastes better after. Chop suey restaurants stay open late, and if they close, you can always go the next night. Chop suey, sex, and my career. My work was the most fun. Sex was second best. I didn't want it when I was working. I wanted to save my sexual energy to put into my work. You've gotta conserve your sex energy in order to do your work. It's the same energy. When I started to write or did a picture, I stopped all my sex activities. Sex divides your mind.

The sex drive is behind everything creative we do. The stronger the sex drive, the stronger the desire to create. When an architect designs a building, he puts his sex drive into creating that building. People who want one thing more want everything more. It's part of the same drive. But there are moments to slow down. I don't like a man that's in a hurry. "I like a guy what takes his time."

I

Perhaps men could be divided into two kinds—those who take their watches off, and those who leave them on.

MAE WEST

Say—I like that. You know, maybe you *could* learn, honey. *[I gather up my things to leave]*

Don't forget your baby oil. But remember what I told you: It's gotta be warm, and you've gotta have a man put it on—all over.

Mae apologized for not being able to drive me to my hotel. "Paul could've given you a lift, but we don't have the Dusenberg anymore."

I said I understood.

Just as I was leaving, she called me back.

"Honey, there's something I want to tell you before you go," she said, reaching out and clutching my arm. "You know, my diamonds I told you all those men gave me? I wanted you to know —I bought some of them myself."

Part II

GETTING
THERE

"You have to go to all the bullfights"

PABLO PICASSO

DRIVE, NO MATTER how intense the desire, how fervent the longing, is only the beginning. Being able to direct that drive toward the realization of a goal is what is difficult. All of the exceptional people who spoke with me regarded themselves as privileged to be able to spend their lives doing what they loved to do, that special work which was for them the ultimate seduction. "Getting to play," Laurence Olivier called it. "It's only when you actually get to do something that you can go on improving."

Talent, even more than drive, would seem to be the most essential qualification for "getting to play." Billy Wilder told me, "I believe if you have talent, the world will find you. Edvard Munch didn't have to go to the Sidney Janis Gallery for a cocktail party."

While the significance of talent or ability cannot be underestimated, I have come to believe that there is yet another factor of the greatest importance. It is confidence.

There is an extraordinary relationship between confidence and success. Confidence allows one to try in the first place and to keep on trying even with little or no encouragement. Success of any kind reinforces confidence, enabling one to continue trying longer.

I have also come to believe that the correlation between confidence and ability is considerably less than might be assumed. Confidence seems to exist almost as a separate entity. Some of the most talented people I have ever met seemed the least confident. With every reason in the world to be perfectly confident, even those of brilliant achievement still expressed some self-doubts.

"Every time I dance before an audience," Margot Fonteyn told me, "I always feel as if I am dancing on a tightrope. No matter how many times I have done it before, I never lose that feeling."

The amount of confidence in the same person varies at different times, confidence not being constant. My own observation based on meeting many famous and successful people is that no one is totally confident. There is no such thing as perfect confidence.

As much as anyone, Picasso in his nineties projected an *ethos* of perfect confidence. "Have you always really felt that way?" I asked him.

"Yes," Picasso answered without hesitation. This confidence, however, did not extend to everything in his life, and he qualified his response. "With women, for example, I did not have perfect confidence."

The quality that Picasso liked most in a woman was devotion to him. In art, he told me, he did not mind being compared to any artist who had ever lived or who might ever live, but as a man, he never liked to think of a woman comparing him to any other man.

While Picasso was showing me some of his own work in his personal collection, we passed an unfinished painting propped against the wall in a corner. Going back, he took another look at it and appeared disgusted. Annoyed, he muttered, "I never could get it. It always eluded me." Even Picasso wasn't perfect, and even Picasso knew it.

Since I usually met the famous after they had become famous, I have often wondered what they were like when they were young, or before they achieved recognition. Picasso was already one of the most famous people in the world when Virgil Thomson knew him but he was less exalted than he was later to become. At lunch with Virgil Thomson, I seized the moment to ask about Picasso's confidence in order to determine whether it was as monumental as Picasso himself had indicated to me near the end of his life.

This was obviously not a winning topic for Virgil Thomson, who had grown tired of the subject. "Hasn't there already been enough said about that man?" he said, almost in a scolding tone. "Picasso was no fun at all. He was a serious person who just worked and worried. Like Joyce."

The gift of talent is not necessarily the gift of knowing how to find one's way to success. Not everyone with talent reaches his goal. Finding one's way to success may be quite a different aptitude from the ability to do the job once one gets there. Doing a good job is not necessarily, as Hubert Humphrey expressed it, "bankable." He told me he thought this was a basic problem in politics:

"The people best qualified to do the job are not necessarily the ones most able to get themselves noticed or best able to get the financial backing and other kinds of necessary support. In fact, it's often just the opposite."

He added that *appearing* confident was essential in politics:

"People don't really want you to share your doubts with them. They want to believe that someone knows the answers. Indecision is taken as a sign of weakness, and it's important that it not show. Often the more arrogant person or the one who is foolish enough to see a simple answer may look better to an audience.

"I was never good at conveying that image of certainty. I always saw too many sides to a thing. I couldn't believe in a 'sure' thing, just high probabilities. But once you have assumed the responsibility for decisionmaking and you allow your own hesitancy to creep through, that very insinuation of uncertainty may sabotage whatever chances the project has for success.

"When an important decision has to be made, you must vote one way or the other. It may be a choice you felt fifty-one percent in favor of, but in the history books you have gone on record with a one hundred percent decision."

The celebrity can seldom afford the luxury of sharing his own doubts, if indeed that is a luxury. Marvin Hamlisch said that whenever someone asked him if he could do something, they never wanted him to show any lack of confidence. "Even if you're not sure you can do it, you don't want to be too forthright and honest. They don't want to hear, 'Maybe, I think I can.' You have to reassure them. They want you to assume all the responsibility. So you say as confidently as you can manage, 'Sure, I can do it.' You've gotta say it sort of offhand. That's important. Then you go home and you find it's true—you *can* do it. You've gotta have chutzpah.

"My mother gave me some advice when I was very young, and I

never forgot it. I'd like to pass it on to you: 'You've gotta have elbows.' "

Edith Head told me, "Bette Davis never stopped to take that last look in the mirror. She didn't have that lack of confidence. She knew whatever had to be done had to be done before that last look."

Bette Davis herself disagreed. "I was thought to be someone of perfect confidence. It was just because I was outspoken. Being outspoken has come to be equated with intelligence. It's often really just foolishness."

I asked Picasso what, after natural talent, he considered to be his most important quality, the one that most directly led to his success. He responded that it was only my assumption that talent was first in importance. He said he believed that confidence was his own most valuable quality, and that talent was second in importance. Early success, he said, enhanced his confidence and allowed him to develop his talent. He credited the encouragement first of his parents and then of his teachers as essential in the development of his confidence. It allowed him to go on experimenting even after he was successful.

"We all start out in life imitating others," he said. "What matters is growing beyond that. With only talent, you may be merely the best copyist." Confidence freed him first from just imitating others and later from imitating himself. He added that success could limit people because success encouraged them to go on repeating themselves.

From that first slap received on the back by the newborn, life is a series of assaults on one's confidence. Picasso believed that those who really need encouragement should not enter into a competition where the odds against success are excessively great:

"I am asked if I would advise my children to be artists. My answer is no. To the contrary. I would advise them *not* to be. Then if they went on, I would be glad for them and hope for the best. But if they did not go on and were so easily discouraged, there would be little chance that they would be able to work with the necessary confidence. They would have to be the ones who felt that they *must* be artists."

Finding that one can overcome adversity can inspire confidence. For Lillian Gish it was a positive advantage:

"The most valuable gift I ever received was from my father, who gave me the gift of insecurity. My mother gave Dorothy and me love. She made all our dresses. My father left us. My mother's love might not have prepared me for life the way my father's departure did. He forced us out on to the road where we had to earn our bread."

Perhaps the most significant disadvantage in sharing one's self-doubts with other people is not that they will lose confidence in you, but that you will lose confidence in yourself. Telling something to someone reinforces it, making it seem true even when it isn't. Every time you tell your self-doubts to someone else, you are telling them to yourself.

Recognition of and for one's accomplishment is obviously a prime motivation toward success, and upon it confidence is built. It is not possible to determine how great a factor the quest for recognition is, but probably less would be done in this world if no one were going to know about it. There is certainly less satisfaction in cooking an elaborate meal and serving it by candlelight to yourself.

Lee Strasberg theorized about those who receive early acclaim and have a headstart because that enhancement of their self-esteem is invaluable in giving them the necessary confidence. If, however, something went wrong and they lost that gift, he believed that they were worse off than others because they had grown dependent on it. They had the most difficult time searching to recapture an early recognition which might then always elude them.

"An early specific genius for something like mathematics shows you the way to go," he said. "It's a straight course; that person is praised. He develops his potential. If he doesn't choose that field and develop that capacity, it may be a life of frustration if he can't find that recognition again."

I remember Charlie Chaplin commenting on "the difficulties in life and the dissipation of genius if you have too many ways to go, too many talents." It is not a serious problem for most of us, and I remember thinking at the time that it was better than not having any choices at all.

There are two kinds of people who display perfect confidence: The foolish can have it because it is easier for those who are ignorant of their own ignorance. Then there are those with apparent perfect confidence who only exhibit what seems to be perfect confidence in order to persuade others.

Sometimes the image projected is not what the person himself is feeling. Otto Preminger's public self was well known for its swagger, but the private self had more in common with the person who feels compelled to go back and make certain he has locked his door or turned off the stove. He expressed it this way for me:

"I have never walked out on a stage without feeling my fly was open, no matter how many times I had checked it. I always had to resist the impulse to reach down and check it again."

Confidence allows you to dare. You don't impose limitations on yourself. Belief that what you do has a good chance for success is essential. Sometimes we believe that a goal is beyond our ability to attain, and our belief makes it a self-fulfilling prophesy. René Clair told me about his "impossible dream" that remained impossible because he believed it to be so:

"In life there are those happenings that don't happen, those I lament. They are the what-might-have-been-if-only meetings. Fate is the greatest practical joker.

"I was always a Marx Brothers fan. When I saw their early films, I dreamed of directing them. It looked like such fun, working with these funny men. But I knew all of the reasons why it couldn't be. Knowing so many reasons was a handicap I did not overcome. How could I even contact them? I was in Paris, and Hollywood was very far away. They would have agents, lawyers, secretaries, a wall of employees there just to keep people away. They were probably committed years in advance. Had they even heard of me? I was certain that the answer was no. So I saved the stationery and the stamp.

"A decade later when I was in Hollywood, I came to know Groucho and Harpo. Groucho said, 'What a shame we never got to work with you. It was a dream for us. There wasn't anyone we wanted more. We looked for you when we went to Paris, but it was August and you were out of Paris for the summer holidays.' They dreamed of working with me at exactly the same time I dreamed of working with them."

Seeing what can go wrong may be a deterrent to confidence, but there are advantages as well as disadvantages to imagining in advance all possibilities, both the positive and the negative. There are advantages to constructive worrying:

During a visit to his Paris home, I asked Roger Vadim about a painting. The picture, which had been painted by Vadim, resembled a Hieronymus Bosch in modern dress.

"That is supposed to represent an optimistic vision of the end of the world," he explained. "There, in front of that house, is a big broken egg, and in this egg is a river and a garden and a young naked girl who is laughing and looking at the bombed town outside. The sky outside the egg is completely polluted and the town is destroyed, but you don't know if it's been destroyed by pollution or bombs. The people there have lost their heads, and there's nothing left of them but their arms and legs. And this giant egg that has arrived on earth is the hope for new life. Then, they break the egg and there is nothing hopeful inside."

Because he was shooting a film during the day, we would always talk through the night, and the painting seemed even more eerie to me than it might have in daylight.

"Why is that hopeful?" I asked.

"It's optimistic because it will help people to think," he said, "and the moment you think about what you are doing, then you can change or do better. People think that being optimistic is being sure that everything will be all right tomorrow. That is really very pessimistic because if you're sure that everything will be all right, you'll just wait, and then you'll get it, man! I think I have an optimistic view of the world because if people become aware in time of what they are doing wrong, then things can be changed."

Persistence is a result of confidence, hope, and energy. As lack of confidence and disappointment drain energy, hope and encouragement sustain energy. With characteristic verve, George Cukor described his philosophy of directing and of life:

"Mrs. August Belmont once said to me, 'Riding on a private railroad car is a taste that does not have to be acquired.' Money is cheerful, indeed, and one grows accustomed to having it, but I happen to work because I like working. Deliver the goods. That's the important thing. Success can't be a favor.

"But there are two things you have to have. I always have high hopes. You can't work without high hopes, my dear. The other thing is, don't let a kick in the ass stop you. It's how you cope that says what you are. I was put off the biggest picture ever made, and I'm here to tell the tale.

"I shot *Gone With the Wind* for two or three weeks. I never knew why I was fired. When it happened, I just coached Olivia [De Havilland] in my home, and she said to me, 'Poor Vivien [Leigh]. It's not fair to her that I'm getting all of this extra help.' I said, 'Don't worry. She's been coming here, too.'

"We've all had a kick in the ass. If it changes you, that's when you're done in. Guts and pride, that's what you have to have.

"It's a terrible feeling when you start something with high hopes and, before you finish, you have the feeling it isn't going to turn out the way you thought. It's like whipping a carrousel horse. But you have to go through with it. You can't have any successes unless you can accept failure. When it goes wrong, you feel like cutting your throat, but you go on. You don't let anything get you down so much that it beats you or stops you. I know what it's like to make a floperoo. I made one even with Kate Hepburn. After we saw it, we went to Pandro Berman, and we said, 'We'll make a picture for you free if you don't release this one.' You feel you can't face the world, but you have to push yourself. After your mother dies, no one cares that much, so get on with it.

"I'm Hungarian, you know. Hungarians are very driven. Adolph Zukor used to go back to Hungary, and all of the directors there would try to win him so they could come to America. You know, Hungarians are terribly clever, and they will try anything. This story may not be true, but it could be. That's what's important.

"There were two leading rivals who wanted to win Zukor. One

of the directors who thought he was full of beans decided to take Zukor to the grave of Zukor's mother. He bought the biggest bouquet in the city, and got a driver and a car, and they went to the cemetery. When they arrived at the grave, they found the other director already there, collapsed over the tombstone, and weeping so hysterically that his tears watered the ground."

When George Cukor finished speaking, he showed me the handsome portrait puppets of Spencer Tracy and Katharine Hepburn which hung in the hall that led to his study. They were created for a film, for stardom, an idea that long ago ended up on the cutting-room floor. Their moment never came. They are still waiting for stardom, for the film to be made that can never be made. But they wait. Talent and opportunity do not always find each other.

How long one can persevere without encouragement influences the possibility for eventual success. Even discouragement can be more stimulating than total neglect. Less persistence requires luckier timing. Those who are stopped more easily by discouragement or neglect need to have their good luck come sooner. Some success along the way increases one's resistance to disillusionment.

King Vidor worked for several years as a maker of short subjects in his native Galveston. Then he went to Hollywood, where he was eventually rewarded with a few assignments—but only as a director of shorts. "And that's not what I wanted to do. I wanted to make feature-length films, and the studios were only hiring directors with feature experience. Well, how do you get to do something if the qualification for doing it is you've already done it? How do you get experience if all opportunities for experience are closed to those without experience? You have to be persistent, confident, and lucky."

Visiting some acting classes in New York and Los Angeles with George Cukor, I noticed that he never discouraged anyone no matter how terrible the performance. He said that they hadn't had enough encouragement yet to be able to withstand discouragement.

"You never know who is going to succeed. I never discourage

anyone because they may not have been good that day. Another day they might be better. I don't feel qualified to judge them for a lifetime because of one poor performance. And, anyway, you never know what you'll be remembered for in life. In my case, it may be Nancy Reagan's screen test." He laughed. "Spencer Tracy was a close friend of her father's, and he called and asked me to do him the favor."

Charlie Chaplin told me that young optimism is fragile and must be protected from discouragement:

"Anyone who takes away hope from the young is a murderer. It is a sin to impart your own disillusionments, to share your disappointments, and to rob them of an openness to life which is the chief blessing of the young. Age shares its bad experiences, using the excuse that they are sparing the young pain, when what could be more painful than not discovering life for yourself? You cannot go to the dentist for your children. You can only make them more fearful of the experience. Everyone has the right to earn his own disillusionment."

The people I saw were seduced by their work rather than by its financial reward, but they did recognize that the price their work brought signified more than mere economic security. Achievement was measured by acclaim, not by money, but money did provide a concrete manifestation of the world's judgment. Money also bought time and the freedom of choice that allowed the person to go on doing his unique work.

"When the world tells you of your own greatness, it is not difficult to hear and believe," Picasso told me. "But nothing gives you more confidence in life than to have what you do be worth a lot of money. Money is very reassuring—not just having it, but knowing that you can earn it. When people pay their money for your work, you know that they mean all the encouraging words. Money is a wonderful inspiration. It is encouraging to see your value rise."

An early advantage is enjoyed by those in whom confidence is instilled by a parent or other influential person who is able to pass on a vision of accomplishment along with accumulated wisdom and knowledge. This kind of influence can last a lifetime.

Several of the famous people who spoke with me referred to conversations they carried on in their heads with persons no longer present who had at one time been important in their lives.

"I would stand back from one of my paintings," Picasso said, "and long after the death of my parents, I would see in the eye within my mind a look of concern and the slight approval on my father's face and the warm look of pleasure on my mother's. I would paint for them, and I could see their reactions in my head." Picasso's father, José Ruiz Blasco, had taken the first steps toward realizing in miniature the dream of worldwide acclaim his son would later achieve.

There was a story I had heard many times in reference to Picasso and his father. As a boy he was supposed to have drawn something which so far surpassed his father's talent that the elder Picasso handed Pablo his own palette and never painted again. I asked Picasso if the story was true. He said no, but he thought it was a good story.

Though Otto Preminger's father was not involved in the world of theater or films, he provided his son with every educational and cultural advantage, and encouraged him in whatever he did. "Whenever I had a problem," Preminger said, "I talked it over with my father, even after he died. I knew so well the way he thought that I could tell him in my head what was troubling me, and he would answer."

Even early disapproval can be encouraging if it is not taken too seriously. Sometimes it is better than being ignored.

Chagall told me that he never drew a picture of a naked woman that he didn't think of his mother, remembering how shocked she was that day in Vitebsk when he was a boy, and she saw for the first time a drawing he had made of a naked woman.

Elliott Gould admitted that occasionally he found himself having to say in his head, "Be quiet, Mother!"

Sometimes the early inspiration that persists in memory was provided by someone who was oblivious to his or her role. Picasso remembered a girl whom he had once wanted to impress:

"There was a girl I met when I was very young. She was just a few years older than I was. She seemed the most beautiful girl I had ever seen, and I wanted her. At night I dreamed about her, but she did not pay any attention to me, except in my dreams. I was too young. When I was in my fifties, I painted something of which I was very proud, and in my head I showed it to her. She was thrilled—in my head, that is. She was sorry she hadn't noticed me before. Of course, by that time I had not seen her for years, and she was probably in her sixties. It was only in my mind that she was forever young and that I still cared."

Having friends who are doing the same thing helps one get through the hard times. "It's easier and pleasanter not to be all alone in the lifeboat" was the way Laurence Olivier put it. I remember when Barbra Streisand told Groucho how she envied the Marx Brothers because they didn't have to go out and perform alone.

Eubie Blake believed that every successful person has visible or invisible people in his or her life who offer necessary encouragement and help. "I was lucky to find the right people early in my life," he told me. "You can't do anything alone; you've gotta get together with other people. I was sixty-one years with Sissle. He took responsibility for contracts, money, minor decisions—everything I didn't want to do. My wife, Avis, handled the house perfectly, and she held up through neglect. She didn't get too bored and lonely.

"I had a show that failed when I was seventy. I ain't sayin' that it made me feel good; but it didn't hurt like it could have hurt earlier."

"The strongest bond is troubles," Lillian Gish told me. "When you go through troubles together, it's a bond that's never broken. My mother and Dorothy and I shared all the early hard times. When you lose those people, new friends can't ever share those memories with you."

Early success nurtures enthusiasm and shelters innocence, but even legends enjoy assurance and reassurance. George Cukor on his way to the 1982 Venice Film Festival explained his reason for going there: "We're all hungry and praise is so nourishing."

It is often said that at the top there are not many helping hands, but that is not necessarily true. Wilfrid Hyde-White told me about a time when George Cukor extended such a helping hand:

"I had an English friend from school days who wanted to be an actor. His name was Rex Evans. He played the piano rather well, but he didn't care at all about that. He just wanted to be an actor, so he asked his friends if they knew anyone who could possibly help. They all wrote letters, but only one answer came back. It was from George Cukor in America.

"When my friend went to Hollywood, he called George, who invited him to dinner at his house. He told George about his hopes and dreams. George said he had a very small part in a film he happened to be directing that my friend might do if he wanted. My friend said, 'Oh, yes!' George said, 'Wouldn't you like to think a little about it?' My friend said, 'Oh, no, not at all.' 'Well,' George said, 'you'll be getting a call from wardrobe.'

"My friend never left his phone. He almost starved to death. He couldn't go out to the grocer. He was so afraid of missing that call.

"Well, finally the call came. He went to the studio and had his fittings. He was told, 'We'll call you when we're ready.'

"So he went home and waited. He got plenty of groceries, lots of tinned things on the way home. After a few weeks, the food was gone, and he was about to starve to death when the phone rang. It was his call.

"He went to the set. Robert Taylor was there in the drawing room. George directed my friend. He showed him very carefully the business he was to do as he sat on the sofa, and just exactly how he should rise and go to the mantel of the fireplace and stand there before he made his exit.

"Well, Garbo arrived for her part. Her acting was always so apparently effortless as though she didn't have to study and memorize her lines the way other people did. They just came upon her and became part of her. I think that was the secret of her beauty, her graceful movement; it all seemed effortless.

"Garbo made her entrance. My friend had risen from the sofa, gone to the mantel and left.

"Garbo said, 'I don't remember him in the script. George, why was he there? What part is he playing?'

"And George said, 'He's playing the part of a friend of mine who needs a job.' "

A common characteristic of the uncommon people who spoke with me was intense concentration on their work. Luciano Pavarotti would walk through the lobby of his New York hotel on the day of a performance, oblivious to everything, get into the elevator, and never push the button. Whenever we got into the elevator together and *I* had to push the button, I knew that it was *La Bohème* or *Trovatore* that night.

"Concentration is everything," Pavarotti explained. "On the day I'm performing, I don't hear anything anyone says to me."

Dame Judith Anderson stressed the commitment and dedication of the professional. She told me about an incident which took place while she was working on Alfred Hitchcock's *Rebecca* with Laurence Olivier and a very young Joan Fontaine:

"Joan came up to me and said, 'Slap me!' I just looked at her. She said, 'Please slap me hard. Really. I need it—for the part.' I just told her to go find someone else to slap her.

"So she went up to Hitch. I saw her say something to him. Then he just hauled back and slapped her, hard. She reeled back and staggered out in front of the camera, looking fragile, hurt, as though her eyes were just about to well up with tears. She was in the perfect mood for the next scene she had to play."

A high level of energy is one of the most important elements in achievement, but it must be channeled constructively or it dissipates itself. Knowing where to direct one's energies is just as important as the energy itself—maybe even more important. Nothing is more tiring than disappointment and frustration.

Conversely, success is exhilarating and can provide extra energy. Chagall told me that he felt energy level rises to meet need, and that there is nothing which gives a greater transfusion of energy than that which comes from doing what you want to do, excelling in it, and being acclaimed for it.

"Enthusiasm is life," Paul Scofield told me in his dressing room in London just after a performance of *Amadeus*. "I think I'm the most fortunate person in the world because I do just what I want to do, and I get paid for it. If my own enthusiasm ever flags or I get tired commuting from the country, there's a new audience every night to recharge my batteries."

King Vidor, who was originally to have directed the film about Charles Lindbergh, told me that *The Spirit of St. Louis* had a serious flaw:

"At one point in the film Lindbergh is seen getting tired and fighting his exhaustion. Well, I remember him telling me, 'You don't get tired. It's the greatest shot of adrenaline to be doing what you've wanted to do so badly. You almost feel like you could fly without the plane. It would be impossible to get tired while it's happening, you're so keyed up. There's no way to tell someone who didn't feel it what that kind of exhilaration feels like.' "

Chicken Little is alive and well. She is the standard-bearer for all of those who have guaranteed their own lack of success by allowing fear to inhibit action. Knowing the sky is falling may not be useful information even when it is, and certainly not when it isn't. Chicken Little, however, has the fear of her convictions.

Often people seem to cut themselves off from any chance of success, big or little, because they are afraid to risk failure. "Nothing ventured, nothing gained" becomes "Nothing ventured, nothing lost." If you try, you may fail, but if you don't try, you *have* failed. When I first told Woody Allen I was going to write a book, he said, "It's a dangerous thing to do. If you don't try, you can always be happy believing you would have been successful if you had tried."

Eubie Blake told me that he never had stage fright, and he was never afraid to try anything. "If you've got a lot to lose, you're taking a risk. I'm a Jones, and a Jones ain't got nothin' to lose."

Laurence Olivier said that he wished he could have given himself certain advice years ago, not because he would have behaved differently, but because he could have *felt* differently:

"Don't waste your time striving for perfection. Nobody will notice when you achieve it. Maybe you won't notice it yourself, and striving for perfection is the greatest stopper there is. If you do, you'll be afraid you can't achieve it, and if you achieve it, you'll be afraid you can't achieve it again. It's your excuse to yourself for not doing anything. Instead, strive for excellence, doing your best.

"Don't let your own high standards trip you up. You have to do your best, but you only find that out through doing. It's through doing that you learn, and learning is very stimulating. As you work, you discover yourself, and your best gets better.

"It's difficult to explain to people who don't feel subtle differences. They say to me, 'You were Jewish in *The Boys from Brazil,* and you're Jewish in *The Jazz Singer.'* But I wasn't just Jewish in *The Boys from Brazil.* I was a Viennese Jew. That was important, but they didn't notice that. Now, in *The Jazz Singer,* I'm the rabbi and I'm Polish. It's quite a difference."

People often say no to themselves because they are afraid to risk someone else saying no to them. In doing so, they set their own limitations. Receiving a no is not very different from not having asked at all, unless of course it stops you from asking the next time.

Marvin Hamlisch described how he consoled himself when a no came into his life:

"You have to be able to take getting a no. You don't have to like it, but you have to be able to survive it. You can't get anywhere unless you're willing to face that big NO. The trick is to find a way to console yourself.

"Now, it's not the same for everyone. You've gotta find your own. When I need to distract myself, I go to Sedutto's for ice cream. Sedutto's is better than sex. When a girl says no to me, I go right to Sedutto's for chocolate ice cream."

I asked him if he gets much chocolate ice cream, and Marvin responded, "I'm sorry you asked. Yeah. Quite a bit."

Every failed dream, every rejection takes its toll on enthusiasm, making it harder to try again, undermining the next effort. Almost any obstacle is more readily surmountable than our own emotions. We live so much of our lives in our own minds, and no one can work so effectively against us as we can against ourselves. The ability of others to discourage us or stop us is limited or enhanced by the power we give them in our own minds.

It has been said that a pessimist is someone who is better informed and more experienced than an optimist. Not knowing all of the possibilities for failure is a kind of blessing. Fear of failing causes one to find excuses for not trying. Everyone is handicapped in life by being told what they can't do—and believing it. If you don't know you can't do something, that may be an advantage. Very often, what people tell you *you* can't do is merely what *they* can't do, and sometimes the most valuable advice is the advice you don't take.

Billy Wilder told me no one should listen to anyone else, especially to him, about the basic decisions that determine one's whole life. "Trust your own instinct. Your mistakes might as well be your own instead of someone else's.

"In Berlin I remember being asked my advice by someone who wanted to leave his wonderful job, where he made a lot of money and knew all the beautiful women, to write a novel. I laughed. I advised him to stay where he was well off, that the gamble was too big, and how did he know he could do it?

"So he quit, and Erich Maria Remarque wrote *All Quiet on the Western Front.*"

Jacques Tati risked all, including his own money, to make *Playtime.* He gained a film but lost his house to the bank, proving himself vastly more proficient at the "show" than the "business" of show business. We talked about the risk of public and private mortification.

"You have to believe in yourself before you can expect anyone else to believe in you," he said. For him the purpose of art was not to make money, but money was for creating art. When there was not enough money available from other sources to make his film *Playtime,* Tati took the risk personally, mortgaging not only his home but his possessions. Many would say it was a gamble lost. Though he did make the film, he lost not only his money and his house, but also most of his personal possessions. Even proper distribution for the film was never achieved.

He showed me his last important personal possession, one that the banks had seen fit to allow him to keep: a painting of a Russian coachman by his grandfather, Count Tatischev, painted toward the end of the nineteenth century. The coachman had a look of pride and resilience, not unlike that which Tati himself had evinced.

Tati's greatest tragedy was that the economic failure of *Playtime* caused French backers to be even warier of anything else he did.

They saw him as noncommercial, making it impossible for him to raise the money for other films he wanted to do and cutting him off from the work which gave meaning to his life. It also meant that he had to face his wife and children with a financial failure that was his, but for which they, too, had to pay the price; and that for him was the most terrible part.

"People ask me, would I prefer popular success or artistic success? Would I prefer to make wide-appeal pictures for a large audience? It is a silly question. What difference does it make which I prefer to do? I can only do what I do and work to do it the best I can. There is no sure formula, or everyone would do that, and then there would be only successes, or no successes, depending on your perspective.

"If what I do coincides with what a lot of people would like to see, then I live in a big house, my telephone is one continuous ring, and everyone wants me to come to their dinner parties and make big talk, and people put money behind their compliments and want to back my next picture. If only a few people come to my picture, and the critics say I'm a genius, and if it doesn't lose too much money, I'm invited to some cocktail parties for small talk. If nobody comes to my picture and nobody likes what I do, there isn't even a 'Hi, Jack.' You don't choose success; it chooses you."

Life is a series of choices. Often the choices we live out are really the choices of others, and we are, in effect, playing parts in a scenario that has been written for us by tradition, custom, convention, and the values of others. Liv Ullmann described it as "a kind of secondhand life." One of the problems is that frequently the important choices are made too early, so that future choices are made within the confines of those early commitments. Sometimes we may not realize how many choices we have, particularly when none of the choices is ideal or desirable; but even among undesirable choices there are still choices, one of which may be preferable to the others.

"I used to say, 'I did it because I had no choice,' " Liv told me. "Only long afterwards did I realize that at the time I had many alternatives if I had seen them. Recently I came to fully comprehend the importance of making one's own choices. Then one truly has freedom."

"And what did you do with your newfound freedom?" I asked.

Liv hesitated for a moment, then said, smiling, "I cut my hair."

We were at Lutèce, about to have lunch, and André Soltener appeared to enumerate and explain the specialties of the day. Liv momentarily contemplated the possibilities, then said to Chef Soltener, "Oh, you choose for me."

Picasso represented someone greedy for life. "You have to be willing to waste some effort," he advised me, in talking about bullfights and life.

"If you want to see a great bullfight, you have to go to all the bullfights. No one can pick out just the great ones. I was a person who never wanted to miss anything in life."

Being prepared is an important element of success. Lee Strasberg stood at the wooden counter of his book-filled kitchen while we ate curry and listened to Bjoerling sing in *Turandot* and said, "Preparing for the moment is all anyone can do. There is nothing sadder than getting the opportunity without being ready for it." He believed that you can't make your moment; you can only be ready for it when it happens. "Jean Seberg was given this great opportunity by Preminger, but she wasn't ready. It would have made someone else, but it only hurt her."

I was at lunch with Vladimir Zworykin in his Princeton home when he slipped the choicest morsel on his plate to his dog, "Lucky."

"He certainly is," I said. "Lucky, I mean."

Responding in a philosophic tone, the inventor of television carried my particular to the general, saying, "Luck is knowing how."

Some months later in Houston, Texas, I was with heart surgeon Denton Cooley, of whom Dr. Christiaan Barnard had said, "He has the greatest natural talent of any surgeon in the world." Dr. Cooley remarked, "I find I'm luckier when I work harder."

Hubert Humphrey told me, "All you can do is prepare yourself as best you can for the moment when it comes, then you have to be in play so you and your opportunity have a chance to find each other. There are many people who could have performed with greatness who never found their moment of greatness."

I told Alan Shepard, who had indeed found his moment of greatness, what Eubie Blake had said to me about the astronauts: "They have hearts bigger than other people."

"Heroism is largely opportunity," Alan Shepard responded. "Everything now takes more people to do than it used to. You really should be talking with Wernher von Braun. It was *his* dream. What I did was nothing. I never felt safer than when I was going into space. I knew they had done everything. Millions of people would have volunteered to do what I did if they'd been given the opportunity. I was lucky to be the one who got to do it. Most people never act heroically just because they don't get the chance to."

Luck was invariably mentioned as a prime factor in success, though not everyone believed in it to the extent Eubie Blake did with his admonition "You can't duck your luck. It will find you out." He went on to define luck: "Luck is getting to do what you love to do. I spent my life doin' what I love. That's really lucky."

Luck cannot always be judged good or bad at the moment it occurs. Sometimes "bad" luck has to be redefined, as King Vidor discovered:

"My luck was my father not striking oil. He was there in Texas at just the right time for it. And he was just the person to do it. He was kind of a business speculator—not exactly a gambler, but always looking for something, always finding some fortune-making scheme. They all sounded pretty good; things like certain trees in the Dominican Republic for the wood, but something always went wrong with the plan. If he'd stayed closer to home, he might have struck oil, and we'd have been rich. I'd never have set out for Hollywood with my camera, and I'd have had a lot less interesting life."

King Vidor happened to be telling me this at the 1981 Directors' Guild Awards dinner. Sid Sheinberg, president of MCA, was sitting at the table with us and heard King's tale of luck. Then he told his own story about the kind of luck over which none of us has any control:

"When I'm in New York, I never walk on the hotel side of

Central Park South anymore. A few years ago I was coming out of the St. Moritz Hotel, and the body of a man came plummeting down from the roof and fell right in front of me. As he fell, I felt him brush my clothes. Another few inches and I would have been finished, too. Someone who was with me said something, and I didn't quite hear him. I turned and said, 'What?' That second's hesitation was what saved me. I haven't walked on that side of the street since."

One can't really do much to get in the way of, or rather, *out* of the way of this kind of luck.

On another occasion, King continued his story of good luck disguised as bad:

"When I was very young, I tried selling used cars in east Texas. It didn't last long. I guess that was my good luck too, that I didn't show more promise at it, or I might have been an automobile dealer in Texas. But I don't really think so. More and more, I believe each one of us has something he's meant to do. You know, the movies and I were born about the same time. I've always felt it was my destiny. I couldn't have escaped it. You have a destiny in life, and luck is finding that destiny. Some people are unlucky and don't find their destiny.

"When I was five years old, I lived through a hurricane. I was in Galveston and ten thousand people died. You have to be lucky just to be alive. It's my most vivid early memory. All of what most impressed me in my life have been visual impressions.

"In a long life you aren't lucky just once. When I was making *War and Peace* for Dino de Laurentiis, De Laurentiis decided *he* was really running the picture. He kept getting me to make little concessions here and there. Each was small, but the sum total was that all these little things put together were changing the film I was making just as surely as if it had been one major decision. The difference was that on what seemed a major decision, I would have stood my ground, but I allowed his chipping away. It was always for the same reason—saving money. A few lire here and there. Finally, I'd planned to put 5,000 extras as soldiers into a small valley so they'd look like more. He said, 'Use fewer extras and get a smaller valley.' But there weren't any smaller valleys around!

"We'd agreed that when I left Italy, I'd go by the United States Line. I always take the American ships if I possibly can. Well, De Laurentiis said, 'I've got you the greatest suite—on the Italian line.' That did it. That was the straw. I'd had it. I knew what he really meant was he'd made some deal to save a few lire.

"Well, there was this rage that had been building up in me during two years of working with him that I should have let out before, but we're taught not to act that way. So I took a stand with the force I should have taken right from the beginning. The reservation on the Italian line was canceled, and I took the U.S. ship. Just before we got in we heard the word: The *Andrea Doria,* the ship I was supposed to have been on, had just gone down.

"You know—if he had given in on the film, I would have given in on the ticket!"

Waiting with me in the Philadelphia TV studios before we appeared on the Mike Douglas show, Bob Hope threw a few punches at a nonexistent opponent and said, "I was lucky I wasn't a better boxer, or that's what I'd be now—a punchy ex-pug.

"Being a comedian is a lot like being a prizefighter. You've gotta always be alert. It's a mental battle. You try to get your best jabs in before the end of the round." He threw a couple of punches as he spoke.

Sometimes what might have been called bad luck was converted into an advantage by the individual. I was at the apartment of Lee and Anna Strasberg during a visit by Golda Meir when the conversation turned to a play about the Israeli prime minister in which Anna might play the title role.

"You're too pretty to play me," Golda Meir said to Anna. "Myself, I was never a beauty. There was a time when I was sorry about that, when I was old enough to understand the importance of it and, looking in any mirror, realized it was something I was never going to have. Then I found what I wanted to do in life, and being called pretty no longer had any importance in my life. It was only much later that I realized that *not* being beautiful was the true blessing, though you might say a blessing in disguise.

"It's better not to be beautiful. Not being beautiful forced me to develop my inner resources. The pretty girl has a handicap to overcome because she receives so much attention and encouragement for something she hasn't really done anything to achieve, except be lucky. She isn't encouraged to develop her own potential. She doesn't start early enough to try to find what she's really capable of. She is passive instead of affirmative, and that puts her into a more dependent position in respect to what life does to her. I came to understand that women who cannot lean on their beauty and have to make something on their own have the advantage. I cannot think of anything more terrible than looking back at the end and feeling that you have not written well in the Book of Life."

"I was an alone child," Alfred Hitchcock explained to me. "I was not attractive or popular, so I was forced to live in my imagination, and I believe that helped me to develop my creative resources. I always had a vivid imagination, and I bring so much in my mind to any situation that I need less stimulation from the outside world. I was always eccentric, and it is a good thing I was successful or, instead of saying I had a unique style, they would have just said I was odd. Success modified eccentricity.

"There are internal people and external people. External people are more likely to spend or waste their creative resources. They are constantly faced with temptations that did not come my way. It was an advantage that the homely, less popular child has— the time to develop internal resources. I was forced to develop my interior self and not be dependent on the others. Then my work brought me a kind of appreciation, even love, you might say, that I never expected. Perhaps that made it all sweeter. It's the cream on the bun."

I was sitting next to Alfred Hitchcock at the Plaza Athenée Hotel in Paris just after he had received the French Legion of Honor. Touching his medal, he said, "It's just a matter of luck. I believe that luck is everything in life. Luck determines our roles. I have been accused of typecasting. But I am not the one who does that. Life typecasts us. Look at me. Do you think I would have chosen to look like this? I would have preferred to have played a leading man in life. I would have been Cary Grant."

Alfred Hitchcock told me that while screening the daily rushes of *North by Northwest,* he noticed an unnatural scarlet cast to Eva Marie Saint's complexion in her first scenes with Cary Grant. For the next day's shooting, they tried to compensate for this with makeup, but the peculiar coloration persisted, and no one could explain it. Finally, Eva Marie Saint admitted she was blushing! Ever since she had been a little girl, she had had a crush on Cary Grant, and now that she was playing the romantic lead opposite him, she was embarrassed. "Do you think she would have been blushing with me by her side instead of Cary Grant?" Alfred Hitchcock said as he finished the story. "Certainly not! I wasn't typecast in life for that part. That wasn't my good luck.

"My good luck in life was to be a really frightened person. I'm fortunate to be a coward, to have a low threshold of fear, because a hero couldn't make a good suspense film. I'm afraid of driving, of policemen, of getting up before a crowd, of women. I'm afraid of you. I'm afraid of other people. That's why I am able to work so well with fear. Because I can feel it. To be a good cook, you have to have a developed sense of taste. I have a vivid visual imagination which allows me to make things more frightening than other people can."

Alfred Hitchcock suggested that we "exchange murders." It was a game he called "Murder."

A man and a woman sitting at a table next to us were deep in conversation. Her earrings were next to her plate on the table. Observing them, Alfred Hitchcock pointed out that they knew each other well. "You can tell she is comfortable with him or she wouldn't have taken off her earrings, which were bothering her." He indicated a man whose feet were sticking out from beneath a table. "See that man? He's wearing very expensive shoes. You can tell a great deal about a man by his shoes."

"And his socks," I added. He asked me to choose a victim. I hesitated. "Well, then," he said a bit impatiently, "choose a murderer." I suggested he go first. He chose as a victim the fattest man in the room, saying he could best identify with him. "Now we need a villain." Looking around the room, he selected a good-looking man with blond hair and blue eyes. "A villain cannot look villainous or no one would let him into their house."

When I met Pavarotti coming back at night just after his triumphant 1981 performance in *The Elixir of Love,* he was wearing a bulky fur coat that gave him the appearance of a big bear. His curly beard blended into the coat. Smiling to himself, he looked quite tickled, which I could well understand. I had just watched the live telecast from Lincoln Center of his performance, which had elicited an overwhelming ovation.

Already knowing the answer, it was a pleasure to ask the question: "Was it fun?" Obviously it was an even greater pleasure for him to answer.

"Yes. Do you know why? Because I didn't make any mistakes. At the top you aren't allowed a mistake. I was lucky tonight."

I said that it was more than luck. For me, an important aspect of good luck has always been being able to make mistakes without having to pay for them. We all make mistakes, but when we're very lucky, we aren't punished and may even be rewarded.

Pavarotti touched his ear. "That is my luck," he explained. "My ear. Everyone says it is my voice which is good. It is, but my luck is perfect pitch. Because of it, my ear can make a correction in any mistake before I make it."

At his Hollywood home on the Rue du Vallee, Rudy Vallee talked with me about the special appeal his singing voice had for women. He told me the secret of *his* good luck: "I had a cock in my voice."

Charlie Chaplin was presiding in his customary fifth-floor suite at London's Savoy Hotel when Martin, an institution at the Savoy, wheeled in a cart with a still-warm custard, compliments of Chef Trompetta. Chaplin put a finger gently on top of the custard, which jiggled invitingly. I remembered something King Vidor had told me—a game Chaplin played which he privately called "high society."

He would be at an elegant dinner party with royalty or some titled guests present. Mashed potatoes would be served by elaborately uniformed servants, whereupon Chaplin, affecting an aloof and genteel manner, would ignore the serving utensils and reach in with his fingers and scoop up a gob.

I asked him if the story were true.

"Not true," he answered. Then, affecting an aloof and genteel manner, he reached in with his fingers and scooped up a gob of the custard.

He picked up one of the plates, with its Savoy Wedgwood design of five little men in their gondola on a blue wave. "Winston Churchill loved this design," he said. "I am fortunate that I have never ceased to appreciate luxury. I have never grown so sure of it that I could take it for granted. In that way I believe I was lucky to have been very poor in early life. But being poor is not lucky if it lasts too long, or if it comes so late one can do nothing about it, or if it takes so great a toll, one's life is spoiled. Certain people are not constitutionally suited to poverty, and it can crush the highest of spirits if those high spirits are accompanied by any fragility.

"My mother was naturally disposed toward happiness, but life dealt so harshly with her that she forgot how to be happy. I wanted my success so that I could give her everything, but by the time I was able, it was too late. What I could give her brought no happiness, because by that time she had forgotten how to be happy. Happiness, you see, is a habit, and she had got out of the habit.

"There is also non-luck, you know. People always talk about good luck and bad luck. With non-luck, one works hard and is adequately rewarded, but nothing special ever happens. There is nothing more terrible than the prolonged anxiety of desperately waiting for something to happen. Working hard and getting fairly rewarded is not good luck, though it requires an absence of bad luck. Good luck is receiving something wonderful out of proportion to what has been earned."

I asked Chaplin if he thought himself a particularly lucky person. He was the only one of those whom I asked that question who answered in the negative. He felt that while he had received many rewards, he had earned them. He did, however, admit that after his poverty-stricken childhood, he had been blessed with an absence of bad luck.

Chaplin gazed out of the window at the imposing view across the Thames, but he seemed to be looking beyond the National Theatre, the Royal Festival Hall, and the other buildings of the South Bank. "I can look out from here and see the dirty gray building where I lived as a boy. Everything was gray. There were no colors."

In Washington, D.C., at a reception in his Georgetown home, Averell Harriman and I were sitting on the sofa talking about his long career in politics. While he was aware of his good luck in life, he had missed something. Long prominent in the background of politics, he would have preferred public foreground.

"It's the wheel of fortune," he commented. "It spins you around, and it's where you are then—all a matter of timing in life."

You cannot know which will be your lucky moment, but it is less likely to occur if it has to come and find you. The person who has bought a ticket is more likely to win the lottery.

Sometimes one has either to send his pride on vacation or get some lucky assistance. Anita Loos, curled up in the little child's rocking chair that was her favorite spot in her New York apartment, told me the beginning of this story about Luise Rainer:

A very young and relatively unknown Luise Rainer was walking along the beach at Malibu with her scottie when she happened to meet Anita Loos. Excitedly, Anita Loos told her that the studio was looking desperately for someone exactly like her. "You must call them," she said.

"Call *them?* Never!" Luise Rainer replied disdainfully. "If they want me, they will have to call *me.*"

"But they're desperate. If you wait, they may not even think of you and just give the part to someone who isn't right for it."

Luise Rainer completed the story:

"I said I could never do such a thing. I was terribly independent, and things had always come to me. When I had finished my walk with my scottie, about half an hour later, I went home and M-G-M was calling me. It was because Anita Loos had called them.

"You ask me if I think it all would have happened if she hadn't made that call. Yes, but it would have happened differently. I would have gone on walking my dog on the beach, waiting out the end of my contract. Then I would have gone home to Austria, which I wouldn't have minded at the time, because I was already homesick.

"I would certainly have succeeded, because this immense urge could never have been stopped. But I would have missed those few years that meant so much in my life. I would have missed the two Oscars, and I would have gone back to Europe for World War II. As it was, my father was put in a concentration camp, but because I was in America, we were able to get him out.

"I was the Queen of Sheba. I didn't know if it was hard or easy. What does the Queen of Sheba know?" She made a gesture with a finger to push her nose up into the air. "It was all given to me. I didn't know there was another way it could be because I had nothing else to compare it to. I departed, leaving it all, without a look back. I didn't really think about leaving permanently. All I knew was my personal life, my traumatic marriage to Odets—it was something I knew I had to escape.

"Not working, I felt like a nun strangling the forbidden impulse within her. Now I only want to do my work. That is the real satisfaction. Being the Queen of Sheba couldn't last."

Everyone knows that fabled story of luck—Lana Turner just happened to be wearing a very tight sweater when she went out to Schwab's Drugstore and was "discovered." It is a romanticized example of good luck which gives everyone hope. Only that wasn't the way it happened. Her career actually grew out of an appointment with producer-director Mervyn LeRoy in his office.

I was having lunch in California with Mervyn LeRoy when a columnist came up to him and said, "I'd like something from you for my column." Before Mervyn LeRoy could say anything, the columnist got in his question. "What was it about Lana Turner when you first saw her that you immediately recognized? Were you able to tell right away that she would be a star? What was it that she had? To what do you attribute your instant recognition of her unmistakable charisma?"

Mervyn LeRoy wrote down a telephone number on a minuscule scrap of paper and handed it to the man, asking him if he would call him at his office. When the man left, Mervyn LeRoy said he wrote only the phone number without his name, and if he were lucky, the man would put it in his pocket and forget whose number it was. He was really tired of being asked that question. "A whole career and I'm asked one question: 'Why did you happen to select Lana Turner?'"

Smiling, I asked him, "And why *did* you select Lana Turner?"
Smiling back, he responded, "Just male intuition."

On the last day I spent in Rome with Lina Wertmüller, I
brought her a gift of a silk scarf. It was an art nouveau pattern, the
sort I knew she admired, but her reaction was far from the pleasurable one I had anticipated. Instead a troubled look of conster-
nation filled the eyes behind the white glasses. She frowned
deeply. Then she grabbed her purse, quickly taking out the first
coin she could find, and thrust it into my hand, saying, "Here, I'm
paying you for the scarf." I accepted the coin, and she added,
relieved, "Now it's not a gift. I'm buying it from you."

I looked down at the lire coin. It represented substantially less
than the tax I had paid on the scarf at Liberty of London. The
worst was yet to come. Before I could pull back my hand, she
pricked my finger with a needle. Then she smiled.

"I had to," she replied in response to my shock. "If you receive
a gift that is anything like a handkerchief, it could bring tears, and
the bad has to be undone. It doesn't matter how little I pay, it
undoes the bad luck." I was glad I hadn't brought her a blanket.

The maid entered with more of the endless procession of
espresso in tiny eggshell porcelain cups. "Be careful of the
chips," she warned. "They make the cups broken to look old."
She laughed. "That is not really why they are chipped. They are
so fragile that they chip almost every time anyone washes them.
But they are so beautiful that even when they are broken, I cannot
bear to throw them away." She went on to explain that she hoped
I did not mind the pin prick, and that she was not superstitious,
but that still one does not wish to jeopardize one's luck. . . .

I was sitting in George Cukor's art deco living room while he
enthusiastically told me about a project he was considering. He
had only just begun with, "This lady inherits a baseball team
. . . ," when Katharine Hepburn marched into the room.

"Don't talk away your luck, George!" she said sharply.

Then, as abruptly as she had appeared, she departed, followed
by Whitney, the resident golden retriever who instantly recognized that she was wearing her outdoor clothes and walking
shoes.

George laughed. "She was my tenant for thirty years, and she always paid her rent regularly. She thinks that gives her certain rights. She's always been indomitable and funny—two wonderful qualities in a woman. She's afraid I'll get to be like the director who tells at great length, in infinite detail, all about the movie he's going to make. He tells about it in such elaborate detail that he no longer needs to make it. Kate has always believed that if you tell your project, it will go away; that you have dissipated the energy that should have been guarded for the creative experience. She won't talk about her projects. She thinks if people use up their creative energy in the talking, it will chase their luck away."

That reminded me of what Henry Moore had said when I started to say something about the book I was writing: "No, don't," he stopped me in mid-sentence. "The dreams will be released!"

Achievement begins with a dream. Making one's dream a reality for others to share is the essence of the creative experience. It is an effort beyond survival and personal gratification. All of the appurtenances of civilization itself are the legacy of those who had dreams that became our reality. What would life be without wishful thinking? Converting illusion into reality and reality into illusion, one finds oneself in the realm of Queen Mab. Shakespeare's fairy queen, who herself travels in a carriage carved from an empty hazelnut, is always more likely to tickle the fancies of those who are already predisposed to fanciful dreaming. I remember Rouben Mamoulian saying to me, "This may be wishful thinking on my part, but then perhaps all things should begin with wishful thinking."

Talking with me about why people fly in his paintings, Chagall said, "Man must look up. And now men actually have walked in the sky. Art is life, but a larger life—like religion."

I stood as far back as I could without leaving the room in order to look from a distant perspective at what Chagall said was one of his favorite paintings. Then I moved close to it. Chagall approved, saying, "Go on, go closer. Go close enough to smell the paint." He laughed at his own little joke. The picture had been painted half a century earlier.

"My paintings are my past and my future," he said. "A Vitebsk in which no one ever dies, no building ever disappears. I left Vitebsk, but Vitebsk never left me. Inside me, it is always as it was. I paint what I dream, but my paintings are my real world. I have created my own world and have been privileged to share it."

There is an element of magic, something more than can be explained, in the shared dream—a vision conceived by one in which many can find wonder and pleasure. "People want you to explain your art to them," Picasso said, "but if it could be explained, it would not be art. Art has a life of its own. To try to explain it would be like dissecting an animal in a laboratory. You can account for all the parts, but you cannot explain why together they have life."

I asked Picasso if there were any people he would like to have known whom he had not known, and he answered, "The people in my pictures."

Alice B. Toklas thought that Picasso could see around corners, according to Virgil Thomson. "Gertrude Stein and Alice were meeting Picasso at a cocktail party. Alice was standing there when he came in. She was very social. Her moustache never bothered her. Gertrude was three rooms away, but Picasso caught just a glimpse of her and, turning to Alice, said, 'Gertrude had her hair cut.'

"Picasso was an eye person. There are eye people and ear people. Of course, there are people who use words, and muscles, too. The eye person sees more than other people, remembers more of what he's seen, and then he creates from that a vision others can share—a unique vision which is something more than reality."

The ear people have their own special ability that enhances their "vision" of sound. Virgil Thomson talked about southern cooks who listened to spoon bread and then put the dough into the oven when it "sounded" right. "It can be heard to make a small crackling sound. If not, more soda is needed." Throughout his life, Virgil Thomson cooked by listening to the sound of the food he was preparing.

"Beethoven was an ear person who heard more than other people and shared that vision of sound. He didn't have the eye of Leonardo, but he did have the ear of Beethoven."

The dream can be dreamed without any clear view of how to achieve it. Picasso said the most important step was the first one, "That you have the dream."

"You have to have a dream so you can get up in the morning," Billy Wilder told me. "But that dream can't stay the same all your life. If I'd been a boy in America, I would have dreamed of being a bat boy. But of course that dream couldn't have sustained me all my life."

For Alfred Hitchcock the great moment of vision was when he first saw his entire film from beginning to end, exactly as he wanted it to be, in his mind. He said no subsequent viewing of the film was ever again as exciting. He would have liked to have stopped there, because once he had seen the film, it was no longer so interesting, and the reality, no matter how well it worked, could never live up to that film in his head.

The vision can change along the way. Indeed, it is certain to do so. Erté, whose 1920s art deco drawings so epitomized their moment, had just returned from Barcelona. In his late eighties and still active as an artist, he had personally known Antonio Gaudí, Barcelona's legendary architect. Erté had visited the Cathedral of the Sacred Family, created by Gaudí to be his masterwork, but left unfinished at his death. Now it was being completed by others.

Erté smiled as he spoke of the prevailing idea that it was being built exactly as Gaudí would have done it. What they were actually building was a realization of Gaudí's blueprints. Had Gaudí lived through to its completion, the cathedral would have been changed each step along the way. Every stage of construction would have been different because of those alterations that preceded it. Erté told me, "The finished cathedral will lack Gaudí's erasures and new lines."

Virgil Thomson cited a dramatic example of how the artist's view can change even when the work is completed:

"Christian Bérard had designed a set in which he had included a slender spire in the background, but he was uncertain as to whether it should remain or not. He fell ill. Still he could not resolve the question of whether the spire enhanced or detracted from the effect he wanted to achieve. His condition worsened. Then, just before he died, he managed to speak. He said, 'The minaret shall stay.' *That* is dedication."

"Our dreams are our real life"

FEDERICO FELLINI

FEDERICO FELLINI ENTERED into the daily game of life with a playful spirit. He pointed out to me that "playful" interviews are the best—not only more fun, but more revealing. I asked him how we could achieve that kind of interview, and Fellini said there were no rules; we would have to find our own way. He compared it to the atmosphere he liked on his sets. "I must always have a playful atmosphere on the set. I strive for flexibility so no one is forced into a mold. It should be impulsive, exploratory fun, like the games of childhood." I responded that it was a very special kind of childhood to which he referred; one with money, power, and freedom. Fellini admitted that people had accused him of behaving like a willful child accustomed only to getting his own way on the set.

"Are they right?" I asked.

"Of course they are," he answered. "Children say 'I want' or 'I don't want.' I don't say 'I think, maybe, perhaps.' I say 'I want.' "

Fellini was a big man, well over six feet tall, but with a larger aspect—that of being even bigger than his physical size would indicate. It was not only his height, but his broad shoulders and chest which gave this impression. He seemed just about to out-grow his clothes.

His voice was softer than might be expected from such a large man, and it caused one to draw closer in order to hear every word. If that didn't bring you close enough, he would draw you closer physically by taking your arm, touching your hand, or putting his arm around you. There was a lot of physical contact.

His conversation was often highly animated, ranging from ex-pressive looks to the rich repertory of Italian gestures that tell all and a bit more. In a high mood, Fellini would act out all the characters in one of his anecdotes.

As a boy of seven, Fellini was taken to the circus, where he was profoundly impressed by the clowns. That visit influenced his whole life. He told me that at the time he couldn't understand why *everybody* didn't want to be a clown. Not only did he think about it all the time, but at the age of twelve, he actually ran off with the circus. He didn't stay long. Thinking back, he wasn't certain whether he was gone several weeks or only several days. He was returned to his parents but felt it was a preview of coming attractions in his life.

"I am now a clown," he said, "and the movies are my circus."

Fellini did not always know that he wanted to write and direct movies. "When I was a boy, I thought the actors made up the dialogue and the story as they went along." As a young man he hoped to be an artist, to be a Picasso or to draw a comic strip like *Flash Gordon.* "I thought I wanted to draw and to write, but I had no idea of directing films. Before you know something even exists, you cannot imagine it, so you cannot want it. When you know, you are curious, but it is never just like you thought it would be. Then, when you experience what you have been made for without even knowing it, you cannot live without it. In my life, finding that I could write and direct films was like the discovery of sex."

Fellini recalled the day of his examination for military service in Bologna, when he stood nervous and naked before the doctors. At that moment, two hundred British planes began to bomb the city. Within a few minutes, the original reason for his nervousness was gone, as was the hospital, which no longer existed. Fellini survived uninjured to run naked through the streets on a day he would never forget.

Fellini's reserved and refined manner was not to be confused with weakness. "One of the most important things a film director must be is authoritative," he said, "and it was something I could never imagine myself being. When I was a young man, I felt shy, and I could not envision myself speaking with power and authority to anyone, especially to a beautiful woman. Now, I am still shy, but not when I am the director."

I first met Fellini at the Conchiglia Hotel in Fregene, about an hour and a half from Rome, near his weekend house.

I was sitting and contemplating my second cappuccino, a bit forlornly, because Fellini was late enough for me to begin to wonder whether he was coming at all. Fortunately, I wasn't wearing a watch, so I didn't realize just how late it really was.

On that sunny Sunday, the bar was completely deserted. Through the picture window, I couldn't see one square foot, or in this case, one square meter of Italian beach that wasn't covered by bodies. The number of sun worshipers seemed to be exceeded only by the number of automobiles. There were so many cars it appeared that every person had come in a separate automobile, and, indeed, that some of the cars had even arrived on their own.

The cars were triple-parked, or just left on the sidewalk or anywhere else that struck the fancy of their owners. It was a LIFO situation—last-in-first-out—and the ensuing melee was inevitable. At the end of the day, drivers would rage apoplectically, as though the unimaginable had occurred rather than a simple fact of life today in Rome—anarchy.

Behind me, I heard the sound of someone striding toward my table. Turning, I recognized Fellini, who sat down beside me.

FELLINI
Forgive me for being late, but I'm not really late. I have been sitting in the next room for forty-five minutes waiting for you to arrive. *[Feigning melodrama]* We have lost forty-five minutes in our life together which we can never make up, but we must try!
I
[As melodramatically as I can manage] I hope we never catch up but always try . . . *[The waiter comes to take our order]*
FELLINI
What will you have?
I
I'd like a *sugo di aranci rossi [Orange juice which looks like tomato juice but tastes like a very rich orange juice]*
FELLINI
I don't know if they have those red oranges here now. It's been

a bad season. But if they don't, I will paint the oranges red for you.

I

That's the best offer I've had today.

FELLINI

Look out there at the sea. It is especially wonderful when the sun is shining. Did I tell you I can also bring out the sun?

I

[It had been rather cloudy. Just then the clouds pass, and the sun shines quite brightly.]
I'm impressed.

FELLINI

[Nonchalantly] I thought I should do something for your visit.
[The red orange juice arrives, looking just like a glass of tomato juice]

I

You painted the oranges just the right color. You're an artist.

FELLINI

Would you like to come to my office and see my drawings?

I

Yes.

FELLINI

I mean to *really* see my drawings.

I

Oh. Well, I'll come anyway.

FELLINI

What is this cake?

I

It's a semolina cake I've brought you. They told me in the bakery that this *torta di polenta* is a great Italian specialty.

FELLINI

I've never seen one.

I

It was in the window of the Pasticceria d'Angelo on Via della Croce, and it looked so tempting. Doesn't it look delicious?

FELLINI

It was very generous of you.

I

It was really very selfish. *I* wanted to be able to have a slice.

FELLINI
Is it an aphrodisiac?

I
Yes, now that you mention it, I believe it is.

FELLINI
It is more likely to be if you believe it is. Our minds can shape the way a thing will be because we act according to our expectations.

I
It's like not letting the phone ring long enough when you don't think the person will be there. When no one answers, it's a self-fulfilling prophecy.

FELLINI
Perhaps it is better that way. I do not like to speak on the telephone. *[Eating the cake with gusto]* You said this is a *torta di polenta.* It sounds like something from the macrobiotic vegetarian restaurant.

I
Imagine that I should be able to introduce you to something in Rome! Will you come to New York and introduce me to something there?

FELLINI
I will. I have the idea already in my mind.

I
I've brought you a tee shirt.

I gave Fellini a tee shirt, a souvenir of my first book, *Hello, I Must Be Going.* On the front it read *Hello,* and on the back, *I Must Be Going.*

I
It's extra large. But you don't *have* to wear it.

FELLINI
I *want* to wear it. You may think of me wearing it. But I'll wear it only with nothing else on *[Holding it up against his chest and posing]* Not even my undershorts. Do you like that?

I
I do. Do I get a photograph?

FELLINI

Of course. Where do we begin with this interview of me? What do you have in mind? The hard thing is beginning. Whatever it is you want to do in life, you must begin it. The picture I make is never exactly the one I started out to make, but that is of no importance. I am very flexible on the set, but I come with a script from which to start. After the first weeks, the picture has a life of its own. Then, it becomes the director of me.

I

René Clair told me that the first shot, the opening of the picture, was the most difficult for him and the one into which he put the most thought. The difficult thing, he said, was "getting the film born."

FELLINI

Understanding what makes a thing difficult doesn't necessarily make it less difficult, and understanding how difficult it is can make it more difficult to attempt.

I

Sometimes the more stumbling blocks you see, the more likely you are to stumble.

FELLINI

You're right. Pictures do not get easier for me to make, but more difficult. With each one, I learn more things that can go wrong, and I am thus more threatened. I realize also that the dream cannot be touched, that the picture in my mind will never quite be the one on the screen. One must learn to live with stumbling blocks.

I

Personally, I would rather see all of them in order to avoid them or to prepare for them.

FELLINI

That's fine as long as you don't let it stop you. Being too aware of all of the negative possibilities can stop you or keep you from starting at all. Finding the right project and beginning are the most difficult. You almost need an excuse to set off on a journey. You always need a *raison d'être* to do something. So many people say, "I'm going to write a book," but . . .

I

Famous first words!

FELLINI

. . . but it's rare and so difficult to just do that. You need a combination of purpose and encouragement. It's hard to work like that if you don't know it's going to be published. Or for me to do a film maybe no one will produce. I need the contract in order to go through the discipline. And the studio means a great deal to me.

I

Bette Davis told me the studio was for her like a bad home. You long to get away from it, and then you miss it.

FELLINI

Yes, the studio provides shelter and control.

What were we talking about before? Ah, yes. Beginning and how hard it is.

I

But fun—and important. Mae West said it's the first moment that always determines everything.

FELLINI

Perhaps so. But where are your questions? Didn't you bring any questions? What are you going to ask me? Don't you have a list?

I

No, but I will make a question for you. *[Pause]* I have it. What did you do on your summer vacation? *[Fellini laughs]* Do Italian children also have to write those essays in school?

FELLINI

Yes, they do. You mentioned Mae West. You were fortunate to meet her. I would have liked to. I admire her very much. She was wonderful. She was so anti-erotic. She always seemed to me to be anti-sex, because she made a joke of sex and made you laugh, and that is anti-erotic. I think that her work was really her sex. It seemed to me that her work was everything, and that she cared so much about it, she probably had no time for sex. A person cannot do everything in life. If a woman chooses to have sex be her life, she must spend her time in that, with *la toilette*, making herself attractive. If she chooses the career, the investment of time and energy is there. Do you know that you look like a writer?

I

I think it's easier in life if you look like what you want to do. Do you think people are typecast in life as well as in films?

FELLINI

Yes, of course. I never tire of looking at faces till I find the right one for a part. For the smallest part I could and often do look at a thousand faces to find the perfect one that expresses what I want it to express. Face is the first thing we have understanding of.

I

Do you think that sometimes it works the other way, and that we come to look like what we do?

FELLINI

Yes, because we respond to the way people treat us and become the way we are treated by the world, which is so influenced by the way we look.

I

Sometimes it seems that actors are affected by the parts they play. They find a part in which they are particularly successful, so they come to play that part in life.

FELLINI

I knew an actor who played the fool so long that now he is one *all* the time.

I

Maybe he was something of a fool to start with.

FELLINI

Yes. That was why he got those parts. But, then, playing those parts brought out that side of him and reinforced it.

I

From the time we're babies, we get more approbation for some things than for others. I think we sense that, and act accordingly.

FELLINI

We all like to please. And we like best those people who see us the way we want to be seen. You should watch me doing what I do, directing. That's when I am most fully alive. You must be here when I make my next film. You see me in my most virile moment when you see me doing what I do. When I am directing, a special energy comes upon me. I can do all the parts and participate in every aspect of the film. My life is making movies. It is only when I am doing my work that I feel truly alive. It is like having sex.

Work is the same as making love if you are lucky enough to work at what you would do anyway, even if you didn't get paid for it. It's like lovemaking because it's total feeling. You lose yourself in it. Work is the greatest attraction there is.

I

And sex is the ultimate distraction?

FELLINI

Yes, that is so. When I work, each film is a jealous mistress. She says, "Me, me! Don't remember the past. Those other films never really existed in your life. They couldn't have meant to you what I do. I will stand for no unfaithfulness! You must perform only for me. I am the one." And so it is. The film now is my total passion, but one day that film will be finished. I will have put everything I have into it, and the affair will be over. It will pass into memory, and I will search for and find my new mistress—my next film. And there will be room in my life only for her.

Tell me, why are you traveling alone? Is it because you prefer it?

I

No, that's not the reason. Of course, it's more fun to share pleasurable experiences—if you have the right person to share them with. But it seems better to do it alone than with the wrong person.

FELLINI

To be alone is to be all yourself, because you are free to develop, not according to others' constrictions. Being alone is a very special thing, and being able to do so is even rarer. I have always envied people who are able to be alone, who have interior resources, because it gives you an independence, a freedom people say they want, but are in reality so afraid of. People are more afraid of that than anything else in life. If they are left alone for even a few minutes, they look for someone, anyone, to fill the void. They are afraid of silence, the silence when you are alone with your own thoughts. Then, you have to like your own company very much. The advantage is you don't have to misshape yourself to conform to other people's ideas, or just to please. I have been trying my whole life to shake off the encumbering baggage with which I was weighted as a child. The intentions may be good, but it doesn't make the baggage less heavy. I was taught "No." "You cannot." "You ought to be ashamed." There were so many admonitions to remember, it was a wonder after all that I was not too incapacitated to button my fly. I was filled by school and Church with an overwhelming sense of guilt before I had the faintest idea about what I was guilty of. Organized religion has too much of superstition and duty—that combination. Real religion should liberate man to find divinity within himself. Everyone hopes for a more meaningful existence.

I spent my life trying to cure myself of my education, which told me, "You can never measure up to the ideal; you are impure." We were affected by a pessimistic and repressive education inflicted by Church, Fascism, and by parents. Sex was something not spoken of. For a time I thought all women were aunts. I was overcome by excitement if I saw a woman in an evening dress.

I

But you discovered that all women were not aunts . . .

FELLINI

Yes, that came to me rather quickly.

I

How did it come to you?

FELLINI

I saw Dora's "house" where the women painted themselves, wore veils, and smoked gold-tipped cigarettes. You have never experienced the brothel, the house of prostitution. It's an experience you have missed in life which, as a writer, would be important for you to have had.

I
But I have.
FELLINI
I find that difficult to believe of *you*. Were you working?
I
Yes, I was in Paris writing an article about Madame Claude's. I was sitting in her salon when a man I knew came in. He was really startled. He was so upset he never even asked me why I was there. He spent the whole evening explaining why *he* was there—Madame Claude had the greatest chef, and he enjoyed the food. He kept telling me he came only for the food. Finally, after dinner, he had to leave. "Really delicious," he said to me, then to Madame Claude, "My compliments to the chef." He wished me good evening in a brightly cheery tone, but I considered the possibility he was going to have indigestion. I assumed I'd ruined his evening.

Our first meeting at an end, Fellini left me, riding away on his bicycle. He wasn't watching where he was going, but where he had been. He looked back at me, waving first one arm, then the other, and then both at the same time. With Fellini's big frame impeccably attired in a blue silk Sunday suit with white shirt and blue tie, the bicycle seemed absurdly undersized and was only partially visible beneath him as he pedaled off.

The next day, I went to Fellini's office on the Corso d'Italia. The attractive 1920s facade saved the best for the inside in the private way that northern Italian buildings have of keeping their secrets. Behind the wall was the garden, intended not to be shown off, but shown in. I went up a few steps to the ground-floor studio, which was an apartment serving as an office.

Inside, the high-ceiling room reflected its occupant, looking just like Fellini. It was tall and sunny; tidy, but rumpled; masculine and comfortably worn. It was not a room of fussy possessions, a state which Fellini explained to me he had achieved only through the greatest exercise of will. With the years, he had found that his interests did not expand, but instead contracted, till in their shrunken state they had come to represent what he felt had become his kind of tunnel vision. The tunnel was his work.

The light at the end of the tunnel was his completed film. When he reached that light, it was his signal to enter a new tunnel.

I was embraced by Fellini and led to an already well-sat-upon leather sofa that felt like an Italian glove. In the style characteristic of a man who didn't do anything in a small way, Fellini strode to a bookshelf. He carefully removed one oversized bound scrapbook. The outside had the well-used look of all of his possessions. One could not have imagined anything new in the room. If Fellini brought anything brand-new to his office, it seemed as if the article would age on the way there. He sat down on the sofa next to me, holding the heavy book in his lap.

FELLINI
What do you think of my office? I try not to have too many possessions. I like things, but it is strange about things: One day you acquire *them*, but after a while, they own *you*. I don't want to be sentimental. Being sentimental is a terrible burden. I get rid of whatever I can.

I
Just your understanding that and not wanting to be sentimental would indicate that you are.

FELLINI
[Laughs] It takes one to know one. Sentimental is romantic. Are you a romantic?

I
I suppose it depends on the definition. I'll tell you what Otto Preminger told me is his definition of the romantic: Someone who doesn't remember anything that went before or think about anything that will come after.

FELLINI
Are you a romantic by that definition?

I
Not yet.

FELLINI
I am. It is the way I feel.

Fellini opened the large book and spread it across his knees, careful to protect my white skirt.

FELLINI

It may be dusty. I don't look back much. I have a wonderful life at night in my dreams. I'll show you, except the pictures are often obscene. Do you want to see them in spite of that?

I

Please.

FELLINI

But my drawings are *very* obscene. You don't care?

I

Of course I care. But tell me about your dreams.

FELLINI

They are not sleeping dreams. It's my mind playing at night. These are really visions, not dreams. A man's subconscious creates the dream, but his vision is a conscious idealization. *[He shows me some of the drawings]* Here are Laurel and Hardy. They were wonderful. These are very old dreams. You see? August '74. *[Turning the page]* I don't remember doing this one! I see in the meadow a great metallic structure, shining in the sun. And a voice inside me exclaims, "Ah, there is the great mechanical nurse!" The voice has the tone of a revelation. But it is also a little bit ironic. I know that the mechanical nurse will take care of Stan Laurel and Oliver Hardy. I was taken to a movie to see them dressed like two little boys, and they were playing near a swing. There it is, the swing, very empty. I say to myself, "Stan Laurel and Oliver Hardy, when they play the roles of little kids, they are very funny." *[Pause]* Now you need the explanation of the explanation.

I

Yes.

FELLINI

No explanation. You don't get explanations with my drawings.

I

[Looking at another drawing] There, you're sitting on the railroad tracks. And that woman, she's wonderful!

FELLINI

She will appear many times in my dreams. Here I telephone her. And she's jealous, because she asked me, "With whom

were you talking? Who is *she?*" She is so jealous and can't bear
for me to talk with another woman.

I

Why are you lying naked on the railroad tracks? Is it because
life with women is dangerous?

FELLINI

I suppose it's because in sexual relationships and in life I feel
vulnerable and am aware of the risks. Yes, life with women *is*
dangerous.

I

The women in your dreams are unusual—extraordinary, to say
the least.

FELLINI

Why do you say that? Just because they have big tits?

I

It's more than that, although they certainly *are* amply endowed,
now that you mention it. Titian's ladies were modest, pitiful
wisps by comparison.

FELLINI

You see this poor naked little fellow? Do you recognize him? It
is Fellini. He is very thin. That's why you don't recognize me. In
my dreams, I never get fat. He is about to be smothered with
love by this larger-than-life, mountainous creature of sexuality.
He thinks that he is going to make love to her. But she is too
much for him, and he will be swallowed up. Poor fellow.

I

But he goes willingly to his doom, like a male spider.

FELLINI

He is lost, the victim of his own libido. But he will die happily.

I

[Indicating another drawing] And this is you, too? I wouldn't have
recognized you.

FELLINI

You find me young and skinny?

I

Yes.

FELLINI

And I had more hair.

I
You've drawn yourself at about twenty.

FELLINI
Yes. That is because I haven't changed inside. That is still the
way I feel inside, the way I see myself. Of course, if I happen to
look into a mirror, I think the mirror is a liar. I've learned to
shave without looking in the glass.

I
What is this one where the telephone is two faces of the same
woman—one ecstatic, one angry?

FELLINI
It is the woman I am speaking with at the other end of the
telephone. She is bitterly jealous because she believes there are
other women in my life. She is right, but she doesn't know, she
only suspects. Women fight over me.

I
Woody Allen told me if he had to die, that was how he wanted it
to be: the victim of a *crime passionnel,* to be torn apart by beautiful women fighting over him.

FELLINI
Let me show you a dream that I had just before one of my films
was going to open. I am the little man in the small boat. The
waves are very high, and there are sharks all around. You can
see how afraid I am. The little boat is being pitched about by
the waves, and I don't have any oars. Then, do you know how,
in my dream, I saved myself? *[Not waiting for an answer]* Sitting in
the boat, I looked down, and I noticed I had a prick as big as a
tree. So I used it to row first to one side and then to the other,
swinging my prick from one side to another. Using it as my oar,
my prick rowed me to safety.

This next one is a dream about my childhood. You see that
young boy standing in the middle of the street completely
naked? That is me. I have gone out into the traffic. The little
cars are whizzing all around. There is so much traffic and no
traffic lights, and I am directing traffic with my prick.

I
Do you think we can ever expect to see scenes like that in a
Fellini film?

FELLINI

[Laughing] People say that we're going very far these days in our treatment of sex in the films. But look at Aristophanes in the fifth century B.C. The actors wore false pricks that hung down to their feet and dragged along the ground as part of their costumes. That was very funny, but if I do that in a Fellini film, my mother won't be able to see her friends in Rimini anymore. My mother can hardly see her friends now! I was going to make her proud of me, but I think I made her ashamed.

I

Do you ever go back to Rimini?

FELLINI

I could go back, but I don't like to go back to Rimini. The real Rimini I want is the one in my head. If I go back, the reality goes to war with the world of my imagination. It is strange how different places and different people are important to you at different times. As a boy, I wanted to impress my circle of young friends—my schoolmates, many of whose names and faces I no longer remember. There was a time in my life when it was my grandmother who was the most important person in my life. I couldn't imagine life without her. Now she comes only very occasionally into my thoughts, and my picture of her is faint. There is also less of her in the image, and more of me, as it depends increasingly on my vague and scattered memories. Sometimes in later years when one person seemed too important to me at a certain moment I would remember how important my grandmother had been to me in her moment, and that helped me to gain perspective.

I

Did it always work?

FELLINI

[Laughing] No, never. The way you think and the way you feel are two different things. I discovered that the life I told about was more real than living it. After a while the only reality I remembered as real was the fantasy, and if someone who shared the experience with me recalled it from his point of view, I felt he was lying.

I

I suppose no two people sharing the same experience are ever really having the same experience.

FELLINI

It's like a man telling about what he was like the night before with a girl. His performance, and everything else, keeps growing. Except in my case where it's all true! I'm the first to believe my stories. What I've imagined seems more real, more immediate, and more an intimate part of me than what more objective observers believe happened. No one can be objective about himself anyway.

I have often been called mad. Madness is an abnormality, so I don't take that as an insult. Madmen are individuals. Each is obsessed by an individual obsession. I have always been fascinated by the idea of the insane asylum. I have visited several and found that there is a kind of individuality in insanity that is rare in the so-called sane world. The collective conformity that we call sanity discourages individuality.

I

When I see a person on the street in New York who is walking along screaming or someone sitting in a doorway talking to herself with all of her possessions in shopping bags around her, I always wonder why there aren't many more people like that— people who have succumbed to what was too much pressure for them in daily life.

FELLINI

It seems to me that sanity is learning to tolerate the intolerable, to go on without screaming. Perhaps, then, those who can't adjust are also the more sensitive. I realized either I would be considered crazy or a film director.

The luxury of being a director is that you are allowed to give life to your fantasies. My fantasies and obsessions are not only my reality, but also the stuff of which my pictures are made. I am lucky to be in a position to bring them to life. In a very real sense, they are my children. So I don't miss having children of my own. But I am a bad father to my films. When they leave the nest I forget. Until then, they are my whole life. Once a picture exists complete, I fall out of love, and I search till I find a new love.

I

Do you ever have trouble finding a new one?

FELLINI

No. Pull a little tail, and maybe there is an elephant at the end. Everything is intuitive and emotional. I do only what I want to do. I don't know what work is. The idea of wanting a vacation is not something I can feel. A vacation from my work would be a punishment.

I

So for you, happiness is your work, and your professional happiness and personal happiness are the same.

FELLINI

Not exactly. My personal happiness is making love seven times a day, maybe six—because I don't like rules. And I don't like routine. But sometimes I am grateful for routine in unimportant things. It leaves my mind free for what is important. *[He turns the page of his dream book]* In this drawing I'm in a basket in the sky. But my basket is missing its balloon. I'm floating high in the air in my basket. You can see the clouds.

And here I am with the Pope. I am about fifteen years old. I really had met the Pope, who called me "Fefe."

In this one I am with God. You can see God as the great maker and destroyer of clouds.

I

You've drawn God as a woman.

FELLINI

Yes, and She is nude and voluptuous.

This picture is of the Cesarina. I will take you to eat in her restaurant. See how angry she looks? That is because I missed a meal in her restaurant. She will forgive me. But not right away.

And this one: Do you know what the naked woman is saying to me as she holds up the big key over the water closet? She says to me, "This is your key. We'll put it in the water closet and flush it down." She has a mind to have a new life with me, and she wants to cut off all my past. She doesn't want me to even remember any other woman.

This is a dancing girl who has taken off all her clothes. She wants to get to know me better. She will do anything to entice me because she wants me so badly.

Look away, *bambina.* This one is too obscene for you. *[He turns one of the pages so quickly that I cannot see it]*

This one, she is so big and beautiful, isn't she? I've lost something, you see, and I'm looking for it in her vagina. You're blushing. You want to stop this interview?

I

No. I want to begin.

FELLINI

It's very difficult to make interviews, because it's a phony situation. One has to make the questions, and the other tries to please the one who is listening, to appear intelligent, interesting, original, and funny. Whenever I hear that anyone wants to interview me, I try to fly, to escape. I do so when I can because I cannot face the sameness of the tired questions, which are always the same. I would like to be able to have numbered questions. The interviewer says "46?" I respond, "46." We have saved so much time.

I

Is there a question everybody asks you?

FELLINI

There are two. The first is a silly question because there is no magical formula I can tell, and because if someone asks it, it is already a bad sign: "How do you become a director?" They do not want to know how *I* became a director, but how *they* can!

The other question I am always asked is, "Are your films autobiographical?" The answer is yes, but not exactly. It's the way you remember things after a while, not exactly as they were.

Giving interviews is boring for me. And it may be boring and disappointing for the interviewer, which is even worse. Then there are the interviews that vanish into The Great Unknown. One day you decide to give up some of the time you had put away for yourself because everyone says this is what you must do. Your project can't stand on its own; people have to know about it; publicity and promotion are essential. So you weaken.

You spend your time with someone who brings his machines or makes funny little secretive notes. You look at his face for some clue as to how you are doing, but it is not forthcoming. You try harder, but there is no laughter, no glint in the eye; you have a better chance that the relentlessly marching tape recorder will giggle. You hope at some point he will get tired. But why should he when you are doing all the work? At some point, you decide: Finished.

You breathe a sigh of relief. The interviewer goes away. But there is always the need for a second interview. No matter what happened in the first, guaranteed, there will be that need for a second one. You have invested so much time and energy, you are locked in. Instead of cutting your losses, you spend more time. Then you wait for some word of the appearance of the interview somewhere in some obscure journal distributed free to ten graduate students at the University of Patagonia, where your pictures don't show. But nothing so wonderful as that. You hope that what you said will not come out exactly the opposite, that it will have some relationship to what you said and the way you said it, that you will not appear to be more of a fool than you are in reality for having given the interview at all, that someone will read it, and that no one will see it. You almost forget that you gave it. Then, long after it could have done your film any good, you remember it and wonder about it. Maybe you can tell me the answer. Where do all the interviews go that vanish? Why do people who interview me leave my office and go join the Foreign Legion?

I

I promise not to join the Foreign Legion, or even to follow in the footsteps of Marlene Dietrich as, leaving her high-heeled shoes behind, she trails after Gary Cooper through the hot desert sands.

FELLINI

Von Sternberg was wonderful, romantic and optimistic like movies and life were in a more innocent time. I wish I had been born sooner, in the time of the beginning of the movies. I grew up watching Marx Brothers films, and was influenced by them, I hope. They were terrorists against conformity and the rational. I loved them. "Good night, Mrs. Calabash." Jimmy Durante was wonderful a long time ago. He had an act called Jackson and Durante. Did you ever meet him?

I

I used to go to his house with Groucho, and Groucho would sing, "Inka Dinka Doo."

FELLINI

You're very lucky. It must have been wonderful and funny to be there with the two of them.

I

I'm lucky, but it wasn't funny. Jimmy Durante was already very ill, so it was sad. Afterwards, Groucho, who was also very old, would be depressed for two days, but he felt he had to keep on going because the visit seemed to please Jimmy Durante so much.

FELLINI

Harry Langdon. Great. Toto was wonderful. With the very great, like the Marx Brothers, the story is not the important thing. It's like saying, "The Coliseum appeared in a film, but it wasn't much of a plot," as if it made a difference. What's important is that it appeared. Martha Raye was so good, and Abbott and Costello. Laurel was wonderful, but so was Hardy. They could be so touching. Buster Keaton was a king. And, of course, Chaplin.

I

Among people in the world today, whom would you like to meet?

FELLINI

I've been very interested in Carlos Castaneda. I find his books fascinating. I would like very much to meet him, though I've never felt drugs are the way. I feel we have to expand our dreams into our real life. I do it by making films. But I don't have the answers for other people.

I

It is very optimistic of you to spend all this time with me in light of how you feel about interviews and their limited future.

FELLINI

At its best, the interview represents human contact. And establishing human contact with another person is the most precious thing in life.

I will tell you my dream of some twenty years ago which sums up the meaning of my whole life. I've never told this to anyone before.

I was the chief of an airport. It was night, a night full of stars. I was behind my desk in a big room there. Through the window I saw all the landings at the airport. A great plane had landed, and as chief of the airport, I was proceeding to passport control.

All the passengers of the plane were in front of me, waiting with their passports. Suddenly I saw a strange figure—an old Chinese man, looking antique, dressed in rags, yet regal, and he had a terrible smell. He was waiting there to come in.

He now stood in front of me but spoke not a single word. He didn't even look at me. He was totally absorbed in himself.

I looked down at the little plaque on my desk, which said my name and gave me the title, showing I was chief. But I didn't know what to do. I was afraid to let him in because he was so different, and I didn't understand him. I was tremendously afraid that if I let him in, he would disrupt my conventional life. I was not open to the unknown, what I didn't understand. So I fell back on the excuse that was a lie that exposed my own weakness.

I lied as a child lies. I couldn't bring myself to take the responsibility. I said, "I don't have the power, you see. I'm not really in charge here. I have to ask the others."

I hung my head in shame. I said, "Wait here, I'll be right back." I left to make my decision, which I didn't make. I am still making it, and all the while I wonder if he will still be there when I go back. But the real terror is I don't know if I am more afraid that he will still be there or that he will no longer be there. I have thought about it constantly through the thirty years that have passed. I understand full well that there was something wrong with my nose, not with his smell; yet I still have not been able to bring myself to go back and let him in, or find out if he is still waiting.

What are you going to call your book?

I

I'm thinking about calling it "The Ultimate Seduction."

FELLINI

Don't you think about anything but sex? I'm only joking,
Charlottina. Don't look downcast. I have an appointment this
afternoon, but tomorrow morning we could have some breakfast at Rosati. We shall sit and look at the Piazza del Populo
together, and maybe some of its ghosts will come and visit us.

Later that night, Fellini remembered that he had an early-
morning doctor's appointment. I suggested meeting at the doctor's office after the appointment to go and celebrate with a late
breakfast.

It was June in Rome, the sky was Mediterranean blue, and the
sun shone warmly as I waited outside. Fellini came running out of
the doctor's office looking happy and free. He was actually running, and he reminded me of a big dog that had been confined in
a place not of his choosing who, when let out, couldn't wait to
shake off the bad experience. Fellini was glad to walk for a while.

FELLINI

I was sorry not to be able to join you at Rosati's this morning. I
wasn't supposed to eat before seeing the doctor. What did you
have?

I

I had cappuccino and some croissants, warm and fresh from
the oven, with cold sweet butter and whole strawberry marma-
lade.

FELLINI

I gain weight even hearing about food. It was thoughtful of you
to meet me at the doctor's office. How did you know it's something I very much dislike doing?

I

If it were something you liked to do, then I really would be
worried about you.

FELLINI

I have a good doctor. He always knows what to prescribe for
me.

I
More sex?

FELLINI

Yes, exactly. For that prescription, I pay him extra. It was only a routine annual checkup, but it is disconcerting. When you are naked in a nonerotic situation, you feel very vulnerable. While I was standing there without my clothes, I saw the doctor talking with the nurse. I could see their lips move and hear the sound of whispering, but I couldn't make out what they were saying. The doctor put his hand up to his mouth to cover his words. When you are a child that happens to you. You hear your parents whispering about you, but you cannot quite hear what they are saying.

I remember once when I was in the hospital and thought I was dying. I lost all my dreams and fantasies. One is left only with the terror of reality.

Being in a hospital reduces you to the status of being a thing, not for yourself, of course, but for the others. They talk about you in the third person, referring to you as "he" while they're in your presence. "*He* isn't looking so good today," they say, studying you like merchandise to be unloaded quickly at the lowest mark-down sale price. They say it, but you are the one feeling it. It is like being a baby or an old person. You are deprived of any small illusion you once harbored of being even somewhat in control of your own destiny. You are in the hands of your doctor, whose priorities are shifting from body to body, and all these bodies are competing for his attention. They are in competition for your doctor's attention along with his own thoughts about his plans for Saturday night, with a pair of shoes he saw in the window of Gucci on his way to work, with what his wife was angry about the night before when she didn't let him sleep, with how to pacify his mistress so his afternoon "vermouth" isn't spoiled by having to talk about giving up his wife and fine flat in Rome. That is a thing not easily come by these days—a flat in Rome, that is.

When you arrive in that world between dreams and reality to which you have been transported not by jet but by injection, in that state the nuns ministering to you seem like black apparitions in the night, more like assassins or bats coming for your blood at worst, your urine sample at best. I imagined giving a urine sample to be dragged away in gallon containers by teams of workmen. One's world becomes simplified, and one's horizons narrow. The great world out there becomes of little importance as compared to the walls of your tiny room. Your interests become fewer in your shrinking world. Suddenly you are the excuse for a great social occasion as your acquaintances, with their forced and uneasy cheer, gather to catch their last glimpse of you. In their eyes, you are suddenly free of all wrongdoing. The perishable fruit for which you have no appetite comes unceasingly and spoils as the flowers wilt and die. In the face of the dying flowers, you see your own future.

I saw in my mind the films I wanted to make but hadn't gotten around to. In my mind they were born complete without struggle. They seemed perfect, better than anything I had ever done—babies as yet unborn, waiting their turn to be conceived and have their life. Everything was of vast epic proportions and the most splendid colors. It was like dreams you have that you feel lasted hours, but they were really only a few minutes long.

I knew that if only I recovered, I would make all these films. If only I recovered I would do everything I had ever intended to do, and more. But as soon as I recovered, I allowed all of the mundane matters of living to intrude.

I

In Dostoevski's *The Idiot,* Prince Myshkin tells about a man he knew who had been sentenced to death, but at the last minute he was reprieved. The man was told he had only five minutes to live. Those five minutes seemed so vast that he felt no need to think about that very last minute. He divided up his time into two minutes to say good-bye to his friends, two minutes just to think, and one minute to look at the world for the last time. Everything mattered, and he lived life intensely as he never had before. He thought to himself that if he could only be spared, he would live his whole life that way, making every single minute count, never even losing one minute. Then, when he was reprieved . . .

FELLINI

It was like it never happened. He learned nothing from it, and was totally unchanged by the experience. I know it well. The depersonalization of illness is the most terrible thing. The healthy don't know what to do in the presence of illness. When I was in the hospital, they brought balloons to a man who had had a massive heart attack. The image has stayed in my mind. He was lying there, and one was not certain if he was wondering why they brought the balloons, or even if he knew they had brought them. It's because they didn't know what to do and felt the need to do something. And they met a balloon seller.

I don't know why I'm talking about this, but after visiting the doctor, I always feel a bit confused, disoriented.

Fellini said that his favorite activities in life were directing, sex, eating, and riding in a car around Rome. Later that morning, I shared the latter with him. It was like watching a film and being in it at the same time.

FELLINI

Do you like to ride around like this? *[Not waiting for me to answer]* Rome is the most seductive place in the world. Look out the window. See the images, the city moving by us. I find it very stimulating to watch everything moving while we are sitting and talking. But it is not without danger. Italian men prove their masculinity through driving. Perhaps it is the only way they can do it. There is so much to see and experience right in Rome, I no longer feel the need to go anywhere else. I used to have the desire to see more of the world, but it went away. Now I like to see other people travel. I get the stimulation of it without the discomfort. Rome is the perfect place for me. Also, I can't work in a foreign environment. I must know what kind of shoes a character wears, or in which shop in Rome he would buy them. Here I know the labels in his clothes. I must understand even my actress's underwear.

Look, there—that is the Palace of Justice. It was built about seventy years ago. But they didn't allow properly for the weight of the building, and so, ever since, it has been sinking into the river. Only recently it began sinking faster, and had to be emptied. Now you can see it's empty, and it has a macabre look. But its best moment was with the rats. I wanted to use the scene in a film, but I haven't used it yet. Maybe I will.

The building has subterranean tunnels filled with rats, and the rats are so big that there are no cats that could kill them. The cats, in fact, would be killed. So, one night—actually about three in the morning when there were no people around—they brought the trucks. The trucks were from the zoo, filled with panthers and tigers. They moved the trucks to the tunnel, and then let the tigers and panthers loose, out into the tunnels. Can you imagine in the blackness, the only light was those glowing green eyes . . . !

There's nothing better than riding around Rome in a car.

I

I like walking, too.

FELLINI

Then we must do that. In the afternoon we can walk along the Via Condotti and see the rich men living their "five-to-seven" lives. If they are very rich, it is four to eight. They are taking their afternoon stroll with their "second wives." They shop with their mistresses, then take their packages and stop for a vermouth or a Cinzano. After that, they go to the "nest," and the man is finished in time to get home for dinner with his wife and children.

[We hear sounds of shouting] Do you hear all that? Do you know what that noise is? It's a protest demonstration against Fellini. It's all the people I don't see, everyone I don't give interviews to. They see me with you, and they say, "Why is he doing it with this American instead of with us?"

We finally arrived at Rome's very grand Grand Hotel, with its rococo ambiance, for a late breakfast to replace the one his doctor's appointment had prevented.

FELLINI

I was a very provincial boy when I arrived and first looked wide-eyed upon Rome. I could never have come in here. I was even

inhibited by cafes on the Via Veneto. I didn't know how much
to tip. I knew only that nothing could be enough. I was worried
about how the waiter would judge me. You don't believe me? I
was shy then. I am shy now, but no one believes it.

I

I believe it. Perhaps most people feel shy.

FELLINI

Sitting here now is like being in another world, another time.
Too many of the times when I come here, it is to try to make a
deal like at that wonderful hotel in Beverly Hills where everyone goes, the Beverly Hills Hotel, and they make deals in the
Polo Lounge. When the American producers come to Rome,
they come here. They spend the days sitting in their underpants in the biggest suites making long-distance phone calls.
They always have a bottle of mineral water on the table. And
when they receive you, they seem totally unaware that they are
wearing their underpants, and they make no effort to put anything more on. I've always thought they did it to make me feel
ill at ease . . .

I

Maybe they think it will make you feel more at ease.

FELLINI

To put me off my guard?

I

They may feel that it makes the meeting seem informal. Or
maybe after eating a few Italian meals, their trousers just don't
fit anymore.

FELLINI

They spend most of your time speaking long-distance on the
phone with someone else, to their people back in the United
States or Japan or anywhere far away. They shout because they
don't trust the Italian telephone. When they do talk with you,
they talk a long time about irrelevant things, everything in the
world that is unrelated to what you came for. Then they throw
in casually the important part during the last few minutes you
are together. Why do American businessmen spend hours
making small talk and telling jokes, avoiding only the reason

for which you are there, then mentioning it in the last few
minutes?

I

I suppose they're worried you're going to say no, and they're
trying to win you first so they'll get a yes from you.

FELLINI

But if you say no to anything, they believe you are only bargaining. They never think you really mean no. Then they want you
to go on television to sell what you do like soap. In the U.S.
they wanted me to do a TV show demonstrating how to kiss
hands. I will not tell you what I told them!

Sometimes I like to direct a program for Italian television
because I can do something different and get a more immediate reward. That can be very nourishing.

I

But not as nourishing as theatrical filmmaking?

FELLINI

No. It is a different experience for me. When people gather in a
theater, there is the sacred aspect of the spectacle. Television
comes and gets you in your house where you are off guard.
When you enter people's houses on their TV sets, you are in a
position of inferiority, and you have lost your position of respect or reverence. They are eating and undressed.

But you cannot always do exactly what you want to do. You
have to be flexible, or learn to be flexible. You can't count too
much on any one thing. When I was making *Giulietta of the
Spirits,* I was counting on a wonderful tree that was about one
hundred years old. The night before we were to shoot the
scene, there was a storm. No tree.

Television offers you the chance to do something you might
not have the chance to do on film, and you can do it faster.
Immediate satisfaction may be better than something bigger
that is too slow in coming. It confirms your sense of self-
importance. It is important to enjoy your success. People may
have been much happier in low vaudeville than as headliners in
the best theaters. Sometimes I have professional satisfactions.
More and more it is only the professional satisfactions that
occupy my attention. When I was very young, I used to think

about being happy. Happiness is not something I think about now.

I

But it's something you feel . . .

FELLINI

Yes, I feel it now as we sit here. But I know it will not last. And unhappiness will return. But there is a consolation in knowing that it will not last, either.

When I make a film or write something, I'm really drawing. *[He is sketching on a napkin]* I do unflattering little caricatures. I can never get anything to turn out in its material form in quite the same way as the picture in my head. I tried drawing you, but it didn't turn out.

I

I would love to have your drawing of me.

FELLINI

You only *think* so. My pictures are funny little impressions; caricatures, not flattering.

I

Picasso drew a picture of me. It was a nude, but I didn't pose for it. Actually, it was only half a picture.

FELLINI

Which half?

I

The right half. He signed it "Pica"—only half his name for half a picture.

FELLINI

I don't draw from life because real life isn't what interests me. I have to draw away from life. I will dream about you, and in that dream my imagination is unfettered. It will not be you I'm drawing, but the picture in my mind of you. Meanwhile I will show you Rome.

I

I think you're the best tour guide of them all.

FELLINI

I will get your testimonial if I am ever unemployed as a film director. The capacity for marveling is the greatest gift. I, personally, believe everything I am told.

I
Elliott Gould told me his motto in life is "We are all children." The difficult thing is to remain a child.

On our visits to the restaurant Cesarina, Fellini cautioned me to behave decorously in the presence of the grande dame herself, not because I was likely to disgrace him, but because to live in Rome and be deprived of Cesarina would be a punishment too cruel to contemplate.

FELLINI
I'm glad you love my restaurant the way I do. My style is to taste a little of this, a little of that. *[More confidentially]* You must be careful what you say to Cesarina—reverent, but not obsequious. Others might call her rude. She has to pass on everyone. I warn you, she doesn't like women. She exists only in the restaurant, you know. There are people like that. They and their place are symbiotic. She is one of those people in the world that I most admire, because she exemplifies what I respect—genius in your chosen field and total dedication to it. She is a combination of Picasso and the Pope. She regards me as her son, her spiritual son. I thought perhaps you would want to try another restaurant rather than come back here again.

I
When I find what I like, I'm not fickle.

FELLINI
I'm the same. And there's something comforting about routine. Not having to think about where you're going to go leaves you free to think about other things. For dessert, there is a wonderful cake.

I
In your film *City of Women,* a man celebrates his ten-thousandth woman with a tremendous cake that has ten thousand candles on it. That wouldn't exactly be a woman's dream.

FELLINI
It wasn't really ten thousand candles. In pictures the illusion is

more important. Real things don't seem real. It is difficult to portray reality.

I

Charlie Chaplin talked with me about the illusion of reality having to be filmed a hundred times to make it seem real.

FELLINI

Yes, that's true. It's fantasy. Ten thousand women! Perhaps the realization of this could be a little tedious, but not in the fantasy. And the fantasy is what's important. Our dreams are our real life.

I

If we're lucky, our real life is our dreams.

FELLINI

You appear to lead a good life. But you travel so much. When I fly, it is only for reasons of work. I'm a bad traveler. I'm always rumpled.

I

I am, too. I never get off the plane looking like Grace Kelly in a Hitchcock film. Perhaps it's because I didn't get *on* the plane looking like Grace Kelly!

FELLINI

It would not suit you to be so preoccupied with appearance. You are too busy doing your work. The happiest people do it for the work, not for the success.

I

Are there disadvantages to success?

FELLINI

Success takes you away from life. It robs you of the contact that gave you the success. What you create that pleases people comes out of you, only you—the extension of your own imagination. But that imagination did not grow in a vacuum. It found its individuality through contact with others. Then came success, and the greater it is, the greater your economic capacity to disassociate yourself. You can travel alone in your car instead of walking or taking the bus. You tell yourself you will save time and energy, and what started as a luxury becomes a need. You become jet set, and you replace doing something worthwhile with going faster. You move so fast, you no longer need to see anything along the way. You get a press agent who makes everyone believe you are superior and worth more than everyone else. And you come to believe it more than anyone. So, whatever anyone offers, you know they are taking advantage of you, the deceivers who would use you. You protect yourself by not letting anyone get too close. You not only have bodyguards, you have mind guards. You develop a coterie of sycophants. Your aura of success becomes a ring around you to keep out the others—those who originally inspired your imagination. What you created to protect you becomes a prison which shuts you in. You're so special, more and more special, until you're all alone. Your perspective from the high tower is greatly distorted, but you adjust to it, and you begin to think that's the way everyone sees things. Cut off from what sustained the artist in your life, that part of you withers and dies in the tower of the castle where you fled.

I

But you don't have to worry. If you understand the danger, you can avoid it.

FELLINI

I don't have to worry, but not for the reason you say. I don't have to worry because I'm not a success. No matter what anyone calls you, you aren't a success unless you feel like one.

I

I can't believe you feel like a failure.

FELLINI

Of course not. I'm not a failure. I know that. But I'm not a success, either. Others say to themselves, "I will figure out the formula for Fellini's success, and I will turn out 'The Son of Dolce Vita.' " But, of course, it doesn't work. They can't figure out a recipe for success because what works once will not work again if you make an exact copy. But I don't have the answer any more than they. Every time I start a picture, I begin my first picture. Each time, before I begin, I feel the same fear, the same self-doubts. Will I ever be able to do it again? More is expected each time. The responsibility grows. And I have only one source on which I can draw, because it comes from within me.

I

But you have one advantage the others don't have in making a successful Fellini picture: You have Fellini. You are you. No one can steal you.

FELLINI

Maybe no one would want to.

I

Do you think you could work in Hollywood?

FELLINI

I couldn't work in America because I don't know it, and I can't depend on others. One of my chief virtues is fanaticism. Otherwise, I would have been browbeaten into doing what others wanted. I would have been changing all the endings—the saddest thing in life that can happen to a director. The businessmen, the producers want to change the ending of your picture. They want to change it even before you have a beginning. They are always behind because they want to copy what has just been done. Producers always want you to make the same film again. After *La Strada* they wanted me to make "Gelsomina on a Bicycle." That's why I turned down the foreign offers to make bad pictures. One of the curses of success is the opportunists— people who want to use you.

I

What else annoys you?

FELLINI

Too much approbation for the wrong things, and also so much intellectual analysis of my work. And seeing so much message in my work. I want to entertain. When I go to see a movie, which isn't often, I go to see a story and have an experience. I don't notice the shots at all. I don't want to have the technique showing. Too much talk about anything kills it.

I

Groucho was always being asked to explain a picture he'd painted, the only one he ever did. He said, "I don't talk about my art or about humor, or about romance or sex, because if you talk about those things, they go away."

FELLINI

An artist can never explain what he has done. It is a terrible thing to try to force him to intellectualize it. Once you've done something, you have to set it aside and go on to the next project. You tend to forget what you've done. With me, I am forced to set aside a picture when I'm finished because it's too painful to watch what happens to it. My picture is abused from the moment it's born—bad copies, theaters where the sound is terrible, cuts. In some movie theaters there is bad projection with focus that is off. The glass of the window between the projection booth and the theater—dirty—with the distance of the screen too far or the walls too white. So, all the effort you have made before is completely wasted. All the mixing, the sound—I take a lot of care in the sound. It has to be like an orchestra—polyphonic. Then you go into projection booths and they have old machines. The sound goes, "Waa-waa, waa-waa." So it is better when you finish a picture to leave it. Because from that moment, the picture will be destroyed by bad advertising, bad posters, bad graphics, bad choice of movie theaters. Nothing goes right because nobody cares the way you do. It becomes only something to make a profit. If I appear at my picture, it's like I am going out to be an accomplice at its murder.

I understand that Kubrick is able to watch carefully over each film. Someone told me he even has plans of the major theaters around the world, and if he sees that the first rows of seats are too close to the screen in a theater in Tokyo, he wants them to take out those rows. But if you take the time and energy for what you have already done, it is not without price. It has to be at some sacrifice to your next project, which is delayed. I am disappointed, but it's absolutely impossible to try to be there in two thousand situations. And I have my next film, so I'm lucky. I consider myself very lucky because I do exactly what I want to do.

I

Can one help oneself to become lucky?

FELLINI

It's difficult to give advice on how to become lucky. I think that one can have luck if one tries to create an atmosphere of spontaneity. You have to live spherically—in many directions. To accept yourself for what you are without inhibitions, to be open. I think that if you tried to understand why one man is so lucky and another one so unlucky, and you made a real research without prejudice, one reason must be that probably the man who is lucky doesn't put too much confidence in his rationality. He accepts, has faith. It is a kind of religious feeling, to believe in things, to believe in life, I think.

In my work I have to leave a part of myself without responsibility—more infantile. I leave that part of myself free in my work. Another part, the intellectual, rational part, is against this and makes a very bad judgment about what I am doing. When I do things without any explanation, but just with spontaneity, even if my rational part is against it, I can be sure that I am right.

I

Maybe it's because the feeling and the intuition is really you, and the other is the voices of other people telling you what you should do.

FELLINI

Perhaps. Equilibrium is difficult. Usually one part pretends to be more right, more important.

I

When you finish a film, do you ever feel let down?

FELLINI

No. Because a picture says many little good-byes to you.

I

Like a love affair . . .

FELLINI

Exactly. After you have finished cutting, then there is the dubbing. Then the music. So, you are leaving your creatures in a very soft way. There is not an ending—just an interruption. You know that your feature is going out from you, day by day, operation by operation. After the good-bye from the mixing, there is the first projection, the first running. So you never have the feeling that you are leaving in an abrupt way. When you are finally separated from your picture, you are practically in a new one.

But when my picture is finished, I don't like to live in the shade of that picture—the ritual of going around the world to talk about what I have done. I don't want to be on exhibition because people expect me to be like my work. I don't want to disappoint them by not being abnormal enough.

Didn't you find it difficult making appearances to talk about your book?

I

People had no expectations, so it was easier. I couldn't disappoint anyone. For you, the pressure is different. Accomplishment and reputation have greater responsibility. Also, it's always seemed to me that it's harder for a man. More is expected from a man.

FELLINI

Sexually?

I

I wasn't referring to that; but perhaps that, too.

The next day Fellini suggested we spend some time in the "country." We went out of Rome to a restaurant which was one of his favorites. Because it was located on Route 13, it was named "R-13." The owners of the restaurant had their own vegetable garden.

FELLINI

These are eggs that have just been laid, still warm from the hen, fertilized by a rooster.

I

Please don't tell me too many details. I'm sort of a city mouse.

FELLINI

The white beans are delicious just cooked in bubbling oil. I'll take some of your green beans. Do you want oil on your mozzarella? Let me give you some of my peppers.

The owners of the restaurant returned with a waiter. All three had more dishes of cold fish, mushrooms, salad, vegetables. These were the appetizers.

THE OWNER'S WIFE

Oh! I forgot the stuffed peppers . . . *[She rushes off as though we might starve before her return]*

I

You said you don't go to the movies much.

FELLINI

I used to. The movies I saw became a part of me.

I

The movies are a great part of the memory of all of us.

FELLINI

When I go to a film, what interests me now is the story. I escape. I have no interest in the camera. If I'm aware of it, that's wrong, though when I'm making a picture, I constantly look through the camera viewfinder. I feel compelled to act out all the parts for the actors. I'm even a very good nymphomaniac. For me, the set is life. I think nothing personal happens to me anymore.

Work becomes more important to me as I get older. When you are very young, there are many competing pleasures. And maybe you need less to make yourself happy because everything is new to you. The world of old age, it is a shrinking world. Smaller things are magnified. It's like childhood. Few people are important to you, but they are *very* important. Little things get bigger. Food is more important. I fear old age and physical decadence. I don't want to live to be a hundred.

I

I've heard that a few times before, but never from anyone who was ninety-nine.

FELLINI

But the man who likes women remains young.

I

Isn't it usually the other way around? That the man who remains young likes women?

FELLINI

Both are true. But the liking keeps you young. It's the same with youth. The old who have the possibility of being with the young remain younger—they get a transfusion. But it's rather vampirizing for the young.

I

I don't think so. I've spent a lot of time with older people. Some of them were rare and gifted people, and I think to some extent all of the people you know well become a part of you, as the movies you saw became a part of you.

FELLINI

We must talk about what we will do tomorrow. We could go to a cocktail party . . . except I don't like cocktail parties.

I

Then it must have been rather tedious for you to do the research for *La Dolce Vita*.

FELLINI

I didn't have to do any research. I don't go to orgies or wild parties, or spend my time with the rich. I can do it all better in my dreams and fantasies.

I

At an ideal cocktail party, whom would you like to meet?

FELLINI

Real or fictional?

I

No limitations.

FELLINI

Casanova and Pinocchio. You know, they had something in common. With Pinocchio it was his nose that grew. Casanova could do it eight times a night. Did you know that?

I

No, I didn't. How do *you* know?

FELLINI

I have it on his own authority. He wrote it.

I

That may not be the best authority.

FELLINI

Who would be better?

I

The women in his life.

FELLINI

As long as I can remember, I wanted to meet Flash Gordon. When I was a boy, he was my hero, and he has remained my hero. I could never, never quite believe that he wasn't real. Does that seem odd to you?

I

Ray Bradbury told me that Buck Rogers was like that in his life. At one point when he was a boy, his friends made fun of him because of his fascination with Buck Rogers, and he destroyed his entire comic strip collection. Then he felt lonely and lost. He decided that those "friends" who wanted him to be just like them, who wanted to take away something from him that enriched his life, were not friends at all. So he stopped knowing them and started collecting Buck Rogers again.

FELLINI

I think I have read everything Ray Bradbury has ever written. I am very fond of science fiction. Fantasy and the supernatural are what interest me. It is my religious belief.

I

What would you like if you could have three wishes?

FELLINI

To be able to eat everything yet be thinner, to have more hair, and to make another film—always another film. But I have found it easier to fulfill my wishes in my fantasies.

Have you noticed the way Rome has recently begun to age badly? Do you see it?

I

Rome is such an old city, it would be hard for me to notice change.

FELLINI

It is aging much faster now, and differently, in a way that is graceless. It has less to do with antique, and more to do with decay. They give reasons like the smog, but I think it is an attitude, a loss of optimism and pride which permeates even the statuary. Rome looks older to me now than it used to be. But perhaps that's just because I'm getting older.

The next evening Fellini and I walked in Trastevere, the old section just outside of Rome, through narrow, winding streets on our way to the home of a young journalist and his graduate-student wife. On the way there, we stopped at one of the innumerable cafes both for the atmosphere and for cappuccino and cake, because Fellini said it was only going to be a small informal supper. Arriving at their apartment, we were stunned by a sumptuous array of food that indicated days of planning, shopping, and careful preparation.

The wine was too expensive. The young woman's elaborately coifed hair represented half a day at the beauty salon. She served in a black cocktail dress and high-spike heels. For the occasion, the finish had virtually been dusted from the furniture surfaces.

After the dinner, it was with obvious pride and anticipation that she presented Fellini with her completed doctoral dissertation, the occasion for the invitation. It was contained, or rather constrained, in two huge volumes. Politely, he leafed through the pages and nodded with approval whenever he observed her observing him. When we left the apartment, Fellini was obviously relieved.

I

I guess you don't like being a thesis.

FELLINI

It's embarrassing to be someone's thesis, especially so many pages. I've never seen such a big work. Imagine, three years of her life! And it isn't even about my films. If it were about my films . . . It's about my days with *Marco Aurelio*—the humor magazine. It was all forty years ago. Forty years ago!

I

Do you know what time it is?

FELLINI

I'm not wearing a watch.

I

I'm not wearing one either. I think it's about 4 A.M. These little winding streets are really dark. There's almost no light and no one around at all. I have a question: Do you think it's safe?

FELLINI

No.

I

I'm sorry I asked.

FELLINI

I told you not to carry a purse.

I

I didn't, but it wasn't my purse I was thinking about.

FELLINI

Once I could have walked anywhere in Rome, with no thought —absolutely anywhere. I had a special immunity. It was like being a sheriff. Now there are a lot of strangers around, new people from all over. We have imported muggers. These new ones, they won't recognize Fellini. If they do, they won't care.

I

We're not alone. *[We hear male voices, but we don't see anyone. Then they come around the corner into view, about six well-built young men in leather jackets, talking loudly. They move in, following close behind us.]*

FELLINI

Don't look like you're afraid.

I

But it's so dark, my bravery will be wasted. Do you know where the car is?

FELLINI

Somewhere around here—more or less. *[The group draws closer and stops, making a sort of semicircle around us. They stop talking. No one is smiling. One of them who is standing just a little out in front of the others steps forward. He stares at Fellini. Fellini stares back. Then suddenly in the darkness we see smiling teeth, and the stiff figures relax. The one in front salutes, greeting Fellini. "Alo, Federico!" Greetings are exchanged. We leave, followed by a chorus of "Ciao, Federico!"]*

FELLINI

They were the ones I know.

I

Yes. I noticed.

"Vlady, invent me something"

DAVID SARNOFF

OMNIPRESENT TELEVISION IS so much a part of everyone's life and has influenced all of us, yet Vladimir Zworykin's name is far from well known. It was his creation, television, rather than his own visage, that became the great celebrity. Television has made Johnny Carson, not Vladimir Zworykin, one of the most famous people in America.

It is difficult to achieve something that satisfies the world. It is even more difficult to achieve something that satisfies oneself. As the "father of television," Vladimir Zworykin made a lot of people happy. When I met the inventor of the iconoscope and the kinescope, however, I found him less than happy with the achievement of his life.

Opening the screen door of his modest Princeton home for me, he asked, "Why are you here?"

"I'm just about to buy a television set," I answered. "Do you have a recommendation?"

"Save your money," he said.

"No, I'm determined, so is there one you could recommend?"

"RCA."

"Are you prejudiced?"

"Yes," he answered. "It's a good company, and they put so much money into it, they deserve a return on their investment."

As I entered, I saw his own television set and said, "There it is."

"I don't know if it works," he said. He went over and turned it on. Then he switched so rapidly from one channel to the other that it was difficult to tell what programs were on. Having tried every channel, he turned the set off. "No, it doesn't work," he said with a look of total disgust.

"They told me television would never be anything—and they

were right. My punishment is my wife likes it. You could say I made television for my wife. For me it doesn't have to work. It entertains her. She watches television. That is my punishment.

"Last year I was very lucky. Thieves broke into my house and they stole my television set. They didn't take anything else, but they took the television set. I could have been twice as lucky; they could have taken *both* sets.

"My child is a test pattern. It is like watching a child of yours grow up that isn't like you. You say to yourself, 'Is this mine?' Television makes more trouble than it cures. It emphasizes the negative and makes for misunderstanding, especially among children.

"Those early years—before eight—shape you very much. I believe I am now entirely the person I was at the age of eight. That is why I worry about television and its effect on the young—watching sex and crime all the time. It is a distortion of life. Bang! Bang! Bang! They know too much too early and have their childhood stolen."

I asked him if there wasn't something on television that he liked. He thought for a few seconds, then answered, "Instant replay."

"Do you watch the news on television?"

"I prefer to read the newspaper," he said. "So much repetition of the news shapes the effect it has. The news on television actually creates news by saying the same thing over and over. It makes everything seem like it is happening more times than it is."

Like the directors who didn't really want to talk about the films they made a long time ago, Dr. Zworykin told me, "I do not think a lot about television. I did that already. I always loved what I was doing until it was done, and then there was only the next time."

Many of those who had the good fortune to choose the right cradles have wondered what might have been their fate without their inherited wealth or their niche in the family business. Vladimir Zworykin was born with more than the proverbial silver spoon in his mouth; it was a gold spoon enameled by Fabergé. Zworykin's childhood household included a nurse for each child, and there were so many servants, young Vladimir never saw all of them, nor could he count them. His family was one of the richest in Russia, but all of his inheritance disappeared in the Russian Revolution and he became a refugee.

During World War I, when the Russian Government failed to send the payroll to his army signal corps regiment, Zworykin was able to support his company with his own allowance until the money arrived. Having been born into great wealth and living with it until he was a young man, he knew well what money bought and what it didn't buy and thus did not have to overestimate it. "It is what you are inside that matters," he told me. "You, yourself, are your only real capital."

I asked if he ever missed the grand style of his youth, a style which the Russian Revolution had abruptly brought to an end.

"No, it never mattered," he explained. "Wealth for the sake of itself is so uninteresting. My real life is in my mind. It does not matter what kind of house I live in. It was always my laboratory that was important to me. I suppose that was my real home. I did not lose my home when the Communists took a house. I lost my home when old age deprived me of a laboratory.

"I do not care about being richer, because there is nothing more I want to buy with money except a big laboratory. And for that I would need the millions of RCA.

"My father was one of the richest men in Russia before the revolution. Now our family house is a state museum. The world has changed very much since I was a little boy there."

"You are one of the people who changed it," I said.

"I am not responsible for the way they use it," he replied, defending his invention of television as though what I had said was not merely a simple statement of fact but an accusation. Changing the subject to one he obviously found more pleasant, he reminisced about his Russian childhood:

"I don't know if you know how the windows were, but in my house there was a place to sit, like a box in front of the window, with something between a mattress and a pillow on it. They sat and looked out the window the way people watch television now, only they saw more. I would sit there, especially when I was very small.

"I would be home a little sick with a cold. It was a luxury to be only a little sick and home like that. Then I would see an old, old man with a long white beard, almost to the ground, trying to run, but hardly able to walk, coming along through the woods toward our house. I could not believe then that anyone could ever be that old, though he was perhaps younger than I am now. When I saw him coming, I knew we were going to have a phone call. This man was the old overseer at my grandfather's house. From our house you could almost see his house, but whenever my grandfather was going to make a telephone call, he sent his man to tell my mother to expect it. Then I would tell my mother there was going to be a phone call. She would say, 'Vlady, how do you know?' At that time, our houses were the only ones that had phones."

Appropriately, at that moment the telephone rang in his Princeton home, and he answered. It was for his wife. "Katuschka," he called, "telephone." He explained to me that it was one of the ladies in her club. Shaking his head with a slightly perplexed look, he said, "It is strange, isn't it, to speak on the telephone with someone and not be able to see them—when it would be so easy.

"Communication has always meant everything to me. At the age of eight, I went with my nurse and a man who worked for my father to see the ships of my father's shipping line. My father was always away doing business. He was what in the revolution they called a 'capitalist.' I was taken to the bridge by the captain of the ship, who would do whatever I said because, even though I was just a little boy, he worked for my father. I was fascinated when he would push a button in one place in the ship and a bell would ring in another part of the ship. Then I discovered Morse code. That was communication. I couldn't get enough of that. I would go home and think about it, and I knew that was what I was going to do—to make communication.

"One of the reasons I wanted to be able to see more than my eyes could see and hear farther away than my ears could hear was that my father was always away on business when I was a little boy. I wanted to be able to communicate with him.

"The life of my childhood was a happy one. I remember going to the river in the summer and watching the servants wash the linen. In the winter I would go skating with my best friend, Basil Vassili. One day, I had a cold and was not allowed to go. Basil

Vassili went skating on the river, fell through the ice, and was lost. After that, my happiness was never so perfect because I knew about the possibility of falling through the ice, which is different from only being warned that it is possible. I wonder what Basil Vassili would have done with his life?"

He indicated a Russian painting on the wall, not one he had brought with him, but a picture he had purchased later. It was a rural scene of nineteenth-century Russia.

"I can look at that painting and hear the piglets squealing. That's the market on Saturday near my home. The Russia I love is the memory I brought here." He tapped his head with a finger. "That Russia lives only here."

Besides inventing the iconoscope and kinescope, which made television as we know it today possible, Zworykin also developed the electron microscope. He had begun work on a device which would enable doctors to view their patients internally, and thus eliminate the need for exploratory surgery. He also had ideas for electronic acupuncture and an electronic translator that would instantly translate any language into any other language. "Anyone could speak with anyone else anywhere in the world, each using his own language, and each understanding the other perfectly."

I met Vladimir Zworykin on his ninety-first birthday. When I wished him a happy birthday, he replied, "Ninety-one is not a day!"

"It certainly isn't," I contributed weakly. While I was speaking he seemed to be mentally calculating something.

"33,146.75 days," he said.

Even at ninety-one, Zworykin did not like to think of himself as retired. "They force you to retire," he told me. It was clear he did not even like saying the word. "It is death to part of you at a time. Retirement is terrible. Perhaps old age is easiest for women who never had a career.

"I have less energy now, so that makes it easier to do less. Your loss of energy as you become old is a help to keep you less angry because you have had your means of working taken away from you." His laboratory had been taken away from him, and though he could have access to it whenever he liked, the keys were no longer his, and he had to ask someone else.

I was invited to stay and have "a real Russian dinner, cooked from memory," as he described it, with him and his wife, and to celebrate his birthday with them.

"I hope you do not mind having dinner at five," he said. "We always have it at five—not because we like having dinner that early, but because of the girl. She has to do the dishes and get home by seven."

We ate borsch, stuffed cabbage with sour cream, and pasca and koulich while he talked about his relationship with Russian-born David Sarnoff, long-time head of RCA:

"Sarnoff liked to eat our Russian food. He was my patron—like an artist has a patron. He would call me and say, 'Let's have lunch together.' I always knew what he really wanted. We would be having lunch, and he would look up and say, 'Vlady, invent me something.'

"Sarnoff would say to me, 'How much will you need?' I always said forty thousand dollars. I never knew the price.

"He had perfect faith in me. The only question he ever asked after that was 'What's it going to do?'

"I remember once I was being honored, and many people spoke about me as a scientist, about what I had done as a scientist. Then Sarnoff, who was introducing me, spoke. He said, 'Do you know what he is? A salesman! He sold us on pursuing his ideas.'

"He was right. What good is an idea that isn't pursued? Having an idea isn't enough. You must take it as far as you can.

"But I was not a natural salesman. I was much better at *un*-selling myself. I always told them every difficulty I could imagine, and that was a great many. I could see everything that could possibly go wrong under any circumstances. Sarnoff told me I must not do this because it would 'confuse' them away from what we wanted. The encouragement of Sarnoff was wonderful, but without it, I would have found another way.

"It's nice to have people say, 'Good work, Vlad.' It is not nice if they say, 'You are mad.' You can enjoy encouragement coming from outside, but you cannot *need* for it to come from outside. You have to be able to push yourself."

I suggested that the ideal is if the helping hand you need is attached to your own arm. He laughed, and even his laugh seemed to have a Russian accent.

"You cannot let your personal life interfere with your work," he continued. "Your work must go on because it is your purpose in life. This is so even when the man inside you is crying. The most terrible thing that can happen to you in life is the death of a child. You don't expect your child to die before you. This happened to me. Yet you go on working. You must, and your work saves you.

"Another tragic experience for the creative person is for someone to accuse you of stealing his idea. Even though not true, it is a mortification. It happened to me, and it was like a scar. More than one person can have the same thought. But the most terrible thing is someone's inventing your thing before you do. You can work years, then one day you pick up a scientific journal, and you get a jolt. You read about your work, and someone has done it ahead of you. It is as if somebody else wrote your idea for a book first."

I asked Dr. Zworykin what was the best moment in his work, the one that was most thrilling for him. He answered, "The moment when it works."

Picasso had said virtually the same thing to me when he spoke of "the ecstasy of that moment when you have the pleasure of attaining what you have been struggling to attain." Picasso had dramatized the concept by reaching up and seeming to snatch his goal from out of the air.

Zworykin continued, "You never know when that moment is coming or when it will come again. I don't know why, but the second time, sometimes it does not work. You invite everyone to see the result you have achieved, then it doesn't happen. But you do not get discouraged once it has worked because you know it will work again. No matter how much you think you know when it is going to happen, it fools you. Then, suddenly, it works. That's what it's all for."

Vladimir Zworykin saw a world of things that have been done and a world of things that remained to be done. He had a special perspective. "I have always been amazed by people who say, 'It cannot be done.' They are so sure in their pessimism. How can they know? I always knew there was more than I could see. People don't need to be stopped because someone says it can't be done. That is lazy. Imposing limitations on yourself is cowardly because it protects you from having to try, and perhaps fail.

"Everyone is born with an idea, but to stop there is not enough. There is really no room for just a theory. Without a laboratory, a theory is nothing, because it is just the first step and it keeps changing. You may learn by accident, but you must be open to receive the message.

"There are many miracles that are no longer miracles, but realities. They already exist in the laboratory and are known to work. But they aren't practical until people can afford to buy them. It isn't a miracle until it not only works but is cheap enough."

I suggested that perhaps the first time is a miracle, but the second time is not, the wondrous achievement being the ability to repeat something over and over again that previously seemed unknowable, to convert the impossible into something routine and commonplace.

"We strive to make the miracle a well-known friend," he responded. "No one ever does anything alone. You are always building on people who came before you. They are your foundation. You must stand on their shoulders."

After dinner his wife asked me if I would like to watch television. That presented a certain dilemma. I had the feeling that I had been asked because it was her opportunity to watch, and that she wanted me to say yes. Dr. Zworykin turned to me not only to hear, but to observe my reaction. It was like a test. I thought if I said yes, he might decide I wasn't worthy of his time. In truth, I didn't want to give up the time with him to watch television.

I answered that I would rather use the time speaking with him but that I would like to watch briefly because then for the rest of my life I could say I had watched television with the inventor of it.

They laughed.

We watched for a few minutes. Then Dr. Zworykin said, "Enough." He turned to me. "We will go into the other room." So we left behind Madam Zworykin, Walter Cronkite, and the bad news of that particular day.

We talked about Albert Einstein, who had also lived in Princeton.

"Einstein was my neighbor," he said. "He was a nice man. They always kept their lawn well." He had known the man, Einstein, not just his extended self.

"What did you talk about?"

"The grass," he said. "He was the cosmos, the universe. I was communication, so we didn't have much to talk about.

"I feel sorry for him, Einstein. So much of what he believed is going to be proven wrong in the next ten years. It is better for a scientist to die before that happens. Dying is less painful than seeing the death of your beliefs. The real death for a scientist is to outlive his theories."

He explained in considerable detail what he saw as the fallacies in Einstein's thinking. While he had this one-sided scientific conversation with me, he spoke much faster. He was in a world where he felt truly at home, the world of science. As he finished speaking, he realized that he had been carried away by his own enthusiasm and interest, and had left me far behind. He felt the need to explain, saying, "Scientific language is my first language."

He said that many people thought Einstein must have been an odd person because he was a genius. "The world has a strange conception of the scientist. Many people think that if he is a genius in his work, he has to be a fool about everything else. Of course that isn't true. Intelligence is intelligence."

Before dinner, Mrs. Zworykin had asked me if I would like to wash my hands. The washroom was as meticulously kept as the rest of the house, but in a corner there was an askew pile of magazines in many languages. On the edge of the sink, one of them was folded open, and slightly damp. The page was full of numbers, symbols, and letters, few of which I recognized, formulas to accomplish that of which I could not conceive, a few foreign words, and a series of hieroglyphics. I recognized some words in the Cyrillic alphabet though I didn't know what they meant. They looked familiar by comparison to the rest of the page.

When I mentioned the journal to Dr. Zworykin, he told me:

"I only read to learn, to learn for what I am doing. There's no time for anything else. I read only technical things. There is so much to learn, you cannot keep up with all of it. You cannot even keep up with all of the journals. Everything goes faster now, and it is getting too complex for any one person. But you are young as long as you are still learning, and you can be doing that as long as your health permits."

As I prepared to leave, he gave me a photograph of himself which he autographed. Some pictures had been taken of us together, but he wanted me to have one of him "when I was a young man." Actually, it was a picture taken in his sixties.

"It is a picture of my spirit," he told me. "Inside, that is the man I am now."

As I rode away from Princeton, I thought about a photograph he had shown me on the wall of his house. It was of Dr. Zworykin and his wife standing in front of the mansion in Murom that had been his boyhood home. The picture had been taken on the occasion of his first visit back to Russia in forty years.

The imposing edifice, which after the Russian Revolution had been converted into a national museum, had in its perfectly manicured setting an aspect of not having changed in a century. But there was one change.

On the mansard roof there was a television antenna.

AT THE TIME something is actually happening, we are not always aware of a memory in the making. I looked forward eagerly to my first meeting with sculptor Henry Moore. What I did not anticipate was the striking image of the day before that appointment, a Sunday in London which I chose to spend with his work at the Tate Gallery.

Some of Henry Moore's figures were displayed in the middle of the floor so that it was possible to stand next to them and virtually become part of the display. As I stood there, a group of children entered. Their tour leader was describing the figures and encouraging the children to touch them. They were gleeful and enthusiastic, and I heard one say, "How beautiful!" just before I realized that all of the children were blind.

Henry Moore was truly fortunate to be able to give such pleasure. I thought about it the next day as I sat with him in his home, walked through his studio with him, and saw those figures that still resided and presided on his land; but no memory would be more striking than that of the Henry Moore who, for a moment anyway, enabled even the blind to see.

Otto Preminger's dining room faced his small but precious Manhattan garden. Dominating the garden with her serenely graceful presence was a rather large Henry Moore sculpture of a woman. Various neighbors, I was told, had expressed admiration for the figure, but had bemoaned the fact that they could see only her back. Otto Preminger had her mounted on a revolving pedestal so that everyone else, on occasion, had a chance to observe the figure not only from the front, but also both profiles.

After lunch, Otto Preminger walked with me into the garden,

where he touched the back knot of her hair affectionately, saying, "I bought her years ago. She is always fascinating. Not realistic, but feminine. Distorted, but graceful. I love her. The whole house would be changed if she went away."

I commented that I loved his figure, too.

"She's not mine!" he responded emphatically. "She's Henry Moore's. If you write about her, you must say she's Henry Moore's. I can see her every day. I can touch her. But she is never Otto Preminger's; always she remains Henry Moore's."

When I visited Henry Moore in Hertfordshire, he was pleased to hear about "one of my girls," as he referred to his figures of ladies. It gave him pleasure to think of them out in the world.

About one and a half hours from London, I realized I was probably getting close to Much Hadham, where Henry Moore lived, because when passing a small church I saw one of his figures in the courtyard. His home, unpretentiously called Hoglands, was a seventeenth-century farmhouse with modern additions. The ceilings were low, and the rooms were not really large, but they seemed so because they opened onto Henry Moore's "park." The acres of greenery outside and his works that dotted the landscape appeared contiguous with the comfortable living room. This was where Henry Moore and his wife, Irina, had lived since World War II when a bomb fell near his London studio, making it temporarily uninhabitable. They had moved to Hoglands then and never looked back. It was a house with many studios that had been added along with additional acreage. As he showed it to me, Henry Moore was, like Chagall, justly proud of the home his work had earned for his works.

Though the interior of the house could not be described as ostentatious, it did contain treasures: works by Henry Moore himself, by Cézanne and Rodin, by anonymous pre-Columbians and Africans, and by nature—rocks, driftwood, and shells. The unifying link in their selection was the taste of their owner, who had chosen each object, one by one, and who took obvious delight in having them about him. In the days when it was all he could afford, he had frequented the London museums. Now he was aware that his home had become his own personal museum.

Sculptors and pianists develop a part of the body which we do not ordinarily realize can be developed—the hands and the fingers. Henry Moore's fingers looked as if they possessed a life of their own—as if they should belong to someone else, a much bigger man, or even as if they didn't really need to belong to anyone at all, and could work on their own. His hands were usually in motion, but striking even in repose.

"This last fortnight's been very disrupted and distracting because of Wimbledon," he told me. Whenever we watched a repeat of one of the matches on the "telly," he displayed the sympathetic responses of the backseat driver or the former quarterback watching a football game. The muscles tensed in his legs, as if he himself were rushing to the net for a point.

During the afternoon, Henry Moore's wife came in to clear a place in front of us for what was going to be four o'clock tea. As she walked through, she moved a few objects, interrupting a thought of his, mid-sentence, and he stopped speaking. Henry Moore looked displeased. He spoke a bit sharply to her, and she hurried away. Pausing for a moment, he turned to me and said, "It's funny, you know, how we copy what we experienced as children, not because we want to, but because it becomes a part of us, and we can't help ourselves. And the older we get, the more often that which influenced us as children shows up in us. My father was the ruling figure in our family. One had to keep away from his chair. His corner was sacrosanct. Now that I'm older than my father was, I sometimes find myself being him. Everyone must have his space."

I had brought my camera, and I asked Henry Moore if his wife could take a picture for me. "Don't you know how to use your camera?" he responded. "I take all my own photographs. I get better work, I don't have to explain to anyone what I want, and why waste money? Here, give it to me, and I'll take the pictures." I explained that what I really wanted was to have my picture taken *with* him. He called in his secretary, Mrs. Tinsley, and she took a picture. "Will one be enough?" he asked me.

Henry Moore made it clear that he could not afford very often to make time to see people. Not bothering to waste any subtleties, he said, "It's seeing you or making a figure."

As I rode away that evening, I wondered what the figure would have looked like that might have existed if Henry Moore had not spent the day with me.

HENRY MOORE
I have to explain—I didn't prepare for this, for you. I didn't plan it at all, so I hope I'll do it all right.

I
You've prepared with your whole life. I can't ask for more than that.

HENRY MOORE
I don't think about what I'll say beforehand. I don't believe in doing the same job twice. If one spends one's time thinking about a task, it takes as long as actually doing it. Longer. I don't think about what I'm going to do before I do it, except with my real work, of course. I think about that a great deal before I begin. Sometimes an idea has to be in my mind for years before suddenly it's ready to be born. Then the time it's born makes all the difference. Born at another moment, it might turn out quite differently. One has to hope it is born at the best moment.

I don't like to make too many advance plans. I always let each day decide. It will anyway. One never knows what each new day is going to bring. The important thing is to be open and ready for it. I think in terms of the day's resolutions, not the year's. I think, what has this day brought me and what have I given it?

I don't do this kind of thing very often—talk to anyone. It's not only that I need the time, but as the time ahead grows shorter, one has to conserve all of one's energy, as well. Energy is precious. With age, it's necessary to think more about conserving all of one's energy for work. Also, I feel it's a mistake for an artist to talk much about what he's doing.

I
Many creative people have said that to me—that the talking dissipates the creative energy. And the luck, as well.

HENRY MOORE
What it does is relieve the tension one needs for one's work. The need to have to get it out is very important. If one can get it

out by telling about it, it's easier, and then one needn't do all that work.

I

It certainly takes a lot less time to tell about it than to actually do it.

HENRY MOORE

Yes, and time, that is the greatest luxury. It's something money *can* buy for you—the choice of how you spend your time. Treasure it. Time is the most limited thing we have, and the most valuable.

But it's also a responsibility. If I don't do some meaningful work each day, something I'm proud of, I feel let down. Of course, some nights I go to bed happy, feeling I've achieved something. Then, the next morning I look at it, and the excitement doesn't hold up.

I

Picasso told me that the most destructive thing that could happen to an artist was to become bored by his own work, to fall out of love with it.

HENRY MOORE

I believe that, too. I could be disappointed for the moment, but I could never become bored by my work. My work and my grandson never bore me. Later I'll show you some of the drawings I've been doing of him since he was born.

Boredom and routine are two different things. It would be terrible to be bored, but it is essential to have a great deal of routine that allows you to do your work. I like routine in the mundane, necessary things because that kind of organization liberates one. My wife and Mrs. Tinsley do that for me. They keep out the outside world, which would impinge on my time and energy. Yet I have never wanted to make myself totally inaccessible. But I don't like routine in what is important to me —in my work. That is where variety and stimulation are essential.

My wife, Irina, was an art student. She is also my best critic. A wife who understands is so important. It isn't that anyone can really help you to do what you do. But the wrong person can hinder you. It's very important to me that my wife is an artist.

She feels what I feel and can understand. She knows when to be there and when to disappear. Another presence can be immensely encouraging if it's the right one, or immensely intrusive if it's the wrong one.

Well, you go ahead and ask whatever you feel.

I

I think it's interesting that you used the word "feel."

HENRY MOORE

Yes. I'm a person who must touch, so I suppose I think in those terms.

I

The idea of getting started has always seemed to me an important one—in the arts, in anything we do in life.

HENRY MOORE

Of course. You're right. The important thing is somehow to begin. Everything grows out of those first few scratches. A piece of marble or stone is just like a blank sheet of paper—the idea has to come from the mind.

I

Writers sometimes talk about "writer's block." Is there such a thing as sculptor's block? I don't mean that as a joke.

HENRY MOORE

If one gets stuck, the important thing is to get some marks down. You must destroy the virginity of the paper or the marble or the stone. Then you can work. Once the novel is begun, it goes on its own. The figures are like that. They are the characters into whom one breathes life, and at a certain point they take over.

I

That's the exciting way, when it happens, but I assume it doesn't always work that way.

HENRY MOORE

No, I'm afraid not. Sometimes after one gets started, the figures go their own way, and it's not the way you wanted them to go. Then you must stop, or you may have to go back and make a new beginning to match the changes. What's important is that you have something that will hold your interest all the way through.

I

Any number of creative people have told me that the hardest thing was to find the right project, one to which they could make that kind of commitment.

HENRY MOORE

That's why these maquettes are so important to me. This is one of my maquettes. *[He picks up a model]* I have used these more and more over the years to help me determine which project I wanted to pursue. I like to start with a small model, or a maquette. Then I can make the final one any size. Everything has an appropriate size.

Take it. You don't know it unless you hold it. That's good. You looked at its back, too. That was the right thing to do. It's meant to be seen from all sides. I'm a three-dimensional artist. I see the world in that way. For that reason, I'm a sculptor.

A maquette is like a story idea for a novel or a film. I shall probably have to do many drafts, so it must retain its interest in order to last through a big one. At every stage it changes. You cannot look at a baby and see the grown man. It would be like seeing a maquette as finished and ticketed for delivery.

If I have a project that's really big, I have to do some little things in between, along the way. Everyone needs their little satisfactions to be able to go on. A postponed reward isn't the same. I always have some little things I'm carving while I work on a big piece. I always thought that if I had to diet, from time to time, along the way, I'd have to have some little cakes.

I

Speaking of little cakes, I've brought some from Fortnum & Mason for our tea.

HENRY MOORE

Not now. We're working. Later. I always have my tea at four. We need to use every minute. When I take time out to do something like this, I'll make up for it by working late tonight. I don't let people or things interfere with working.

You mustn't let anything stand in your way. I find it important to start in the morning. I know I must permit no interruptions or the day will get away from me without my getting what

I wanted. If I accomplish something in the morning, then in the afternoon I can sit and read the paper without guilt.

For me, somehow, I'm resigned to the fact that afternoons aren't for work. Up to teatime, all right; but after that, I want to go back to work. I *must* go back to work. I'll be working late tonight to catch up for today. You see, if at the end of the day I haven't spent at least a part of it where I've accomplished some work that satisfies me, I'm depressed and the day is a ruined one.

I

I'll be hoping tonight is especially productive. If not, I'll feel guilty, too.

HENRY MOORE

Check with me, and I'll let you know. These last days, Wimbledon ruined my schedule. Do you have television where you're staying? Did you watch Bjorn Borg?

I

I watched a little. But I'd rather play tennis than watch.

HENRY MOORE

I love television for the sports events because I couldn't see all of them if I had to go to them. I couldn't take that much time off from my work. I love sports. I was very good at sports at school. My sister and I won the mixed doubles in the grammar school. I was always a good athlete. You have to be as physically fit as an athlete to be a sculptor. *More* fit!

I

More careful, too, I imagine. Sculpting seems dangerous.

HENRY MOORE

I'm a practical person. I know I have to be careful. If I chop off a finger, it wouldn't be good for my work. *[He observes me writing down an impression of the room]*

I see you write with an old-fashioned fountain pen. That's good. The point shapes to your hand. You shouldn't let anyone else use your pen. Your pen is an extension of your hand. What's important is finding what works for you. If you want to do something in life, get as familiar with it as you can; get familiar with the tools and the atmosphere in which the work is done. Go to a sculptor's studio. Go to an artist's studio. See that what you want to do can be done by people who are just people. See people who are doing it, whatever it is. Make the work you want to do in life as familiar as you can, even before you have much chance to do it.

I

When I was at NASA in Houston, Alan Shepard told me that one of the most important elements of astronaut training was simulation. They did everything to simulate space conditions, so that when the astronauts finally got into space, everything would seem familiar, even boring. The ideal was that even the moon would seem mundane. It was a strange feeling talking about the moon with someone who had been there.

HENRY MOORE

I admire the astronauts. I'm very interested in them. They are like athletes, and I've always admired athletes. Society tends to overrate intellectual creative endeavor, but anything physical is mental, too—the discipline and the control. I'd love to go to the moon. *[Wistfully]* All those textures on the moon . . .

Texture is so important. I love shape. *[He picks up a small piece of driftwood from the coffee table]* What do you think this is? A mermaid? A giraffe? These are my inspiration as much as the naked shape of a pretty girl—and a bit less distracting.

We'll have to make a place for the tea things. There's hardly room for your cup. I hope all this clutter doesn't bother you. What was Picasso's house like?

I

Lots of clutter. Picasso said too much order made him nervous.

HENRY MOORE

This table is full of little things I've been given or collected. I often find ideas from bones and pebbles. Any form, any shape in nature can start you off. It does with me, anyhow. And a lot of my sculpture's been influenced by my liking for bones be-cause they're nature's sculpture.

Here's what looks like a pebble. The person who brought it yesterday is a great collector, and he has several thousand early Mexican, pre-Columbian sculptures. And this, he tells me, could be 2000 B.C. You see, it's a pebble, but the sculptor has made that part into a head, has made this part into a breast, and this into a hand. It is seeing forms in nature. *[He hands the piece to me]*

I

She feels good, too.

HENRY MOORE

It's nice to hold, yes.

A sculpture should be based on touch. In form we learn, as human beings, from feeling as well as seeing. I mean, a child learns what is soft and hard when feeding at his mother's breast. It knows the kind of roundness and so on. It knows when it falls later on that a fall is hard.

I

There's one figure of yours I know most intimately. It belongs to Otto Preminger. I don't know if you remember her . . .

HENRY MOORE

A reclining figure? Standing? Sitting?

I

She's rather like this. *[I pose]* She has a little knot of hair at the top of her head. I understand one isn't supposed to describe your work as "beautiful," but she's beautiful; in bronze, larger than I am.

HENRY MOORE

Really? Well, she's not that tall, I think, but I should be pleased for you to say that. You see, there's a mental sense of monumentality which some artists have, and others don't. I love the grand scale. The greater energy of the grand scale is so stimulating. But if it can't be very big, I prefer very small, like my maquettes.

I've always known from the beginning that I had this sense of bigness or monumentality, which Michelangelo has above all people. In fact, I became conscious of wanting to be a sculptor by hearing a story about Michelangelo at Sunday school when I was about eleven or twelve. The Sunday school superintendent always gave a little homily, a little moral. He was telling how Michelangelo was carving in his studio. The studios, he said, in Florence, were often open to the street, like a garage, or like a workshop. And a passerby stopped and watched Michelangelo working. Michelangelo was carving the head of a laughing faun —an old satyr. He was laughing with his mouth open and teeth showing. After watching for about ten minutes, the passerby said, "Michelangelo, an old faun wouldn't have all its teeth in." Michelangelo just listened, then took his hammer and chisel, and knocked two teeth out. The Sunday school superintendent said, "And there, children, is the greatest sculptor that ever lived listening to a complete stranger; listening and realizing that there was some sense to what he said, and acting like it. So, children, always be ready to listen to what people tell you because it may be something which is helpful to you and sensible."

I didn't remember all that, all the stuffing. We don't always get out of a thing what we're supposed to. We take what catches our fancy. I remembered that there was a sculptor named Michelangelo. My father at the time was subscribing to a new encyclopedia for children in installments. And it just happened by luck that there was an article in one of the fortnightly parts on Michelangelo. From then onwards I knew that I wanted to be a sculptor. And when people said, "Henry, what are you going to do when you grow up?" *[Chuckling]* I said, "I'm going to be a sculptor."

I

You really never know when the important thing in your life is going to happen, do you?

HENRY MOORE

No, you never know when a thing just strikes a spark and lights a fire there. Youthful impressions are so important. I remember the combination of the moors of my boyhood and the mines with their slag heaps. As a boy, I collected sticks and bones. I was always interested in shape and form, and texture, too. I would like to run my fingers along something, not just to look.

What's the first childhood impression that comes to *your* mind?

I

A scoop of strawberry ice cream on the street. I was left holding the empty cone. It was before I'd even had the first lick.

HENRY MOORE
Do you think it influenced you?

I

Perhaps it made me live more in the present. I don't tend to save things for the future.

HENRY MOORE
Why?

I

I'd been saving the ice-cream cone. I was postponing the pleasure so I'd still have it to look forward to. I remember pushing it down with my tongue—and then it was gone.

HENRY MOORE
Life is made up of many little things—a dripping candle in a wine bottle. I think those things stay with us all of our lives. Maybe you gained by it.

I

Maybe. I hope so, although it didn't seem so at the time.

HENRY MOORE
The way we see things at the time and the way we remember them are often two different things. It's like what you said about Otto Preminger's figure of mine. When you told me the size, I knew that you hadn't remembered correctly. You thought she was almost your size, but I knew you were wrong. You remember her much larger than she is.

I

It's the impression she made on me. I suppose it's like remembering houses you knew as a child as being much larger than they were; or adults you knew as a child as being very tall even if they were short, because they were all so much taller than you.

HENRY MOORE
The period in which you are young, like the geographical place in which you find yourself, influences you for the rest of your life. I was influenced first by the land, and then by the discovery of the city and its possibilities. Where you are is important—where you start life, that is. Access to seeing the great things is a help. For that, living in a city like London or New York is an advantage. It's not that you copy. But the great works of art

become a part of you. Your mind and your eyes, they take it all in and file it away. And for me, it went to my hands.

Touch is so important. I was the seventh of eight children in the family. I had a sister younger than me, but she died when she was about fourteen. Anyhow, my mother suffered from rheumatism for as far back as I can remember. She'd sometimes say, "Look, Henry, lad," and she'd show a swelling on her knuckles and say, "That's giving me gyp."

I

"Gyp?"

HENRY MOORE

A Yorkshire word which means terrible pain.

When I was about six or seven, my mother would call, "Henry, lad," and I knew what it meant. She wanted me to rub her back. She'd invented a rubbing oil or she'd been given a recipe for it by somebody. I know eucalyptus was in it and some ammonia, because it made tears come to my eyes. She'd come along and bring this bottle. She'd say, "Henry, lad; rub my back. It's giving me gyp." And she'd pour a bit into the palm, and I had to rub her back gently with it.

I was a bit embarrassed always. But this taught me what women's backs are like because in doing this, when you come across the shoulder blades, it's hard; when you come across the behind, it's soft; when you come down the backbone, and so on. I do backs very easily now. I mean, I can make a back in no time. It always comes all right; it's always a good back. And this is because of Mum's. I would massage her back for hours. She said that I had good hands. I think that the tactile image stayed in my fingers. My fingers remember it. It comes out when I'm sculpting a woman's back. I can do good hands and toes, too.

I

Your mother lived to see your success.

HENRY MOORE

Yes, she lived to eighty-four. She saw it, but she was not very impressed. She watched me as I used to carve in the summertime, out of doors, hitting away for an hour or so. And she said, "Hey, lad—whyever did you choose that?" Because her point was that people had been educated to get away from manual labor. I mean, she'd lived and worked hard manually all her life.

My father had been a miner for a period, though he was very intelligent, remarkably gifted. If he'd had my intent of mind, there's a chance he'd have done unbelievable things. Because he taught himself. I got to grammar school by scholarship, which I failed the first time, and he made me take it a second time. He could help with my algebra and my geometry, and he'd left school at nine. And all self-taught. He passed his mining-engineer exam and could've been qualified as a manager. Then he had an accident to his eyes, and that disqualified him. But he taught himself all this from books. He really was a most unbelievable type. And how he worried over his children, trying to get them to be represented better and not have the kind of rough life that he'd had. So my mother looked upon getting away from manual work as the ideal.

I

And you became a manual laborer.

HENRY MOORE

Yes, and she saw me working away. She'd shake her head sadly and say, "And you could have been a teacher." Because, I mean, people may think that miners work, but Michelangelo worked harder than any coal miner ever worked in his life. Michelangelo was known to be carving right through the night. I've carved for exhibitions fourteen hours a day. I did coal-mine drawings in the war, and I was down in the mine for a fortnight.

Michelangelo wrote, "A sculptor has to work." I keep mentioning Michelangelo because he is the unique hero of sculptors. I mean, to do the *David* at twenty-four from a block of marble that somebody else had given up. Yet he was one of the great minds of the world. So this idea that physical labor and intellect are divorced and not together is nonsense. Some of the painters like Leonardo are among the great intellects. I mean, he invented all sorts of things long before their time came. He had ideas for a flying machine and everything else. Yet to paint a fresco is a physical labor as hard as mixing cement. In fact, it's a bit like mixing cement.

Michelangelo must have been the toughest physical competitor. Tremendous.

I

If you could have met Michelangelo or Leonardo da Vinci, what would you have asked them?

HENRY MOORE

Oh, I don't know. . . . *[Thinking for a moment]* No. I wouldn't have asked them one single question. Because their lives were enough to tell you what they were like. I mean, one doesn't *have* to ask Michelangelo, "Do you think sculpture's important?" *[Laughs]* If he hadn't thought it was important, he wouldn't have spent that effort on it. Of course not. There's no need to ask; the work tells you.

I

I've always thought it would be fascinating to be able to talk with buildings and inanimate objects . . . to chat with the *Mona Lisa* or *David*.

HENRY MOORE

Oh, yes, it would be. Future generations will have records and films of famous people nowadays. And they'll *know* what they were like. Now we have to romance about a lot of people. I'm very pleased that I met people like Picasso. Rodin I didn't meet. I would have liked to have met Rodin. Braque's been here. All that period. One knew them by being interested and being in the art world.

I

I suppose one of the dividends of your own success was meeting other people whose work you admired.

HENRY MOORE

Yes, and I'm grateful for that. Of course I am. And I try not to be unhelpful to young sculptors. You cannot tell anyone how to do anything, but you can give clues. You owe it to offer this help —to put something back. Not everyone can take your help and apply it. A person must first have the dream of wanting to make something of himself and then finding what it is he wants to be. You hope a few can. You do it for that hope. When you are young, a little encouragement means a lot. You get a great thrill from the first bit of success that you get.

I

What was that "first bit of success" in your life?

HENRY MOORE

It was the first time I could earn my living without teaching.
That was a great thrill. I'd always believed that I would have to
teach. My parents wanted me to be a teacher—steady work, you
know. "Be sure you can make a living." I can still hear my
father's words in my head. My father said that I had to be able
to do that to have security. He wanted me to be a teacher in an
ordinary school as my older brothers had all become. But I
wanted to go to art school. I didn't want to teach, but I believed
that I'd have to do it part of the time. Then I found that I could
make it just with my work. My mother called my work "playing."

I

That's the luckiest thing that can happen to anyone—when
your work is your play, and it brings success on top of that.
Then to get paid for what you would do for free . . .

HENRY MOORE

Not for free; I would *pay* to do it. It can be a way of earning a
living. But it isn't for that purpose. An artist should be enjoying
himself. To sell his work and get paid for it—that's double
reward.

I

Who most encouraged you to be an artist when you were very
young?

HENRY MOORE

Miss Gostick, who was my art teacher in grammar school. She
had such great enthusiasm. There is nothing greater than enthusiasm. Miss Gostick invited me to tea. I wanted to win her
favor and impress her. I had to do well for her. I just couldn't
disappoint her. I was around eighteen when Miss Gostick, who
had remained my friend, found out about ex-servicemen's
grants, and she helped me apply for one at the Leeds School of
Art. I first went there and took the drawing exam, and then
another exam to get to London. I knew that living in Yorkshire
I couldn't see all the things I wanted to see. The Leeds art
gallery had no contemporary works in it at all. But in the

evenings I used to go and look up books in the city library. There one came across books, in particular Roger Fry's *Vision and Design*. One knew that one well had to come to London and see the British Museum, see the National Gallery. I wanted to go to Paris, too. I knew that Paris was the center, as it was then, of the whole art world, and one must know something about it.

It was great luck for me when I won the scholarship to the Royal College of Art in London, the most important art school in England. Fortunately, the head of the Royal College of Art changed the year I went. When I was at the Leeds art school, the Royal College was a place to teach teachers to teach teachers to teach teachers—a snake eating its own tail. Kind of an ending. But a new head was named the same year I went on scholarship. His name was William Rothenstein, who was the son of a rich wool merchant in Yorkshire . . . *[A cat enters]* Hello, there!

I

Who is that?

HENRY MOORE

That's Mittens.

I

Mittens has the most marvelous white paws.

HENRY MOORE

Oh, yes. We call her Mittens because it's as though she's dripping snow. A wild cat had kittens in the old studio that I've made now into my drawing studio. Me and my wife used to take milk down to them. Two of them died, though. On about the third week, this was the only one left. And the mother cat brought her and put her down on the doorstep. And went off, and we didn't.

I

She abandoned her kitten on your doorstep, but she left knowing . . .

HENRY MOORE

It would be all right. So that's how we got Mittens.

Anyhow, William Rothenstein, being the son of rich parents and wanting to be an artist, had traveled a lot and lived in Paris for fifteen years or more. He was a friend of Degas. And Oscar

Wilde. His closest friend was Max Beerbohm, and so on. So when I went to the Royal College, instead of it being this old-fashioned teaching establishment for teaching teachers, he came and changed it. I was lucky to have that change because he was very friendly and helped me. He gave me the job of teaching in the college, from being a student. I didn't have any period of finding work.

I

Timing and luck are so important in life.

HENRY MOORE

Yes, yes. It just worked beautifully. I was there four years and then went to Italy on a traveling scholarship from the college. Rothenstein later became Sir William Rothenstein. He did a great thing for me. He held Sunday evening salons. I met Ramsay MacDonald there, and that was an important meeting in my life.

I waited for him to say something. He said a few words. They were perfectly ordinary. I don't know what I expected. Something awesome and profound, I suppose. Then I realized that I didn't have to be awestruck. He was only a human being.

That's a great thing to come to. Don't be stopped by what is in your own head. It's something you can take away from this visit—not to be awed by me, although you don't seem overly impressed.

I

It's only the way I look, certainly not the way I feel. I agree with what you said. I've always thought the inhibition barrier that matters most is the one in your own mind.

HENRY MOORE

I'm very grateful I found out that people who are only ordinary human beings can get pretty far. I'm also very grateful that I was too poor to get to art school until I was twenty-one. I think that they generally killed off all freshness. I was old enough when I got there to know how to get something out of it. Perhaps we go to school too early, before we know how to use it. Maybe it would be better if we went to school later, after we did something else first. Anyhow, I was set enough so that it couldn't make me like everyone else. If I'd been unlucky, I would've come from a well-to-do family.

You must always be open to your luck. You cannot force it, but you can recognize it.

I

Do you think it's better for an artist not to start out rich?

HENRY MOORE

Probably, but not necessarily. Cézanne is one of the greatest artists of the last hundred years or so. He can be thought of and ranked with the old masters—he's really our latest old master. He had a private income. And probably in his case, it helped him a lot. But it doesn't really make any difference to the artist. Just the fact that you're able to do it is like being born with a private income. You don't *need* to earn anything. I didn't need as much success as I have. I wasn't at all dependent on it.

I

Recognition of your work, along with the financial security, took a while.

HENRY MOORE

I lived half of my life without great fame. I've been living in this house since World War II, and you can see it's not a fancy house. It's a good, comfortable house. I can only eat so much for lunch, and I've been able to take care of my family. So money doesn't change one's life so much as you might think. When one doesn't have it, one thinks having it will make some great difference. That's because when one doesn't have it, one thinks about it a lot, and its importance is magnified. It's like sex, in that way, but when one has it, one doesn't think about it. That's the greatest thing money buys; not having to think about getting it anymore.

I

And, as you said, time.

HENRY MOORE

Yes, and it gives one freedom, which is everything to an artist. Even when I didn't have money, I didn't take commissions. I've taken only two commissions in my life. One of them was a madonna and child, and I loved the subject. That was a long time ago, and even then they didn't tell me exactly what to do. I hate commissions. I don't need any push from the outside. I don't work toward a deadline. No one can want it done more than I. I don't know when it will be right, but I do know when it *is* right. When I didn't make enough money from the work I really wanted to do, I taught in art school so I could be artistically free.

I

Would you have gone on if you hadn't been so successful or if your success had taken longer to arrive?

HENRY MOORE

I would have had to. I couldn't have done anything else. This is what I am: *[He indicates his surroundings]* my work. People liking it or not liking it doesn't change it for me. But it did make it easier for me to have more time, to have more space in which to work, to use more expensive materials, and, very important to me, to work bigger. And, of course, it's more fun when people like what you do.

But it isn't so much failure that stops the artist as it is success. One is so encouraged to repeat oneself. An artist must take the line of most resistance to keep growing and changing after success.

I

Does success bring happiness?

HENRY MOORE

Not necessarily. To be happy, you have to do things when they bring you pleasure. It's important to get things when you want them. My first year in London—that was my greatest happiness. It was not the best thing that ever happened to me, but I was able to feel greater happiness. Perhaps life subdues you as you are shaped by it.

When I rode in the top of an open double-decker bus in London, it was as close to heaven as I've ever been. I had a horrid little room by other people's standards, and by mine now. But I saw it as paradise. I couldn't bear it now, but I shall never be happier anywhere.

I've never been to a psychiatrist. I wouldn't think of going, because I'd be afraid if I found out what makes me tick, I'd stop ticking or tick differently. I don't understand what makes my

work come out the way it does, and if I hear it being analyzed, I
stay far away. I'm always afraid, I suppose, if I got into too
much analysis of what I do, I might be unable to work. It would
be rather like thinking about walking—right foot, left foot.
You'd stumble! And working is my life. If you took that away
from me, it would be worse than killing me. I've inherited the
Yorkshire value of work from my father. Being idle wasn't what
my father believed in.

I

I was at the Tate yesterday, and it was the longest line I'd ever
seen for anything, a film or any kind of entertainment. And I
noticed with your family group that everybody had to touch the
figures even though there was a sign prohibiting it.

HENRY MOORE

The problem at the Tate is that there is so much to see and feel.
So much of it deserves to be in isolation from other works, so
that one could see it alone, uninfluenced by the group which
influences audience perceptions. It may be good to see a Marx
Brothers comedy with an appreciative audience, but it is also
good, at least sometimes, to be alone with a work of sculpture
and thus be unaffected by the feelings of others.

I

When I was waiting to appear on a television program for my
book, Bob Hope was waiting to be on the same show. In talking
with me, he used a phrase, "the collective individual," to refer
to the audience when it is a group that reacts as one.

HENRY MOORE

In comedy it's a wonderful advantage, because laughter is contagious.

I

[Indicating the view out the window] A sheep out there just moved!
When I first looked, I thought it was part of your sculpture.

HENRY MOORE

It is. A moving part. The sheep give life and movement. The
sheep are in my style. They aren't mine, did you know? I let
someone do it as a favor because he wanted to use some of my
land for his sheep. I thought it would be good for the grass.
Then I noticed how they looked just right with my work. The

sheep really look wonderful, just the right scale. Horses are too big.

I love the land. We always had some kind of little cottage in the country. I always needed to spend some time in the country. My sculptures were mostly intended to be seen outside. The sky is the perfect background. It's space with no distractions. I like working in the open air and seeing my things in the open. I think that I was probably influenced in this by being poor when I was a boy. Our house wasn't big enough to work in, and there were always too many people, so I would go out and draw or carve in the garden. It was the only way I could get the space I needed. I was shaped by this.

Having enough space to work in is a great luxury; not to have to move something in order to do something else, not to have to interrupt your work to achieve order. It was very difficult to work without space. Always having to clear away something was a terrible distraction. The interruptions sap your energy, frustrate you, and diminish inspiration.

I

I understand perfectly. I don't have any space, so I have a carpet of papers.

HENRY MOORE

But everything you do where it's harder and you overcome makes you stronger.

I

As long as it isn't so hard that it takes all of your energy, stops you, or changes you.

HENRY MOORE

Do you like my trees? I love my trees. They're wonderful in all seasons, but I love my trees particularly in the winter because that's when they show their anatomy. Look at that tree. Really *look* at it. In the winter, it's like a naked person. That's when I like to draw it. Then I know all its secrets. I can never understand anyone's embarrassment over anything that is part of nature, such as nudity.

My wife planted all of them. We never expected to see them like this. I'm lucky to have lived so long, to have enjoyed late success.

I

Cézanne had late success, too.

HENRY MOORE

He never had an exhibition until he was about sixty-seven. He had no real success. He was longing for it, to be made a Royal Academician at the salon. But he didn't show a facility and talent to begin with. I mean, in the early work of Cézanne. It was his late work. The watercolors are the most facile, wonderful things—what wonderful technical ability they show! But there are people who are like that, who start without much evidence but with such an ambition or a determination, such a longing or necessity for it in their lives, that they do it eventually.

I

I think the word "longing" expresses it.

HENRY MOORE

Longing, yes. But some people show the promise early. I mean, Picasso is the opposite of Cézanne. At nine or ten his father taught in the art school in Barcelona, and Picasso was brought up in a painting family whereas Cézanne's father was a banker with no trends towards helping his son in that way. Picasso showed terrific talent when very young. So did Raphael. So did Michelangelo. There are people who come at it easily. And there are people who come at it by terrific effort, but they can be just as great.

I

I wonder if it makes any difference in the pleasure they get from what they do, whether it comes to them easily or through great effort.

HENRY MOORE

No. We're talking now about the people who contribute more than the ones that are clever in copying other people—the ones who contribute a new point of view. Art is to expand. I mean, Beethoven made music much richer and took it further than what it was before. Cézanne has taken painting further. He was very interested in understanding nature. Not in a photographic way.

I

Like you perhaps?

HENRY MOORE

Yes. I do not make replicas of real things, but the embodiment of what is felt in the mind when the thing is seen. The work must possess a life of its own apart from the life of the object represented. I consider myself both realistic and abstract simultaneously. I can't imagine not being both. But I don't particularly care for purely abstract art, which is why I don't do it. If people see my work as abstract, that's their problem. Of course, I don't mind if people say my work is beautiful, but it isn't what I strive for. I prefer power to beauty.

I

Your work is in such a wide range of sizes. How do you determine what size is the right size for a particular work you're creating?

HENRY MOORE

There is a right physical size for each idea. If you have a sculpture with architecture, it needs to be very big, because modern buildings are so big. I prefer my work set in a landscape—anywhere rather than in or on a building.

Every day one learns a bit more about looking and understanding. I mean, one can't look through the window without seeing how flat the ground is. The shadow from the trees makes it flat. And then the distance, too. The trees that are near you and trees that are further, and so on. Now, I could find some reason for drawing that just to show this sense of three-dimensional reality. Cézanne was a three-dimensionally minded artist. He wanted to understand the visual world. And, therefore, he wanted to know why certain colors come forward and others go back. I mean, blue goes backwards, and yellow or red hits you.

I'm not a painter, although I like color, and I like drawing. I'm not a painter because I need the actual reality. I want to know that I've made what I set out to make as real as *I* am. *[Laughs]* As real as a chair. Whereas a painter may not have that. He may be interested in tones. Matisse, for instance. Matisse often doesn't worry about the form, though he can. Doesn't worry about the drawing. It's distorted, that's all. But for me, Cézanne is the painter that I learned from. Because . . . how can I explain it? You can tell when Cézanne is painting Mont Saint Victoire, the mountain that was about two or three miles away from where he lived. You know it's two or three miles away when he paints it. If he paints a gardener, the gardener is sitting next to him. And you know that the gardener is that close. It's not a flat pattern. I always want to go behind paintings and see their backsides.

I

Besides Cézanne, are there other painters who have influenced you?

HENRY MOORE

I admire Turner. I particularly admire space in Turner. He paints real space for the first time. It's an amazing achievement. He achieves three-dimensional space on canvas.

I

You speak about Turner and Cézanne in the present tense, and rightly so, I think. The work has an immortality. It must be a wonderful feeling to know that your works will have their place in the future's present tense.

HENRY MOORE

You never know about these things, but you hope. It does give one a good feeling to think that one's works will go on.

I

Is there anything you haven't tried that you still want to do?

HENRY MOORE

I do what I want to do—my work. Actually it gets more and more stimulating. I mean, your eyes get more and more sensitive. Every day, through your eyes you can understand something or get pleasure or get a thrill. People think they see, but they really don't. No matter how many people see something, each pair of eyes sees something different. You should see what you live with the way you would if you were a tourist or a visitor. You must be a tourist in life. Train yourself—the Romans didn't see the Coliseum. I can't imagine what life would be like if I were blind. It'd be the most terrible thing. Of course,

I should think it was a pretty big misery when Beethoven realized he was getting deaf.

I

Perhaps for him that was worse than being blind.

HENRY MOORE

For him it was worse, yes. Well, it depends what people are. Of course nobody's equally gifted in their senses. I mean, you don't have someone who's just as good a musician as Beethoven and yet just as good a painter or sculptor as Michelangelo. Course you don't. You could have somebody tone-blind being a great painter or a great sculptor. It doesn't mean that you have to be cultured in or sensitive to every kind of art.

I

It seems to me that being sensitive to the arts and being able to appreciate them is a gift in itself.

HENRY MOORE

Course it is. And through art, you can help people not only to share your vision, but to increase their own sensitivity, their own perception—to expand their horizons. What you can appreciate and to what extent determines the richness of your life. You need a long life. I'm still learning, you see. There is so much to observation and experience, I don't think I could be bored for a second. I have never in my life been bored.

I like to disturb, not lull, people. If they think, feel, are disturbed, even irritated, it's all right. But not if people say "How interesting" in that way that they do when they don't really feel anything about what they're seeing. Or worse, if they say "How beautiful."

I

I'll try not to describe your ladies that way, but certainly this one figure I admire so much is quite a romantic conception of a woman.

HENRY MOORE

Oh, well, women matter much more to me, women's forms, I mean, more than men. I hardly ever draw men. I only draw them when it's a family and it's got to have a man. An ensemble.

At the Leeds art school we weren't allowed to draw a nude

woman until the second year. And what excitement there was then! Before that we'd had a male Italian model, because all models in those days were Italians, and he had a moustache that you could see from the back sticking out—the two points of this moustache. And I began to hate him. We had him for a whole year, the same model. Dreadful.

I've always liked women better than men. For me there's more meaning; there's something, well, more emotional about women. I mean, my mother meant much more to me to look at than looking at my father. Nine out of every ten drawings that I make are of women. And my figures, they're female. That's just me. That's just my makeup. That's what I'm made like. Yes. But men are necessary as a complement to women, *[Laughs]* but not in themselves. *[Indicating a female figure that is standing outside in the garden]* You see that girl out there? She's ready to go on a journey. She has her ticket.

I

How do you feel about their going away?

HENRY MOORE

I enjoy knowing my girls, but I don't need to keep them by me.

I

Do you travel much yourself?

HENRY MOORE

I travel for my work. I go to Italy, where I love it, to be near the marble, the Carrara marble. Sometimes I go to Germany when one of my big works is being cast, to watch over it. If I travel, I like to travel with a purpose. I like to go to a marble quarry or to see one of my works that has been placed in its setting, or perhaps for an important exhibition of my work. I don't actually travel because I'm really always with my work. I don't really have to travel. The world comes here. [Alberto] Moravia was here last week. Charles Laughton came here once. Lauren Bacall came. I'm glad she's working again. It's terrible not to be able to do what you do. Edward G. Robinson came. He had a wonderful art collection. Great taste. It was *his* taste, I think, not just what people told him to buy. Terrible, buying the big names for the signatures. *[We are served tea]* Is your tea the way you like it?

I

It's perfect.

HENRY MOORE

Here. You must eat one of your own cakes. There are so many. Why did you bring so many? We had a big lunch.

I

I was at Fortnum's and they all looked so good, I couldn't make up my mind. So I just kept adding cakes, and they had to keep getting a larger box. I didn't know which you would like, because nothing I read about you showed you in relation to anything but your work. One would almost believe that Henry Moore the artist doesn't eat.

HENRY MOORE

I'm quite normal. I like everything that's good. One of the great rewards and pleasures of financial success has been my being able to own the work of other artists. We have two Degas here. We've got three Seurat drawings there. We have a little Cézanne, only about a foot by ten inches, of a bather. We've had it twenty, thirty years. And I love it. In fact, there you see me having put the Cézanne figures *[He indicates a sculpture]* in the round, although the painting is, of course, a flat painting. I did it for someone just to prove what I think about Cézanne— that he has a monumental sense of three dimensions.

I'm a sculptor because I love drawing, and I've liked drawing ever since childhood. The lesson in elementary school that I liked best came on Friday afternoon, which I looked forward to, not because of the end of the week, but because of the drawing class. I *still* draw. I'm drawing down in my graphic studio this afternoon because I knew I was going to have an interrupted day. I draw whatever I'm sculpting at the moment. I draw because I want to study something. If I were the Minister for Education, I would make drawing an important subject. Not because you want to make great artists, just as you don't teach grammar at school because you want to make another Shakespeare. You teach subjects because they're part of understanding the world. Drawing from life is the best way of making people see. The face is the first thing we have for understanding a person. It is the first image we have, and really, most of the time, we never go far from that. I've said somewhere that if every husband was made to draw his wife, he'd understand or know what she's like much more than if he just looks. Might make a few divorces. *[Laughs]*

I

It would take away mystery.

HENRY MOORE

No, no. If something is important, you should *want* to understand it. In my opinion, you shouldn't avoid trying to know, to understand. The difference between human beings and animals is that the human beings appreciate things and try to understand them. And we have an intellect. We should use it. We should use everything we've got.

I

Ideally, with understanding you enhance your appreciation.

HENRY MOORE

You *have* to understand. And if a thing loses its interest, I understand it must be a very simple thing. Let's see—what *is* art? What use is it? I was asked this by some person watching me carving once—standing and watching for ten minutes, and seeing me work very hard. And he said, "Mr. Moore, what use is that?" He wanted to know what use it was! I tried to answer him. I didn't answer as well as I could have later because art is *not* for use. Music, painting, poetry, the dance—whatever art you think of—is not to make a living; it's not for use. I mean, an animal going into a green field begins to eat. It doesn't stop and look and say, "Oh, what a beautiful green that is!" Of course it doesn't. Human beings want to *know* what kind of world we live in, what a wonderful world it is. And music, painting, *all* our senses are there to keep us alert and to appreciate life and the world.

I

Now when there are so many economic problems, it's commonly said that it isn't as important to have money for the arts as for medical research; but I believe the arts have a role in maintaining health and well-being.

HENRY MOORE

If life is only to keep alive once you've started it, if it's got no other purpose than that, *[Laughing]* then it's no better than a worm or any what's-it.

I don't draw as much as I would like because it's important to save something for last. When one is young, one doesn't think one will care about things when one is old. But life is not like that. When you're old, that's what there is, and every day is just as important as in youth—maybe even more important. That's why I'm happy I saved drawing. I could have drawn more. I could draw more now. Sometimes I'm tempted. But I realize that I must ration drawing so that I have something to look forward to in my old age, when I can no longer sculpt, especially the big pieces. The big pieces demand the physical attributes of an athlete.

I

But you've been able to sculpt much longer than any athlete could have been active.

HENRY MOORE

Yes, from that viewpoint it's better to be a sculptor than, say, a dancer. Their bodies go out. It's good if you can save something in life for later, even though when you're young you want it all at once. You're greedy for everything at once. But life doesn't give you the choice. I went to Greece for the first time when I was in my fifties. It meant so much to me. I was glad it had been saved. Maybe by then I even saw more.

I

You mentioned liking to read as a boy. Do you still read a lot?

HENRY MOORE

I don't read novels anymore. No. Now I don't mind reading biographies. There's one book that I read almost every two years. And that's *Conversations with Goethe* by Johann Peter Eckermann. It's full of the wisdom of a person that's gone through and knows so much about human life. Not many other novelists have given their opinions outside their novels in the way that Goethe did. Otherwise the newspaper and so on take up as much time as I give to reading now.

But in the early part of my life, the novel was more important than painting or sculpture when I read Dostoevski and Balzac, the French novelists, Thomas Hardy. I think it probably made

me more of what I believe and think than anything else. I went
through all the great novelists. As a young boy it was Scott I
preferred to Dickens. I liked the romantic. After Scott, which
was probably until I was about sixteen, I must have discovered
the Russian novelists—Tolstoi, Dostoevski, Turgenev, and so
on. About two years, that was. Then, after that, came Thomas
Hardy. Later, when I was about nineteen or twenty, came D. H.
Lawrence. And these were coloring one's life more than what
painting and sculpture were doing. In character, that is. Because you don't get character out of painting and sculpture.
You don't get your beliefs in life out of them, or the same kind
of message. Michelangelo's *David* doesn't tell you that it's better to be honest or not.

I

Your air raid shelter drawings say as much as any novel.

HENRY MOORE

They were drawn from memory. I would go to the shelters and
then return home to draw the next day. I couldn't sit and draw
the people in the shelter undressing the children. It would have
been unfair to invade their privacy that way.

I suddenly became aware that he was looking with great interest at the side of my head. As if in answer to my thought, he
explained:

HENRY MOORE

I was just looking at your ear. You have an exceptionally fine
ear. Perfect ears are rare. *[With some difficulty he rises]* Come, I'll
show you my drawing studio. This cane is such a bother. I hurt
my ankle last year, and it still bothers me. They say when you
get older, things don't heal as quickly. But as long as I can
work, it doesn't matter.

From the house we went out to his drawing studio, passing
through a sheltered area along the way. Here he stopped and
pointed up. "Look," he said. Looking up, I saw the smallest nest
I'd ever seen. Inside and peeking over the edge were incredibly
tiny heads.

HENRY MOORE
Shhh! Don't disturb them.

I
What kind of birds are they?

HENRY MOORE
Swifts. The parents built the nest inside the house instead of outside because the weather's been so bad this year. Look down there. Do you see all that? *[The floor below the nest is dotted white—it appears as if an eagle's nest were above]* I saw one of the little ones this morning balanced on the edge of the nest with his tail outside the nest. And he did all of that on the floor, outside the nest. I want to ask you, why? Why? Is that instinctive or learned? Did he just know to do that to keep his home tidy, or did the mother teach them that?

I
I don't know. I've never interviewed any birds.

HENRY MOORE
Think about it. Which do you think is true?

I
Maybe both.

Part III

THERE

"I've become a body of films, not a man—I am all of those films"

ALFRED HITCHCOCK

THE FAMOUS PERSON LEARNS how to hide behind a public character, his extended self as represented by his work—the words of
the writer, the images of the artist, the sounds of the musician,
the discoveries of the scientist. Although the character that he
evolves to send out into the world grows out of his real self, it is
not exactly like that real self. It is a part of him, but not all of him.
As Mae West told me, "I'm all of Diamond Lil, but Diamond Lil
isn't all of me." The extended self usually has at least an exterior
confidence and sometimes a bravado that far exceeds that of the
private person. The private person may or may not be shy, but he
is always more reserved, more hesitant, more self-doubting, and
more complex than his surrogate public self. He is self-conscious,
though usually in the positive sense that he is conscious of self.
He may seem oblivious to it, but he cannot avoid an awareness of
the eyes that are upon him.

The world expects him to be "interesting" and "entertaining,"
so he develops a proven repertory of conversation and anecdotes
that he can draw upon when, as Laurence Olivier put it, "one has
to sing for one's supper." For Groucho's public self, his rule was,
"If it gets a laugh, leave it in." King Vidor described the extended
self as "the one that doesn't have to go to the bathroom." It is a
suit of armor for the protection of the frail human being who lives
within the larger-than-life public person.

Most celebrities enjoy meeting other celebrities. Celebrity is a
bond, and, clearly, it is stimulating to look about and see yourself,
not only in the company of those you have admired, but as Bill

Cosby observed, "Suddenly you're one of them!" He described the first time he realized *he* was "one of them":

"I was a hot young comedian, and Groucho asked to be on *The Tonight Show* when I was doing it. I really knew I'd made it when I was taken into the dressing room and there was Groucho Marx—in his underpants."

At "The Night of One Hundred Stars" benefit at Radio City Music Hall, almost two hundred stars appeared. The most exciting place to be was not in the thousand dollar seats, but backstage in the green room. There the stars had congregated from all parts of the world for the charity and also to see and meet each other. The first people to bring out autograph books were Helen Hayes and Brooke Shields, representing the special confidence of age and of youth.

James Stewart approached Orson Welles and said, "Excuse me, I'm Jimmy Stewart, and it's a great honor to meet you. I've always admired your work."

Orson Welles, visibly pleased, responded, "You certainly don't need to introduce yourself. There isn't anyone in America who doesn't know you."

In such a situation, the most luminous stars become the most respectful fans. It surprised me when Groucho would meet a famous Hollywood contemporary of his for the first time who had been at one of the other studios. "If you weren't in a picture together, and you didn't eat in the same commissary, you'd probably never meet," he explained. Meeting famous people sometimes put famous images into jeopardy. I asked Fritz Lang if there was anyone in the world he would still like to meet, and he told me, "I don't want to meet any more famous people whose work or accomplishments I've admired. I'd like to hang on to the last of my few illusions, if I still have any."

King Vidor recalled the arrival in Hollywood of author John P. Marquand:

"I remember when Marquand came out here to work on the screenplay of his novel *H. M. Pulham, Esq.* He arrived looking like an eastern banker—dark gray flannel suit and vest. He said he wanted to 'go California,' so we went out and bought him a wardrobe of the sportiest casual clothes we could find. He got fancy tennis clothes, the kind to walk around in, not to play in. Then we started to work on the screenplay of *H. M. Pulham, Esq.*

"Right away I realized he didn't know anything about doing a screenplay. Well, I could understand that because it's a specialized thing. So I said, 'Well, let's just talk about your novel.' Anyway, he didn't seem to be very familiar with his own novel. I felt like asking him if his wife wrote it!

"It's always strange if a writer doesn't sound like his work because you expect a writer to be able to use words effectively. Often an actor isn't like the characters he plays. When an artist or composer isn't exciting as a person, even though his painting or his music is, you aren't as shocked as if a writer doesn't say anything. Some of the people who have done great things are impressive, like works of art themselves. Some of them aren't, because what you call their extended self does the work but doesn't come to the cocktail parties.

"I guess I've disappointed quite a few people in my time. People expect you to be not only interesting, but to be like your work. If they meet me and someone thinks, 'Oh, he's not like *The Big Parade,*' they're disappointed.

"It was Marquand who introduced me to Lindbergh. You know, it's funny how in life, for some reason, it's the one that got away that you always remember—a fish, a girl, a film. The film that got away from me was the one about Lindbergh that was based on his book. I'd always really admired Lindbergh. He was the one person I most wanted to meet. Then the chance came to meet him.

"Marquand was back east reading for The Book-of-the-Month Club, and he'd read an advance copy of Lindbergh's book. He called me and said I really ought to come east right away and meet Lindbergh, because the book could make a great film. I got right on a plane to New York, and I cried in the lobby of the Pierre Hotel when I read that book.

"Marquand introduced me to Lindbergh, and we got along just great. The two of us spent a lot of time together. Lindbergh and I ate a lot of Chinese food, which was what he liked.

"It was interesting the way no one ever recognized him. He'd been the most talked-about man in the country, in the world. But no one recognized him, not even once. He just wasn't a visible celebrity without his aviator's cap and goggles. But he didn't mind. He said he preferred it that way. I guess he'd had enough.

"We really spent a lot of time together, and we talked mostly about the picture I was going to make from his book. I pretty much had the whole picture worked out, and we had a gentleman's agreement. I *thought*.

"Then, one day Leland Hayward appeared, acting as an agent. He offered Lindbergh more than I'd planned to spend on the entire film. And Lindbergh just signed.

"I didn't hear from Lindbergh. He seemed to have lost his big interest in Chinese food. I called *him*. He said sort of apologetically, 'I did it for my family.' Then he said brightly, 'Couldn't you just do it with Leland Hayward?' Now, of course, Leland Hayward was working with Billy Wilder. My first thought was, Lindbergh doesn't know much about business. My second thought was my first thought was wrong. Here was Lindbergh getting rich while I'd just wasted my time and enthusiasm and money.

"They made the picture with James Stewart, which was just the opposite of what I had in mind. Jimmy Stewart was in real life a general in the Air Force. He represented something quite different. He was a person who knew how to get along within the mainstream and to rise to the top. Lindbergh was a person who was always something of an outsider, always a little out of order, not quite fitting in, more of a loner and an individual than a leader.

"Younger was important too. At that time Stewart was too old for the part. But even more important, I felt he had to be an unknown. Stewart brought too much of Jimmy Stewart with him. It was such an established identity, and all those pictures he'd made before came with him to the part. I couldn't believe I was seeing Lindbergh. Afterwards I don't think Lindbergh was exactly happy about the picture, but then he had all that money.

"With anyone else I would have produced a contract and had him sign it. My lawyers would have been talking with his lawyers. But you couldn't do that sort of thing with that kind of man. You couldn't be so small as to ask for a signature on the dotted line from a man like Lindbergh, the hero. So that was how I happened a year later to be sitting in a movie theater in Westwood watching a film of the life of Lindbergh and reading the credit, 'Directed by Billy Wilder.' I'd been hero-struck by Lindbergh, and I'd confused the public hero with the private man."

Brendan Gill, who had written a book about Lindbergh, listened to my account of King Vidor's experience and offered his own theory:

"How Lindbergh would have hated that phrase, 'Lindbergh, the hero'! We all probably live at least two or three lives during our lifetime, if we live long enough. At forty or fifty, the person we were at twenty or thirty may have died within us.

"I never knew a person of greater integrity than the younger Lindbergh. Never. He once tore up a check from Hearst for more money than he expected to see for the rest of his life because he wouldn't do anything he didn't believe in or be associated with anyone he didn't like.

"Perhaps integrity is easier for the young. Perfect integrity may come more readily when life's possibilities seem limitless, when there are sure to be many more checks in a bright and seemingly infinite future."

King Vidor talked with me about the concept of the extended self from the standpoint of the private person inside the public person:

"People are always calling and inviting you to come and be honored. They want you to come to some out-of-the-way place, and they don't mention expenses. They want you to commit a date months in advance. They forget you belong to a flesh-and-blood body. It eats. It sleeps. They might as well say, 'Just send your reputation.'

"It's a very self-centered concept, the belief that the celebrity has become a part of your life and belongs to you for those days. They never leave you to have some privacy or get some rest. They come in shifts, but there's only one of you. You become a kind of toy for a few days.

"I remember one film festival that went on for hours. I asked where the men's room was. The reputation doesn't need to go to the men's room at all, but *I* thought it might be a good idea. Well, it was right behind a screen over to one side of the stage, and the only way you could get to it was to cross in front of everyone. I thought I had better use it before I was up there on the dais. I didn't when I found out that to get there, I had to pass in front of the whole audience. I might have gotten a round of applause."

Gloria Swanson told me that people seldom appreciate all of the difficulties involved when they ask a celebrity to make a public appearance. "They say I can go somewhere just for two or three hours, but they don't understand that I have to fly there, and I have to get ready for it. I need a week to do their day. I have to look like a star and be a star. They think you can be everywhere at once. They need you for this cause and that cause, and they're all good causes, but I'm a good cause, too."

Prior to meeting Marlene Dietrich for the first time, I called her Paris apartment.

"Miss Dietrich's residence," a voice, unmistakably hers, answered in French. Before I could say much more than my name, she interrupted with, "I am her maid. Miss Dietrich is not in. She is out, out of the country. She will not be back for a very long time." If she suspected a call was for her extended self, she did not want it.

During the Oscar rehearsal at the Dorothy Chandler Pavilion, I happened to be sitting in the audience between Laurence Olivier and Cary Grant. They were carrying on a conversation across me, but, happily for me, neither accepted my offer to change seats. Laurence Olivier was to receive the special Oscar that year for lifetime achievement, but he had not been well and was concerned about his ability to make the acceptance speech. He was not feeling confident about the way he looked, nor certain that he was even going to be able to make it up to the stage when called upon to rehearse.

Sitting there, we could hear people in the audience whispering and sighing, "Oh, look—there's Laurence Olivier!" Here was a celebrity even among celebrities. At first Laurence Olivier appeared oblivious to the attention he was attracting. Then, unable to ignore the whispers drifting our way, he said to Cary Grant with a sigh of his own, "Oh, if only I *were* Laurence Olivier!"

Cary Grant replied, "If only I were Cary Grant!"

The person behind the larger-than-life image doesn't always

feel larger than life. He is painfully aware of the frailties of the self beneath the extended self.

When Laurence Olivier was called to the stage to rehearse, he had difficulty rising, and said softly, "I wonder if I'll make it." He was assisted up the steps. His short speech was a bit faltering.

On the night of the awards, only one night after the rehearsal, as he stepped forward to receive his Oscar, he suddenly appeared to glow with radiant good health. He strode toward the microphone confidently, having seemingly shed more than twenty years, and his speech was worthy of HAMLET. When it was not rehearsal, but the real thing, his extended self took over so totally that even physical pain was forgotten.

Facetiously, I had asked Picasso, "Are you *really* Picasso?"

He laughed and responded, "I'm *almost* Picasso."

Douglas Fairbanks, Jr., told me that every time one of his old films played on television, it was interesting taking a cab in New York City. The drivers would look back at him with some faint glimmer of recognition and then ask him his name. "When I say, 'Douglas Fairbanks, Jr.,' the cabbie says, 'I just saw your son on television.'" The film actor's extended self is frozen in time.

Clark Gable's lack of respect for his own romanticized image endeared him to Anita Loos. One day she caught him nonchalantly washing his false teeth in the M-G-M fountain. When he realized she had seen what he was doing, he just laughed. His lack of concern with the preservation of the glamour of his extended self only enhanced her appreciation of the private man, though not everyone might have felt the same way.

The extended self often transcends the personal feelings of the private person. As a woman, Maureen Stapleton felt emotions her professional self would have eschewed:

"Personally, I always thought every other girl in the room had it over me, and that the boy I was with would rather go off with any other woman in the world than be with me. As I grew older, I got more certain of it. I envied every woman in the world who was more beautiful than I was, and that was just about *every* woman in the world.

"But it's funny, professionally I couldn't imagine envying anyone. I know I'm not Helen Hayes. I know I'm not Zoe Caldwell.

But it doesn't matter. I'm thrilled by what they do, and I'm happy just to do the best I can."

The public person lives an imagined life in the minds of others. He thrives or suffers as that proxy self outside of him glows brightly or diminishes. It is difficult for him to escape reviews and media response. All of us are reviewed in life by parents, teachers, peers, and others, but seeing it in print gives it an appearance of truth and permanence, as well as importance.

Marilyn Monroe drew two self-portraits which she gave to Lee Strasberg. They represented "the two Marilyns," as she expressed it—her extended self that the world knew and her private self, the little girl within. In the first picture, she is her screen image, glamorously attired in silk stockings and high heels; in the second, she depicts herself as a waif, shoeless, with falling-down stockings.

Sometimes the one most influenced by the extended self is the person himself. This is especially true of actors and actresses, though it can be equally true of any public personality. From time to time, an actor plays a part from which he takes away something that influences him not only in future performances but in real life as well.

"It's not easy being fabulous," William Holden admitted to me. "You really should be talking with Billy Wilder. He says all those clever, cynical things I'm supposed to say." William Holden talked about Africa where he said it was refreshing to be with dumb animals because they hadn't seen *Sunset Boulevard* and didn't expect him to be that character. "I try not to let people down, but I see the disappointed looks on their faces." When he came back to Hollywood, he said he knew how wild animals felt when they were put in a cage with people staring at them. It made him restless and anxious. He wanted to go back to Africa where he felt free.

I first met William Holden, or rather his voice, in the dark at the premiere of *Towering Inferno*. The man sitting next to me in the theater said, "Excuse me, I'm going out for a smoke." The film had just begun, and William Holden was speaking on the screen at the time. I realized that it was the same voice that had just spoken to me in the theater.

He went in and out innumerable times during the showing of the film, apparently unable to sit and watch his screen self for very long, excusing himself each time, saying he was going out to have a cigarette. Whenever he appeared on the screen, he gripped my arm, apparently unaware of what he was doing. It wasn't during the moments of dramatic intensity, but whenever he appeared on the screen. After each one of his scenes, he would turn and ask me, a perfect stranger, "Was I all right?" Even though he had appeared in so many films, he explained later, "You never feel confident that you've done a good job until everyone has told you so, and even then you don't know if you can believe them."

King Vidor talked about his friend John Gilbert, whom he said was profoundly influenced in his daily life by the parts he played on the screen. King had watched the real person change, becoming more and more like the character he portrayed, until finally the private person and the public person were one.

He also knew Greta Garbo well in the days when she and John Gilbert and he and Eleanor Boardman were a regular foursome in Hollywood. This social arrangement lasted until the day of their planned double wedding at William Randolph Hearst's San Simeon castle. On that day, three of the four waited in vain with their guests for Garbo to appear. King told me the story:

"Garbo had two drives, and they were both equally strong. She would do anything to get attention and anything to get away from it. She was always that way. Everything she did was individual— every gesture, every movement, every look, even the way she wore her clothes. Not the clothes but the way she wore them. It seemed like she was going out of her way to be noticed, always wearing some strange conspicuous thing that guaranteed you would look at her even if she hadn't been so beautiful.

"She was naturally the most visible person I'd ever known, and she did everything to enhance it. But if you looked at her, she'd get upset and might run away. She ran away from her own wedding.

"Actually, she never even got there. It destroyed Jack Gilbert. It *really* destroyed him. We always went out together; Eleanor

Boardman and I, and Jack and Garbo. We did everything together, and finally we decided to get married together."

King believed that the half of this double wedding that didn't
take place probably cost John Gilbert his career. When Garbo
didn't appear, Louis B. Mayer, who was one of the guests, tried to
console the jilted bridegroom by saying, "You're better off without that tramp," and Gilbert hit him. "You're finished!" Mayer
snarled from the floor, rubbing his sore jaw. Shortly thereafter,
Gilbert's movie career did, in fact, end with the coming of sound
pictures. King speculated that it was this incident with Mayer and
not Gilbert's voice that had ended his career. "Jack had a good
voice," King explained.

"Garbo wasn't shy. She wasn't shy at all. She would walk
around the house nude. I'd be there with Jack. Garbo liked to
walk nude through his garden. She was Swedish, so she didn't
think anything of it. She would appear completely oblivious to
anyone looking, like it never occurred to her we might, or like she
didn't care. I did quite a lot of looking. So did the Japanese
gardener. It was enough to cause accidents. I almost walked
through a closed french door once because I certainly wasn't
watching where I was going.

"She would talk a lot. She could really go on nonstop. The
thing about her being silent wasn't true. I knew her about a year
before I heard anything she said, I was so busy watching her face,
looking at her eyes, and just listening to the sound of her voice. I
think it must have been about a year before I actually heard *what*
she said, she had such a beautiful voice.

"When we played tennis, at first she hardly knew how, but she
was enthusiastic. I taught her. You learn a lot about a person
playing tennis with them. For instance, Chaplin cheated. He
cheated blatantly, in an obvious way like he wanted you to notice,
and then if you called him on it, he got angry and never spoke to
you again.

"I think what happened was Garbo didn't like spending the
energy on people when she didn't want to. So when the press said
she was so silent and wanted to be alone, she saw a good thing
and latched on to it. It was a convenient image, and it suited her
to put it on like a nice dress. But it fit so well, she never took it off.

She heard and read all those things that were said about her, and she believed them. Maybe she also understood that you have to be careful about breaking your image for people. They meet you with a whole package of expectations, and if you aren't like the way they expect to find you, you see those disappointed looks on their faces. That isn't fun, so you fit yourself as much as you can into the mold you think they expect. You have to be careful about that, because one day you find you've really become the part you've been playing. You have to be careful what you pretend to be because you may become just that."

George Cukor had his own ideas on the subject of the extended self, which he spoke of in terms of "star quality."

"To have star quality—in the movies, on stage, in politics, whatever—the star must project an image of having a secret. It's a secret everyone wants to know. Now, there doesn't really have to be a secret as long as people *feel* it's there. It's the *appearance* of a secret that counts. It's like sex appeal; a curiosity about the person, an intense need to know more. There has to be that element of mystery.

"There was never anyone who had more of that quality of having a secret than Garbo. Every man wanted to know more about that secret, and women were as fascinated by her as men.

"I remember when Garbo came to dinner at my house. Molnár was there, very anxious to meet her. He had a play, and we were talking about making a film of it with Garbo.

"The maid came in to serve. She had been with me for a long time, and she was used to serving a lot of famous people. She knew how she was supposed to behave and how not to behave. I hadn't mentioned that Garbo was one of the guests. The maid saw her and just froze there with the silver tray, and stared. She completely lost her aplomb. Only Garbo ever produced that reaction. Garbo sat looking like a frozen, haughty statue. She was, of course, perfectly aware of the reaction to her."

The film that Molnár wanted to make with Garbo was based on the life of Empress Elizabeth of Austria. He had asked George Cukor if he would be interested in directing it. George decidedly was.

Being a close personal friend of Garbo's, George had invited her to his house so that the three of them could have dinner together. Molnár was thrilled to be meeting Garbo. After meeting her, he was even more thrilled.

The first course was served and eaten without Molnár even speaking. The entrée was served and finished with Molnár still too dazzled to speak. Dessert was served. George kept encouraging him to discuss the script, but Molnár seemed too entranced even to speak, let alone "sell" his screenplay.

Finally, prodded by George, Molnár began to tell Garbo about it, prefacing what he said with abject apologies for the inadequacy of his work. He said that the original idea was not of sufficient interest, that the character of Elizabeth was not suitably fascinating, that there was not enough dramatic conflict, and so on. He went on pointing out all of the faults he could think of or imagine, and when he had completed his "presentation," Garbo left, scarcely understanding why she had been invited.

Thus Molnár's film, *Elizabeth of Austria,* directed by George Cukor and starring Greta Garbo, joined what film historian Herman G. Weinberg called "the Heavenly Films"—those films we never saw and never will see because they remain the dreams of their creators. "But they are dreams that disturb our sleep because of what they might have been."

The extended self of Greta Garbo had overwhelmed Molnár, whose loss of confidence in the face of her larger-than-life image had caused him to un-sell his script.

"After Garbo left," George Cukor continued, "Molnár, who was impressed by her beauty as we all were, told me about how he had followed Garbo in the street one day in New York. He saw her and wanted to speak, but the aura of inhibition around her was just too much for him, so he did this thing he'd never done before. He couldn't believe he actually found himself doing it—he just followed closely behind her for several blocks, watching her. What he noticed—Molnár was quite an observant fellow—was that Garbo didn't behave at all like other women. She never looked at dresses or objects in any of the store windows, nor did she ever glance at her own reflection in the windows. She walked at her regular rapid pace, always appearing to know exactly where she was going, until she came to the Steinway showroom on Fifty-seventh. She lingered, stopped, and stood with her face almost pressed against the glass.

"With Garbo, her public and private personalities coincided more than with anyone else I've ever known. And she was aware of it, although she knew how to appear oblivious to it. She held her head high and seemed untouched by the mundane realities of life. You couldn't believe her feet actually touched the ground when she walked."

George Cukor considered Joan Crawford's extended self more real for her than her private self.

"The time she really came alive was when the camera was on her. As the camera came in closer, she had an expression on her face of wanting it intensely. She glowed from within. Her skin came to life. Her head fell back. Her lips parted. Her eyes were glistening. It was utterly sensual, erotic. The close-up was ecstasy as, yielding, she gave herself completely to the camera.

"Joan Crawford and her camera. It was the greatest love affair I have ever known. She was married many times and had many lovers, and I was never in her bedroom, but I'm certain no man ever saw the look on her face that she had as the camera moved in."

George Cukor had another theory about star quality:

"It's being irritating. The stars have an irritating quality. It's something negative, an essential fault. If they don't irritate you, you don't remember them." As he spoke, George touched the ring he always wore that his friend Somerset Maugham had bequeathed him. "Maugham, Olivia [De Havilland]—with all that sweetness of Melanie—Kate [Hepburn], Garbo—they all had it, the irritating quality."

Bette Davis knew she had led an enviable life, but she believed that if women envied her, it was only because they didn't know what it was like to be Bette Davis on a day-to-day basis. "I'm the one who didn't get the man, which is the more interesting character on the screen, but in real life sometimes I wish I could have just been the girl who got the man." The kind of man she had envisioned in her romantic dreams rarely appeared in her real life. Her theory was that it was because he could not hurdle the inhibition barrier that both protected and isolated her. Instead, her celebrity tended to draw those with more nerve or ulterior motives. She believed that it was her extended self that attracted the wrong men.

"People start to expect you to be certain characters they saw in the films. They think I'm a difficult person because of the parts I've played. They're disappointed in you if you don't say those lines. They don't want you to be out of character. So, everywhere I go, I have to take all of those bitches with me."

George Cukor had known Bette Davis from the very beginning of her career. I mentioned her to him and he commented, "She's no Planny-Annie." I asked him to explain the phrase. He said, "It means she's not a bitch."

Laurence Olivier reflected on the public image of the screen actor, the romantic leading man who is frozen forever in cinematic time:

"I haven't got the right to grow old. People are too disappointed. They do not want you to get old. It's like some unpardonable crime. Your public image belongs to them, not to you. I sense real anger, sometimes even in my own friends, who seem to resent the decline of my physical self. Sometimes I hear them saying to each other, 'He used to be so handsome.' With strangers, I feel that terrible disappointment when my real self does not correspond at all to what they remember on the screen. I am no longer Heathcliff—if I ever was."

Edith Head thought that the day had passed when the Hollywood costume designer was expected to be a magician, imbuing each star with a special aura of glamour. She believed that glamour has been lost and that we are all the poorer for that loss. "When I began doing costumes, a waitress had to be dressed like a star. Then it changed, and a waitress had to be dressed like a waitress. Now, at the Oscars, a star wants to look like a waitress."

Ginger Rogers, about to make a television appearance, caught a glimpse of her reflection in a mirror, and paused to fluff up her hair. Shirley Eder and I, who were standing with her, heard two members of the production staff poking fun at the "fuss" Ginger Rogers had made about needing her own special hairdresser.

Ginger Rogers also heard them, and said to us, "I *am* my hair."

She was right. Her private self had not been invited to appear on the television special. They had invited the public person whose halo of blond hair was an integral part of Ginger Rogers. She understood that she owed it to her public to live up to their expectations.

Salvador Dali always spoke of himself in terms of his extended self. Talking with Groucho and me at the Russian Tea Room, Dali invariably referred to himself in the third person: "Dali can do things I couldn't do" or "I am a great fan of Dali's" or "Dali is the greatest," he would say.

Jascha Heifetz apparently did the same thing, according to Goddard Lieberson:

"Heifetz came to talk about himself in the third person. He would say, 'Heifetz performed very well today' or 'Today Heifetz missed.' Heifetz didn't do this in his earlier days. It was later when this separation of identities took place between the man and the great performing artist that many believe Heifetz's playing came to seem much colder and more detached."

A curious instance of separating the extended self from the private person was exemplified by Juan Perón's explanation of the excommunication of the Argentine president during Perón's own presidential term. According to his reasoning he, the person, General Juan Domingo Perón, had not been excommunicated by the Catholic Church, "only the president of the nation. They excommunicated the office." Convincing me was apparently of great concern to him. To further document his argument, whenever I arrived to interview him, coincidentally there would be one or several Catholic priests who were there visiting or just leaving.

The extended self exists in the eyes of the beholders. Charismatic personages are not assumed to have mundane thoughts, especially at exalted moments. Speaker of the House Thomas "Tip" O'Neill, whom I met at a New York party, made this point. He had known the man, Jack Kennedy, as well as the President of the United States, John F. Kennedy, and he knew that even a President at one of the great moments in his life could have a thought less lofty than might be expected:

"When Jack Kennedy was senator, there was a man in Washington, George Kara, who didn't hold any special post in the government, but whenever there was an important event or great party, he was always there. People called him the 'Ambassador.' Well, he was more than there—he was prominently there. He always had the best seats, next to the most important people. Whether it was the governor's box, ringside for a fight, or first-base seats for the Senators' games, George Kara always had the best, but nobody knew how he got them or what he did. I remember I was at this relatively closed gathering—some of the Senate and House leaders, a few other people—and Jack comes up to me and says, 'What's *he* doing here?' Well, a few nights later, we were at a black-tie affair, very elegant. I was standing with Jack, and there *he* was again. Well, it went on that way. We'd be somewhere and Jack would say, 'What's *he* doing here?' But I never had the answer. After a while we got sort of used to him. We would have thought we were in the wrong place if we didn't see him there.

"Jack won the presidential election, and finally the day of the inauguration came. I was very close to Jack Kennedy. He had eaten dinner at my home with Millie and me. I was seated in front along with Rose Kennedy and some of the closest members of the Kennedy family, and there was an empty seat next to me. I wondered who would be sitting there. I didn't have to wonder long. The 'Ambassador' sat down. I started to say something, but he spoke first. He said, 'Shut up, Tip, or they'll kick us both the hell out of here.' Finally Jack was standing up there, and he looked at me and smiled and then the smile disappeared as he saw who was sitting next to me.

"Well, it was the solemn moment. There he was being sworn in as President of the United States. It was a great moment in his life and in the life of the country. But I knew what he was thinking. After the inauguration that night at the ball, everyone milled around congratulating him. Spirits were high. Millie and I went up to him, and there were a lot of people gathered around him, but he saw me and moved towards me. I told him what a great speech it was. We shook hands; he looked at me. I knew what he was going to say, and he did. He said, 'Tip, how did *he* get the seat?' "

Elliott Gould called from the lobby of my building to see if I wanted to have a chocolate milk shake with him. I did. Lolly, the telephone operator who had put through his call, being an enthusiastic fan of his, rushed out to the front lobby to talk with him. I stepped out of the elevator and saw them engrossed in a cheerful and animated conversation. As I walked across the lobby, I heard her telling him about bits she had enjoyed in his films. When I arrived, he put his arm around her shoulders and gave her a squeeze.

We went out to have the milk shakes at Rumpelmayer's. Elliott was disturbed about a lot of things going wrong and a lot of things not going at all. He had just finished shooting a film and was between projects. One film for which he had high hopes did not look as if it were going to materialize. One of his films was getting poorer distribution than he had expected; he was about to have to move to another house; he was without a secretary and needed a new one; and his wife, Jennifer, while fixing coffee at their house in California, had spilled a pot of boiling water on her leg. Notwithstanding a double chocolate milk shake, Elliott was clearly downcast as he walked back and left me at the door.

In the lobby, Lolly, the telephone operator, almost bumped into me. Bubbling with enthusiasm, she was leaving for the day, but she stopped to say how handsome Elliott was, how nice, how funny, what a thrill it was meeting him. In ebullient spirits, commenting on what a wonderful afternoon it had been, Lolly disappeared into the distance. I stood there thinking how ironic it was that on that afternoon she had enjoyed meeting Elliott Gould more than he had enjoyed *being* Elliott Gould.

What had happened was that Elliott felt like his private self, the person who had to shave twice a day, while Lolly had encountered his extended self, the sum total of all of the roles he had played added to the connotation of many pleasurable evenings with fresh popcorn at the movies.

Certainly, the most readily identifiable public figure among film directors was Alfred Hitchcock. In addition to having a unique visage, he became an instantly recognizable celebrity all over the world because of his television programs. He told me what great pleasure it brought him to draw a gleeful gathering even in the middle of Tokyo, where local politesse customarily required the Japanese to avert their eyes from a passing celebrity. He thought that television had thus given him a satisfaction that he would otherwise have been denied.

"I'm naturally a ham," he said, "and because of television, I was able to have what is usually reserved for heroes or actors. They have quoted me as saying 'actors are cattle,' and looking down on them. But actually I envy them."

Significantly, Hitchcock observed that he had become his extended self even for himself.

"I've become a body of films, not a man. I *am* all of those films. It's not just that way for everyone I meet. The funny thing is, it's that way for *me*.

"I began, I suppose, by trying to satisfy the ego of that young man, myself, whom I scarcely remember. Now, I probably wouldn't even recognize him if I met him on the street. I have seen myself so much on the screen, in films and television, that I now see myself as a photograph."

Many of the famous people who spoke with me expressed some self-doubts, and a few even apologized in advance for what they feared was a discrepancy between their private selves and their public images as projected by their work. As Sartre had predicted, they believed I was coming with a preconceived impression of what they should be like and thus might be disappointed if they were not "in character." Some of them were uncertain themselves as to what character was expected of them by the world.

"Perhaps I should wear a cloak," Fellini said to me. "I would do it if I thought that was what people expect Fellini to be like. But my problem is I have never been able to decide who my own character is."

The extraordinary reassurances of an admiring world helped to create a citadel of confidence around Picasso and Mae West. Some, like Sartre, Chaplin, Henry Moore, Fellini, Groucho, and Henry Fonda—none of whom had suffered any shortage of accolades—told me, in one way or another, that I might be disappointed in talking with them. What they were saying, in effect, was that they thought I had come to meet their extended selves, and that they were uncertain whether they could adequately personify the myths with which their celebrity had imbued them. As even Picasso expressed it, "We are all afraid of being unmasked—that is, of having people discover that we have some weakness, that we are not as great as our image."

"I'm nothing without my writers," Jack Benny told me. "You really should interview them. I've always envied Groucho because he's just as funny, even funnier, offstage than on." What Jack Benny did not know was that Groucho was not perfectly confident, either. Not long after I first met him, I remember Groucho asking me, "Do I disappoint you?"

As Luciano Pavarotti made his grand entrance at the Italian Embassy residence in Washington, the party in his honor following the world premiere of *Yes, Giorgio* was already under way. The personification of vitality, love of life, and confidence, he nevertheless whispered to me, "I do not want to disappoint." The thought was his alone, for nothing he could have done could possibly have disappointed the black-tied and bejeweled throng; but he was aware of the monumental scale of expectation.

Sometimes an actor is so successful in a part that the character he plays comes to have a life of his own—the actor's life. At the 1983 American Film Institute gala honoring director John Huston, I was seated next to Leonard Nimoy, who was elated because he, himself, was about to begin directing the third *Star Trek* motion picture. The young actress who had played the title role in John Huston's film version of *Annie* was there to speak at the tribute. Dessert consisted of chocolate Maltese falcons, exact replicas of the original statuette that had appeared in the film. A chocolate falcon was presented to each table, where they were supposed to be eaten; but like Easter bunnies that are too beautiful, it was only with difficulty that they were broken up. The adult guests were as gleeful as children, but "Annie," already a seasoned show-business veteran, seemed unmoved. Her precocious reserve reflected the total professional.

Suddenly, she recognized Leonard Nimoy, and the trappings of sophistication fell away. She was once again a little girl as she shyly approached our table, greeting Leonard Nimoy not as Mr. Nimoy but as "Mr. Spock."

When she left, he talked with me about what it was like to have created a character who was so much a part of people's lives that it was in greater demand than his real self.

"I was invited to a lot of parties, but I found out they didn't want *me*. They wanted the other one. I was invited, but they wanted me to wear my ears. It's pretty awful to find out they only want you with your pointed ears. Even for years after *Star Trek* was canceled, it was still that way."

At a United Jewish Appeal dinner honoring Bob Hope as "Man of the Year," Jack Valenti introduced me to Bob Hope and former President Gerald Ford. In making the introductions, he said only, "This is Charlotte Chandler," not bothering to introduce the other two. I was reminded of being with Groucho, who was never introduced. Only those meeting him or those with him were introduced. Just as there are few celebrities of such magnitude that they are known monomially as was Groucho, with no need for a last name, there are few who are so visible that, in introducing them, no name at all is necessary.

One afternoon when I was having tea with Bette Davis, I invited Marvin Hamlisch to join us. From the first moment, it was as if they had known each other for years because they were so familiar with each other's work and public images. On arriving, Marvin and I walked down the dimly lit hallway of the Lombardy Hotel. At the far end, framed in the proscenium arch of the doorway, with the light behind her, was Bette Davis. She was wearing a red dress, not tight, but clinging softly in the right places, with a draped effect that followed her every movement. Her shapely legs were accentuated by sheer nylons and high heels. She was leaning sensually against the door, loose, soft hair casually framing her face.

"I always like to have the door open and be waiting for the person who's coming so they don't have to arrive and meet a closed door," she said.

Marvin replied, "Coming down that hallway, I felt like your leading man in one of those films . . ."

"I know you from the Mike Douglas show," Bette said. "You have so much enthusiasm and energy."

It was only after a lot of tea and cookies had been consumed that I realized I had not thought to introduce them. But that would have been redundant.

Celebrities frequently recognize a responsibility toward their images as perceived by the public. Calling on Joan Crawford at her immaculate white Fifth Avenue apartment, everything seemed protected by plastic, even Joan Crawford. She was not wearing shoes and asked me to take off mine before I entered. I complimented her on her beautiful dress, and she responded, "People expect to see Joan Crawford, not the girl next door. If they want to see the girl next door, let them go next door."

As I left, she invited me to take some of her matchbooks. They were white, as was everything else in the apartment, with her name simply but elegantly engraved on the outside. The matchbook had a special sheen and was done on the most expensive paper. I took one. "Don't take *one,*" she said, "I have a lot of them." I accepted the offer and took several more. As she said good-bye to me, she laughed, though I didn't think I had said or done anything funny. In the elevator, I looked more carefully at the matchbook. Inside, besides the matches, was printed the word "Fuck!"

When I walked with Groucho, strangers would frequently come up to him and say, "Hi, Groucho," and talk with him, and he would invariably insult them. Later, he would say to me, "It would have been a lot easier just to say, 'Good morning,' but they would have been disappointed. This way they'll remember it all their lives."

The way others see us obviously influences how we see ourselves, but it is also true that the way we see ourselves influences the way others see us. The people who talked with me did what they did not just for the image the world would have of them, but for their own image of themselves.

Margaret Dumont told Groucho, "I get my character from my underclothes." She said you can always tell a lady by the quality and quantity of her underclothes. She believed that wearing only the best silk helped her to feel her dowager character.

"You are shaped in your life by your shape," George Cukor told me. "I wasn't a very beautiful young man. Of course, I'm not a very beautiful old man, but it doesn't matter now. It did then. The way people see you, their physical impression of you, is everything when you are very young, and they quickly let you know how you stack up. That establishes your picture of yourself in your own mind. Even if an ugly duckling turns into a swan, which happens mostly only in fairy tales, in real life ugly ducklings are more likely to grow up to be ugly ducks. You don't change your picture of yourself even if the world does.

"There wasn't a lot I could have done about it. I was never going to be a beauty contest winner, but I could have eaten less, the way I do now." Whenever I ate lunch with George, he would always insist on ordering for me, and it was always enough for three. He would order the most fattening food on the menu—an apple pancake as an appetizer, and cake or pie for dessert that *had* to be à la mode, preferably with hot chocolate sauce. Then he would order for himself—a lean hamburger with no bun—and watch while I ate.

I was eating lunch with Sir John Gielgud at the "21" Club, and he was reminded of the days when he ate at London's Savoy Grill at a time when he really couldn't afford it:

"People might have said, 'He's doing that to be seen.' But that wasn't the reason. It wasn't just because I liked the food either, although I certainly liked their food. I did it for my self-image. One's self-image is very important because if that's in good shape, then you can do anything, or practically anything. Of course, it's better not to believe you can fly out of a window like Superman. But whatever you can do to keep up your own spirits is worth a great deal. Sitting there in the Savoy Grill made me feel like I was someone. That made it easier to face the world."

When I mentioned that he had been called "the weeping knight," he hesitated a moment, and then his eye, only one of them, filled with tears. The waiter who was serving us gave me a strange look, evidently assuming I had just said something terribly cruel to this very nice man. By that time Sir John's other eye had filled with tears. "It's funny, isn't it?" he explained, "I've always been able to bring tears to my eyes. It always came to me just like that. It never had anything to do with feeling sadness. It must be something to do with ducts. In life you have to find what you *can* do, but the best thing is if you find what you *must* do. My whole life has been spent playing other people, so that's why I'm not really an interesting person. I didn't really have a life of my own, you see."

"I ain't really Henry Fonda"

HENRY FONDA

KING VIDOR DROVE ME to Henry Fonda's Bel Air home, letting me out at what was the top of the driveway rather than taking me right to the house. I walked down a hill to the front door and started to ring the bell. Before my finger touched it, the door was opened by Henry Fonda.

"I was watching for you," he said. "There's nobody else in the house now, and it's always so terrible to ring and have to stand outside the door forever waiting and wondering if anybody's at home."

Looking around for my car, he asked incredulously, "How did you get here? Did you walk? Don't you know nobody walks in southern California?" In Beverly Hills and Bel Air, a pedestrian may indeed be viewed by local police as a suspicious character.

I explained that King Vidor had driven me there but that he hadn't wanted to intrude on our meeting.

Henry Fonda nodded. "We were in Europe together more than a year when he was directing me in *War and Peace*. Sometimes when people are forced to be together like that, when it's over they don't want to see each other. I wasn't ever sure he thought I was right for the part." Smiling, he added, "And I think he liked Audrey Hepburn better."

He showed me into the living room, and we sat on the sofa.

HENRY FONDA
I hope you won't be disappointed. You see, I'm not really a very interesting person myself. I haven't ever done anything except be other people. I ain't really Henry Fonda! Nobody could be. Nobody could have *that* much integrity.

I

I suppose for many people you're the sum total of all the parts you've played.

HENRY FONDA

That's right. All those people sitting in the dark watching me. They have this picture of me that isn't the one I see when I look into the mirror to shave.

For strangers who meet me, I'm all of those parts I've ever been, all added up together, with a little more of Tom Joad for good measure.

I

Tom Joad is one of those characters who, after we've been introduced to him, becomes a part of our lives, more real than people we've actually met and known. Sometimes it's difficult to believe we've never met Scarlett O'Hara and Rhett Butler, or Sam Spade, or Dorothy and Toto . . .

HENRY FONDA

Clarence Darrow is like that for me. He seems like a good friend.

I

For many people, you *are* Darrow.

HENRY FONDA

Well, when I'm doing a part, it's more real than the real world for me. I'm more comfortable in my part than I am in real life. I'm not really an outgoing social sort of person. I'm sure not much at parties. It's not that I'm against parties. It's just that I never know what to say if I don't have lines somebody else wrote for me. There are people who know all the bright and witty things to say, but I was never one of them. I don't have small talk. I never knew how to do that.

When I was young, I sometimes thought maybe I ought to write down some interesting things to say to people at parties so I wouldn't bore them. But that never worked; maybe because I never got around to doing it. I might've had a good time if I could've been invisible, but I don't like to *have* to participate. People think if you don't make conversation, it's because you think you're too good. I was just never that certain that what I had to say would be of interest. I've always just liked being with the few people I was at ease with. But on the stage, I wouldn't be nervous unless I'm playing someone who's nervous.

I

Don't you *ever* get nervous before a performance?

HENRY FONDA

Oh, no! *[Laughs]* Actors I work with call me "the psychotic," because I'm not nervous. You know they're joking, but it's not *all* a joke. There's always a little truth in a good joke. I guess sometimes they don't like it.

I

They must hate you!

HENRY FONDA

In a way they do. They don't really, but they say, "I hate you, you son of a bitch. You're not nervous? How dare you not be nervous!" Well, for me it's therapy for a man who doesn't really like himself or is very self-conscious, which I am. Always was. And shy. I learned it some fifty years ago. It's the reason I've stayed in the theater and become an actor.

A lot of actors are people who want esteem and don't have enough of their own. They often have trouble expressing their own emotions, but when they get up on that stage they can express the emotion that's right for the character they're playing. It's a real luxury to be able to express emotions you wouldn't get a chance to express in real life.

I

Are you one of those people who can express more emotion onstage than in real life?

HENRY FONDA

Sure. In real life, I get impatient and angry and I blow up. I don't forget easily. I cling to the wrongs people have done to me. Sometimes I'm sorry about a rage I got into. But on the stage or in a movie I can act ways I'd be ashamed to act in real life.

I can't wait for that curtain to go up. Because I'm able to be the guy the playwright conceived, who's funny or brilliant or whatever. And it ain't me! It's the old make-believe, let's pretend. There's no reason to be nervous. I can't wait to be the person who's *more* than I am. If I'm making any sense . . .

I

Of course. Acting can be a fantastic escape, but at this point in your career, people expect so much from you, it would seem the pressure could be tremendous.

HENRY FONDA

I guess. I don't think about those things. I just think about how much fun I'm gonna have being whoever I'm playing.

I

And it stays fun even when you play the part over and over?

HENRY FONDA

For me it does. Maybe *more* fun. I really enjoy long runs. I'm not going to do it anymore, but when I was younger I didn't think anything about it. I played *Roberts* for four years without missing a performance. And almost immediately afterward we went into rehearsal for *Point of No Return.* Did that for two years. And almost immediately after that we went into rehearsal for *Caine Mutiny Court-Martial.* Played that for over a year. So I was, for all practical purposes, in the theater for seven and a half years without stop. Anyway, it's great that in the theater you get to do it again. As good as opening night in *Mr. Roberts* was—and the people who were there will never forget it; they wear it like a badge—it was better 1,760 performances later. And Josh Logan, who wrote and directed it, is the one who said it was. To hear it from him meant a lot. The compliment that means the most is the one that comes from someone close to you, someone you respect, when you know it's true. I knew it was, because I grew in the part. If you do a graph about acting in a long run, it should never be a graph that does this: [*He makes a sharp upward motion with his hand*] It should be very gradual. I have to tell this story when I explain this. It may be apocryphal, but I like to think it's true.

George S. Kaufman did a play that finally opened, and it's a big hit. About the third month, there was a notice on the bulletin board that said, "There will be a rehearsal tomorrow at one o'clock to take out the improvements." Now *that* kind of improvement *must* be taken out. You have to be very self-disciplined not to let it happen to you. If it's a comedy, that's to begin to hear a laugh that you never heard before, and to work for it. You lose other values trying to find the laugh that you got a glimmer of at one time. You get out of the rhythm that you were in originally.

I

You have the audience rewriting the show.

HENRY FONDA

In a way, yeah. It's particularly difficult in a comedy that's full of laughs. And in a long run, you can very easily become mechanical. The most terrible thing you can do is stop listening. You're looking at the person who's talking to you, and your face is the way it should be, but you're really thinking where you're gonna have supper that night. Or something else. And you automatically get your cue, and you come into character. But for me I can always tell, "They're not listening anymore." Listening is as important as saying your own lines because it's the first time that person ever said those words to you. Your reaction has to be fresh and new. So for me the excitement is the challenge to make it the first time every performance, even if it's the 1,760th. You have to remind yourself—except I don't have to because I just feel that way. But I don't hesitate to remind the rest of the cast who need to be reminded. They don't always love it the moment you do it, but they know you're right, so they're grateful. The audiences are seeing it for the first time. And you, by God, owe them that fresh first performance, that illusion of first time. That's for me the most important thing, and that's why I enjoy doing it again, always wanting to keep it fresh, and do it better. After we've finished, I think, "Shoot! We'll never get to do it again!" There are the ones who say to me, "How can you play a play that long? I couldn't stand it." Well, they shouldn't have to play it that long, because they ain't any good. They don't keep it as good. They might have been brilliant opening night or for a month or two. But if they begin to let down, or become automatic, or just matter-of-fact, and stop listening, they oughta turn in their Equity cards and change jobs. Too many actors do that. I think they oughta be spanked.

I'm hesitating now because I hear myself kind of patting myself on the back, like I'm different from other people, and better than other people. I don't mean that. But, as you can believe, I'm very proud to have Josh Logan or anybody tell me, "You son of a bitch, you just get better." I don't mean as an actor, I mean in a part. It's what I want to do, and to have people tell me that makes me proud, and it's gratifying. It's knowing that I'm proving I'm being successful. I was lucky to have success early, but I never knew when it might disappear. I didn't believe it could all last this long.

I

I went with George Cukor to New York University. He taught his first acting class, and the thing that really shocked him was that the students didn't listen to each other. They were standing there reciting, and they knew all the lines that were coming. They didn't realize that reaction can be more important than action. Not listening was what he said distinguished the amateurs from the professionals.

HENRY FONDA

Was he able to get it across to them?

I

After five days, it was remarkable to see what happened, the incredible improvement.

HENRY FONDA

I don't think I'd enjoy teaching, but I enjoy directing theater and do it often. Some of the things I've just been saying I say as a director, if necessary. I try to be articulate about my own feeling for each part. When I'm directing, I have to have greater feelings about all the parts. You have to try to make it so real that the audience isn't ever reminded that you're an actor. I, as an audience, can go to plays and become totally involved with the play because it's so good I stop remembering that they are actors performing. On the other hand, there are many actors, in a brilliant play, whose wheels you can see turning. Maybe they were good the first month, but by the time I see the play, you can see the technique working. Hide the technique— don't let the working wheels show. The cogs. That's sort of basic for me in acting. And beyond that, it's just helping an actor who needs help to understand the character. Generally, that isn't difficult because you cast somebody who not only understands the character, but who's right for the part, type-casting. Some people think it's a negative thing, but you have to do it with someone who's the right type.

I'm going to be crying myself to sleep a lot for a while. *First Monday in October* was a marvelous play. It's about the Supreme Court, and I was a justice, roughly based on Douglas. It's taken them a year to come up with some backing to make the film, and just last week they got the money, and I'm not available! I suggested Walter Matthau, and he just jumped at it. And I don't wonder.

I

His good luck. Timing is important.

HENRY FONDA

Timing is everything on the stage and in life. But you can't do everything. It's just unfortunate when things come in bunches like this, and they overlap. I've never known why that is; a dry run, and you can't make anything happen just when you really want it and need it. Then, you get everything at once. You can go on for years and do a lot of crap that you're ashamed of just in order to keep working, and then suddenly all the good things will pile up. You know, it's not for the money when I do something I don't love, but it's that I want to keep working.

I

Do you know in advance when you've really got something great?

HENRY FONDA

Oh, I read *Clarence Darrow* and didn't hesitate a minute. I knew that *Oldest Living Graduate* would be what it was.

I

At the party that was given for you after you were honored at Kennedy Center, I was sitting next to Earl Wilson. And he said, "It's hard for me to really enjoy a play. I go, and I know which are better and which are worse. But usually I can't really get involved in the play because I know all the actors. When you know them so well and they get up there on the stage, there's no way you can get out of your head, 'That's so-and-so and I know him well, and I had dinner with him, or I saw him the other day,' and you don't believe the part." He said you did it for him in a matter of a few seconds as Clarence Darrow—that he didn't think of you anymore as Henry Fonda; he only saw Clarence Darrow.

HENRY FONDA

Yeah. Well, that's good to hear. I had a letter from Albert Maltz, a playwright, just today, who said, "I have now seen you play three old men. They were all three totally unlike each other."

I

People think old is old, and lump old people together as if they weren't individuals anymore, as if getting old made them alike.

HENRY FONDA

Yeah. Well, that's true. But I was lucky with those three parts. They were different people. Getting older slows you down, but it doesn't make you a different person. I'm old enough to speak from experience. But it's strange to go past a mirror quickly and catch a glimpse of your own father, who died almost half a century ago. When it happened for the first time, I realized how much I resemble him. And I realized I was middle-aged. The worst thing about middle age is the thought it will pass.

You know, when I'm on the stage, I always feel younger than I am, even when I'm playing someone older. If I'm sick, I get well while I'm onstage. I'd want to be working in the smallest part in the smallest theater in the smallest town as long as somebody would let me do it. It could be the smallest audience. *[Laughing]* Maybe for no audience at all. I guess if I'd been rich I would have paid them to let me do it. I'm lucky enough to be in a job I love, where my work is my play, and I get the rewards and satisfactions and gratifications that I get.

I

Was there anything else you might have found as satisfying?

HENRY FONDA

I can't imagine because I didn't have any ambitions. I didn't grow up dreaming about being an actor, particularly in the movies. But, for what it's worth, I was majoring in journalism at the University of Minnesota. I had to work my way through college and wasn't able to do the things that a journalism major would try to do, which would be to strive for one of the publications, because I didn't have any free hours at all. I was a resident worker at a settlement house. I had to work so many hours at the job to support myself, I was always tired. Anyway, I was discouraged and didn't go back after the second year. So I wasn't prepared for anything. I didn't know what I was gonna be doing. I had to be luckier than people who know where they're going.

I'm a lucky person. Do [Dorothy] Brando, who later had a son named Marlon, was very active at the Playhouse in Omaha, which she'd organized when I was away at school. I got into it without knowing what she wanted me to do. The idea of getting onstage and performing, for this self-conscious young man of twenty—no way! Without going into a long story, Do Brando was a friend of the family's, and she told my mother to tell me about a tryout. I assumed that she knew I was home, not going back to school, and looking for work. And this was a job. I didn't know what kind of job. If I'd known, I really wouldn't have gone. And I found myself cast in this play without being able to say, "Don't do this to me, wait a minute!"

Well, I didn't think about acting even after that first part. It was very gradual. What I was becoming fascinated by was the theater backstage: the ropes and the curtain that went up, the lights, sweeping up, and building scenery. I did that for a year. Then the second year, the director cast me as Merton in *Merton of the Movies,* and that's when I began to realize what acting could be. And after three years, I went to New York. That's how naïve I was.

I

Sometimes it's better to be naïve. If you know all the hard things ahead, you might not be able to continue trying.

HENRY FONDA

I think you're right. I think if I hadn't been naïve, I probably wouldn't've had the nerve to go. Or if I'd gone and not had any kind of luck for a long time, I would've given up. But as it was, I never thought of giving up. You know, there were many, many days, even weeks of not eating well. Sometimes not eating at all. But I was never alone. That's important. It's a world of difference if you're not alone. There was always a group of us who were in the same lifeboat. We were trying to get into the theater, living together and sharing rents, and that kind of thing. Josh Logan, Jim Stewart, Myron McCormick. Anyway, that's the way it happened to me. I don't know what started this line of thinking. . . . I don't know how to bring it to a stop.

I

I think what you said about not being alone in the lifeboat is interesting. Laurence Olivier told me much the same thing.

HENRY FONDA

He's great. He came backstage to see me in London. Well, it *was* a kind of lifeboat. I was never alone. That was lucky. I, again, was lucky when I got East and fell into the University Players, which was a summer theater on Cape Cod made up of undergraduates from Princeton and Harvard, and girls from Smith and Vassar and Radcliffe, and so on. All of them acted in their university or college drama groups, and they all felt that's where they wanted to go after school. They were creating an opportunity for themselves while they were still undergraduates, to get new experience. We had our own theater on Cape Cod. The first two years, they were all going back to school. So the first year or two I was more alone, although I did get a job in Washington, D.C., in a repertory company that did plays for children. Eventually, we always shared an apartment, either all four of us or any combination of us. We were together in struggling, getting small parts. Each time Jim would get a little bit bigger part, I'd get a little bit bigger part; Josh would get a chance to stage-manage, and then he got a chance to direct. It wasn't overnight, but it was gradual, and you helped each other through the bad times. And you shared each other's encouragement. There were plenty of bad times, too, for all of us.

I

You also had the advantage, even if you didn't get encouragement at a certain moment and somebody else was getting it, of knowing it could be done. Knowing it can be done helps a lot.

HENRY FONDA

True. Being a struggling young actor, I was hardly affected by the Depression. Everybody I knew was young and wanted to be on the stage. And for struggling young actors, there's never enough work, and it's always a Depression.

I

You mentioned luck as a factor.

HENRY FONDA

A lot of it's luck, yeah. You get as much experience as you can so that you're ready when the luck works, so that you're there at the right time when somebody is looking for your type. That's the luck. The part that isn't luck is being prepared when you do get the break. How to make the luck happen—I don't know how to do that.

It's amazing to me today that there're so many good young actors. Where does the luck come from? Where do they get the opportunity? You know, fifty years ago I played over two hundred major parts, the best parts written for young actors at that time, in stock companies all over. How does an actor get that experience today? There's no way. Summer theaters are as professional today as Broadway. And you have to have a reputation; they have to know who you are and what you can do before they cast you. I'm glad I don't have to get started now. You know, fifty-five years ago, they would take a young guy that looked like he had straw stickin' out of his clothes still and apple-cheeked from Nebraska, if he looked like he might be right for the part. I just happened to be in a place at a time when they were looking for that guy.

Anyway, be ready when the guy sees you that says, "He'd be right!" That happened when June Walker saw me in a play at Mount Kisco in a summer theater, and she'd already signed to do *Farmer Takes a Wife* for Marc Connelly. She told Marc Connelly about me, and Marc sent for me. I came down and had a meeting with Marc in his hotel room, read a page or two of the script, and he sent me over to the producer's office and said, "I'll call him up and tell you're coming, and he'll give you a contract." That was a seventeen-day contract. In other words, if they didn't like me after a few days of work, I could get fired without being paid anything. So it wasn't really anything except a good chance. It wound up to be my first film, because Fox bought it and brought me out to re-create the part that I had done on Broadway. And I thought, "I don't care about movies, but if they're gonna give me all this money for a part I've already done in the theater, I'll take it and run." Actually, I had a lot of fun doing it, and stayed and did another movie, and then a third one before I went back to New York. But I hear myself starting to tell the chronological story of my life, and I really don't want to. I've been asked to write an autobiography, but I can't possibly stop to do it. I don't have the time. For everything you choose to do, you're choosing not to do something else. I may have two open weeks in 1981. I gotta paint, too, 'cause they want to give me a show. I'll show you some of my paintings before you go. The show is in the fall. It's not my idea. There was a letter from a man who wants it to tour for two years in every major museum and gallery in America with maybe fifteen of the things reproduced for sale. And he's talkin' about a lot of money for me. But I don't have that many paintings, you know. I've given away most of my paintings. Anyway, I'll probably do something because I find it hard to say no to anything that sounds at all interesting.

I

Maybe one of the things that you do is you don't say no to the opportunity when it comes along.

HENRY FONDA

Well, I did say no to something. About the autobiography I said no. I knew that was something I didn't want to do. I've learned that much about myself.

I

You said you had fun making films. Was there any aspect of it you didn't like?

HENRY FONDA

Kissing. Love scenes in front of people were always hard for me. They used to tell me I should open my mouth for the kiss, but that seemed too personal for me. I hated screen kisses. It's not like a real kiss at all. People think, wasn't that exciting kissing whoever it was. No, it wasn't. Not with all those people gaping. You had to think about not smearing her lipstick. I figured I looked foolish. I didn't have the movie-star good looks of a Ty Power.

I

Is there anything you've learned about yourself that you wish you had known when you were starting out?

HENRY FONDA

Oh, I don't know that I could categorize or list them, but I will always regret that I didn't finish college. Although I know that I would not have done myself any good at trying to finish the way I was going. I just didn't have time even to study properly. I had a job at the settlement house. I not only had to come back from the campus at the end of the last class; I'd have a group on the playground in the good weather, or I'd have a group in the gymnasium or in a small room for basket weaving, a Boy Scout troop or something. And every night I had three basketball teams in succession from about seven to ten-thirty. By the time they'd gone through the showers and everything, it was eleven o'clock. So I was never able to get back to my room to do my homework until eleven o'clock. And, I'd be so tired, I'd fall asleep over my French translation or whatever it was. I wasn't doing well, and I always wanted to do well. If I'd tried to stay for two more years, it wouldn't have been any better for me than the first two years were.

I joined the navy in 1941, and went through boot camp here. Then, after a year on a destroyer, I was sent to Washington, and eventually to officers' training school, and then to a school called ACI, or Combat Intelligence. The pick of everybody they could find of officer age was chosen to go to ACI. It was a crash course: sixteen weeks, all day long. Now, I'm telling you that it was difficult. I graduated at the top of the class. So I know I had the potential to be a student. I don't mean a scholar, an intellectual, but a student. I never had the chance when I was in school. I like to be good at what I do. I'm not a good loser. If I'm not good, I don't do it anymore. I'm not good at golf, so I don't play golf. One of the things I wish is that I hadn't wasted so much time worrying about things. The worrying never did me any good. I used to worry, would it last? I'd think this is too good to last. Will I ever work again? There was a time about twenty years ago when each time I used to wonder if I'd ever get a film again. That was something I really worried about because I couldn't imagine not acting.

But what have I learned in my life that I wish I'd known earlier? I don't know that I could say, "Here, here, and here." *[Pause]* I'm hesitating saying it now, because I know that I never would have changed the life that's happened to me. Ten or fifteen years after I became successful, I was on a tour in South America, just as a tourist. And I bumped into what they call a "dig"—archaeologists up near Cuzco, Peru. To me, it was so fascinating. If I'd known about archaeology before I went into college or during college, I think I could have gone in that direction.

I
Did professional success bring you the kind of happiness and pleasure you thought it would?
HENRY FONDA
Well, certainly it has. I don't know that I needed this much professional success to be happy. Obviously the way we live, you couldn't ask for anything more comfortable than this house, and I appreciate it. But I don't think I would be *un*happy living less comfortably or less opulently or whatever the other words would be. I would be perfectly happy as long as I could work.

I didn't dream about being as successful as I am when I went into the theater. Just to be able to continue work as an actor, without being a star or wealthy, I would've been happy the rest of my life. I'm not particularly wealthy, but I'm obviously wealthy enough to afford this. But that ain't the end. It's marvelous to be able to be in a position to help people who are close to me and need help. Success hasn't taken away from my happiness, that's for sure.

There are people who tell you that success won't be as much fun as you think it will be. Well, they're right. It isn't. It's *more* fun. Opening night of *Mr. Roberts,* it was all my dreams come true. That's it. The really nice thing about a night like that is it isn't over when it's over. It becomes a part of you and stays with you all your life. But my personal life hasn't *always* been as happy as it is today. Since I've been with Shirlee, which is seventeen years, my life couldn't be happier. And all the other years weren't *un*happy; but I had unhappy marriages. There was some happiness during those marriages, but they were all short. I don't think there was another marriage longer than . . . Well, with Frances, the mother of Jane and Peter, that was thirteen years. And that was a good life until she became sick. So there have been personal unhappinesses, too. I've been so happy since, I guess I shut out a lot of what's painful to remember.

I

It's good to be able to forget some of the hard things that happen, if you can.

HENRY FONDA

It's good to be able to, sure. I've been so happy in my life these past years, I really haven't remembered some of those bad times that happened a long time ago. Strange to think of a hick from Nebraska like me being married five times. I'm ashamed of being married so many times. It makes me seem like a fool and a failure. It's embarrassing. I'm an old-fashioned man. I always admired my parents' marriage. They used to go out on a summer evening holding hands to have ice-cream sodas. I thought I was going to have that kind of marriage; you know, for life.

My wives were always more dissatisfied with me than I was with them. But I couldn't change. I am what I am, and they were dissatisfied with that. That's pretty personal. I'm again hearing myself thinking and saying trite things like, "You shouldn't dwell on unhappiness." But I guess I've had my share of unhappiness and I've survived by shutting out what was unhappy. A lot of tragedies have touched my life. Suicide is something I could never understand. I could never imagine wanting to give up my life. But when it's happened to people you cared about, you can't help wondering whether there wasn't something you could have said or done that would have changed it. But I couldn't be happier today. Let's talk about something else.

I

Have there been disadvantages to your celebrity?

HENRY FONDA

Yeah. I think anybody who is in that position would admit there are disadvantages. We can be put upon easily, but you're able to live with it. What I hated was if a girl expected you to be some kind of a great lover because you were a movie star. I was never a star. I was always an actor. The most terrible thing for me would have been to have a girl like me because I was Henry Fonda the actor. I liked it better if they didn't know who I was and hadn't even seen my pictures.

As for me, of course, I haven't had the bad times that Elizabeth Taylor or Richard Burton, or Tyrone Power, or Robert Taylor had. I don't know how unhappy it made them. If it did, I'm sure it was momentary, like the bad moments when you've had to pull a girl from underneath your bunk in a train or something like that.

I

I guess there are worse things.

HENRY FONDA

Yeah, there are worse things. No, the worst things I can think of —and they're not really that bad when you start to talk about 'em, you know—are autograph seekers outside the stage door of a theater. They're not really the fans that appreciate your work. They're professional autograph seekers. What they do with them, I don't have any clue, 'cause you sign the same person's autograph book a hundred times. You recognize them. They're always the same people. They have a whole stack of photographs of you.

I

Groucho used to sign "Mary Pickford."

HENRY FONDA

[Chuckling] Only Groucho could do that! It's not that bad, but it's a bore to come out of the theater with your wife and maybe a group of other couples. If you stop to sign, they're expected to wait. And if you sign one, you've got to sign the rest of 'em. There can be anything from ten to fifteen. And if you sign those, that attracts a crowd, and pretty soon you're besieged. So the other people just stand there and wait? No, I don't think it's fair, and I try my best when I can to say, "I'm very sorry, I can't stop now," and go through. Well, that's not a *big* deal.

I

It's not really such a high price for celebrity.

HENRY FONDA

I guess I am a celebrity. I don't think about it. I know I'm recognized, but generally when I'm recognized, it's not bad. People on the street, whose faces will light up, and then they become self-conscious themselves. First they think, "I know him." Then they realize, "Oh, that's Henry Fonda." Sometimes they will say, "I saw it, and I just loved it," and that's all. Sometimes they don't remember, and a man will come and say, "Did I go to college with you?" They know it's a familiar face, but they don't know where to place it. That isn't bad. It's kind of nice. And of course, the nice thing's to have people stop you, as they often do, particularly in London. I'll tell you this one.

A man, very well-dressed, stopped me on a very good shopping street in London. He saw me coming and just stopped. Then I got to him. He said, "Oh, Mr. Fonda, I've got to tell you; I saw Clarence Darrow last night. It was *so* marvelous!" And he went on and on. He says, "I've spent the morning in bookstores trying to find books about Clarence Darrow." I mean, I wanted to hug him! That's the nicest thing anybody coulda told me. I gave them something that made them so curious and interested in the man Clarence Darrow that they wanted to know more.

A disadvantage is you have to keep changing your private number a lot. I get calls now from people who get the number some way. You know, you can't get 'em off the phone. And you don't want to be rude. I don't think we should take too much time talking about the disadvantages of being a celebrity!

I

You said that actually you're a person who's self-conscious. Yet you do make some public appearances as Henry Fonda, for instance at the Kennedy Center.

HENRY FONDA

I loved that night, but I did not have to get up and do anything. There were five of us. Much more difficult is the AFI [American

Film Institute], where you eventually have to get up there and accept it with a speech. I don't remember now what I said. I didn't really prepare anything more than in my mind I knew I wanted to talk about my father and mother. I'm sorry they couldn't have been there to appreciate that.

I

I think one of the sadder things that happens is not being able to show your success to the people you care about.

HENRY FONDA

Yeah. I wish they . . . Anyway, I got away with that. And the last one, the AFI tribute to Stewart. I was the host, and I got a lot of comment about that. I don't like people getting up there and reading cue cards and a prepared speech that aren't real words, and it's so obvious that they're not. So I said I'll do it, but I don't want anyone preparing my speech or to have cue cards. So I wrote it and learned it enough so I didn't need to be cued, and it made a difference. People commented, "You son of a bitch, you didn't use cue cards!" A big deal! I never go to Oscars, but it's so obvious when a Dustin Hoffman doesn't have to have cards. And I think one or two of the other acceptance speeches were without cards. There are people reading from cue cards that say, "Thank you very much." Anyway, I don't go! Particularly, I don't like to get up and acknowledge an award of any kind. That's difficult for me. But I'm better than I was fifty years ago, that's for damn sure. I think I had about five tributes in one year, and I finally said, "Enough already!"

I

But if you like the thing that's being supported, it means that just your being there can do more than many people could do working all year.

HENRY FONDA

That's right. So I have lent myself. I sent my body. I have "allowed" them to give me tributes. *[Chuckles]* And a tribute, of course, is something to be proud of. It's not like saying, "You're the best actor last year." That I can't buy at all. A lot of it isn't right, the way they campaign for that Oscar. The millions of dollars they spend with full-page ads in both trade papers every day, for months. Just like it's a campaign to be made President or something. I don't compete against other actors. I like to compete against my own best performances. The real reward is working with stimulating people.

I

I know John Steinbeck was one of the people you most admired.

HENRY FONDA

Why, I adored John. And I got to know him toward the end. I hadn't known John when I did *Grapes of Wrath.* I met him after the film had already been released. I was honored by the Holland-American Society. My ancestors were Dutch—before that, Italian, but then Dutch—and came to America in 1620. And when they honored me, John Steinbeck came. He had been an invalid, and I knew that. He came, I don't mean outta bed, but he came to that reception. And I was in tears when I saw him in the reception line, with his Nobel Prize hanging there, because you were told to wear your ribbons. That was one of the most moving moments in my life.

When he died, his widow asked me to come back East. I was here, and I did fly back to read his favorite poems at the services. So, I can't say that I was that close, but I certainly was his friend, and I adored him.

Andrew Wyeth is also someone I appreciate knowing. He's not that intimate, but I've visited him five or six times.

I

On the way over here, we were talking about Andrew Wyeth. He wrote King [Vidor] a letter telling him that *The Big Parade* was the major single influence on his art and that he had seen it 188 times.

HENRY FONDA

Is that right! Well, Andrew Wyeth, he's not only an idol, a god to me, but he's a friend. And he's a dear, dear man. I own one Andrew Wyeth, which he gave me because I did some things for him. I went to Chadd's Ford for two or three days to be there to narrate a documentary on him. He certainly didn't need to do anything for me, but he sent me a drawing. It was all wrapped when it came. Framed and wrapped. And on the wrapping, the brown wrapping paper, my name printed quite large, like this, and up here, "A. Wyeth," about that big. I cut it out just like that, and it's pasted on the back of my drawing. It's just probably a preliminary sketch to something he eventually did, an egg tempera. It's just a part of a fence and a post, and that's about all. I've been to almost every show, and since I've met him, I go to the openings, wherever it is. I feel very close to him, even though I don't see him that much.

I

Sometimes you can meet someone for one minute or one time in your life, and it means something to you and can be important.

HENRY FONDA

Of course. You know, the others are the ones I've worked with in my business over the fifty-five years I've been at it. John Ford's certainly a giant in this business, and I did eight films with him. That was a very special relationship, and a friendship. We not only worked together as director and actor, but we got drunk together and went fishing together, and everything. Played cards together. I was probably closer to Ford than any of the other directors. I worked three times with Henry Hathaway and was very friendly. He just lives up the hill, and we see them a lot. And Bill Wellman, before he died, was a neighbor, friend, and I did *Ox-Bow Incident* with him. Very fond of him. But the others are pretty much one-time experiences. You know, Preston Sturges and then Willie Wyler.

I

And Alfred Hitchcock.

HENRY FONDA

Hitchcock, yeah. I didn't really know him after that one experience. He was a real professional. He knew just what he wanted, and he worked hard.

I

Mervyn LeRoy told me that he never saw anybody work harder than you do.

HENRY FONDA

Well, I don't think anybody should be amazed by that. I think you should expect that. Laurence Olivier never stops. The good ones don't stop. Oh, God, Brando is just incredible. He doesn't always get the challenge that an actor needs. And you get mad at him because he sort of throws it over his shoulder, 'cause he's not challenged. But when he's challenged, nobody can touch him. His mother was a darling woman. A very good actress, incidentally. She and I worked together in a Eugene O'Neill play, *Beyond the Horizon.*

I didn't know [Spencer] Tracy more than to be friendly when I saw him, which wasn't very often, so he wasn't a friend. But I have nothing but great admiration for Tracy. I thought he was an instinctive actor who was never wrong.

I

Tell me about the instinctive actor.

HENRY FONDA

Well, I don't know how to talk about the instinctive actor. It's what I think *I* am. And I don't try to analyze myself. Jane, who calls herself a method actress, can talk about *the* method for hours, and will if she's pressed, even if she's not. She says *I'm* a method actor. I'll accept that if she says so. I don't know what it means.

I

Did you find it a different kind of experience working with your daughter, Jane, rather than just with an actress playing your daughter?

HENRY FONDA

I thought working with my daughter would be strange. For *On Golden Pond,* I was worried that I would be distracted by our real-life relationship which, while it's that of father and daughter, is not the same father-and-daughter relationship as in *On Golden Pond.* It turned out to be such a professional relationship that I wasn't aware of the real relationship. And Jane told me the same thing. She wasn't aware of me as her father outside of the film. Jane produced the film, too. That kept her out of trouble. *[Laughs]*

But I think any actor has a method. Maybe they don't even know how to analyze it or articulate it, but there is a method. What *the* method is, I don't know how to talk about it. And if I have a method, it's to, as I've already said, not let the wheels show. Certainly a lot of it's instinct. A lot of it, I'm sure, is technique that I have learned without even being aware that I'm learning technique. But you also, in learning a technique, have to learn to disguise it. That's the most important technique.

I know that the first time I did *Merton of the Movies* for the Playhouse, I was so young and so inexperienced, that I *was* Merton.

Merton of the Movies is about a young grocery clerk in some small midwest town who dreams about being a movie actor. Eventually he comes out here as a bumbling kid, and blunders onto a set. He's so naïve and funny that they begin to photograph it, and he becomes a star, not knowing why.

I
You are a bit Merton of the movies.

HENRY FONDA
In a way. Anyway, my short hairs would stand up. You know what I mean by the tickle in your skin when you're excited? If you're scared or something? I felt that onstage playing Merton. And I would kneel on the floor before my cot in the back of this grocery store to pray to God to make me a good movie actor. It was so real to me.

Now about five years later, I played Merton again in a stock company on the Cape. And I wasn't able to feel that same tickling of the skin and the short hairs rising because I was playing Merton now with more technique than I knew five years before. I wouldn't even go out onstage to take the bow at the end of the play because I thought I was so bad. I hadn't been able to recapture this feeling that I'd had five years before. Actually, I was probably a hundred times better. At the end they had to push me onstage. It was an ovation. I got brilliant reviews. And I was beginning to learn that there is a way of learning your craft and using technique, and not having to feel your skin flush with heat or get cold with fear—whatever I was feeling, you know, as a kid, a young man. I'm trying to talk about instinctive acting.

I
The feeling that's important is what the audience feels.

HENRY FONDA

Well, certainly it is. But I confess that I don't think of an audience so much as I do of myself. I get as much joy and satisfaction out of a first run-through performance or a dress rehearsal with nobody out front. Like I said, I think I could play in an empty theater. But it does give another dimension to have an audience.

I

It's interesting that it's not an essential dimension for you.

HENRY FONDA

It isn't.

I

Except that it allows you to keep doing the thing you want to do.

HENRY FONDA

Of course it does. I don't know what would have happened to me if I hadn't found my way as an actor. All those times that a decision to go this way instead of that way led to things that you didn't have any idea would happen two or three years later.

In the middle of the summer, the set designer in the theater in Surry, Maine, got a temperamental fit and quit. And the producer was stuck. He had to go to New York and find another. I just happened to be there as a gofer, the only job available. And I went to him and said I had done a lot of scenic design, and built and painted sets. So, he just grabbed me, and I wound up doing the sets. From that, because of some sets I did then and people talking about them, the next year I couldn't get arrested as an actor, but I had my choice of jobs at every summer theater in the East as a scenic designer. And I chose Mount Kisco because it was forty-five minutes from Broadway. Close. More apt to have producers and agents come up to see things. And that summer I was a scenic designer, an opening came for a part that I had played in a stock company in Baltimore. It was a small part that had a little scene in the first act and a little in the third act. That's the part that everybody remembered when they went home 'cause it was a very funny comedy part. And on the strength of that, I came back the third summer playing all the leads at Mount Kisco. That's the summer June Walker saw me and told Marc Connelly. So I went up to Surry to drive a station wagon, and it led *directly*, although it went around the block, to my getting *Farmer Takes a Wife*. Now, if I hadn't gone there, who knows what my life would have been? Whether I'd've stayed in the theater and ever been successful—not necessarily this successful, but enough to make a good living at it—or whether I'd've finally given up—who knows? Sold shoes or insurance. I wasn't prepared for anything else. Maybe one reason I stayed with what I was doing was I didn't have any choice. It never occurred to me not to, you know, through all the years that were difficult when I first went to New York. And there were difficult winters. Summers were always taken care of. I always had the University Players in the summer. Sometimes weeks and months between jobs I didn't really eat well. Sometimes a dime's worth of rice would boil up into a big bulk, and you lived on rice, with no salt or sugar on it. Just rice! Now, whenever I see rice thrown at a wedding, I feel I oughta be picking some up.

I

Were you depressed?

HENRY FONDA

Never depressed! I'd write my mother, "Don't despair. I have a gut feeling it's going to happen tomorrow." And it wouldn't. When it finally did, she lived long enough to know that I was in rehearsal for *Farmer Takes a Wife*. She didn't live long enough to know that I opened with it successfully.

Anyway, I never thought of giving up. And there were friends of mine—not Jim Stewart or Josh Logan, but other close friends—who said, "Why don't you face it, Fonda? You know you're a scenic designer. Stop fighting, trying to be an actor. You can be a scenic designer, and very successfully." And I was grateful for the chance to make a living, but I never stopped thinking I'm really an actor.

I

People often have a lot of negative advice to offer. If you were to listen to everything you're told, it really could stop you.

HENRY FONDA

Yeah, yeah. I know they meant well. It breaks my heart to think about people who wanted to do this as badly as I did and didn't get to do it. It could have happened to me if I hadn't been lucky. A friend of mine was very active with me at the Playhouse in Omaha. When I left to go to New York in 1928, I was twenty-three. He might have been a year older than I, but he was married with at least one child, and he had a good job with a trust company in Omaha. But a hell of a good actor. He was the third actor with me and Dorothy Brando in *Beyond the Horizon.* He said to his dying day, "When you went to New York, part of me went with you. I wanted to more than anything in the world. I didn't have the guts. But you had the guts." And he said "guts." He didn't say "courage." But it's the same thing. I didn't think it was courage. I was foolhardy. I didn't know what it meant to go into the theater. I just assumed you get paid for it in New York, and I went to New York. It was some time before I got paid for it.

I

Do you think any of your parts have influenced you as a person?

HENRY FONDA

I don't know that they have, no. Again, I get credit for an awful lot that I don't deserve. I get a lot of credit for being Clarence Darrow and Justice Snow in *First Monday*—two top lawyers and justices. I ain't anything like those guys. But I loved being able to pretend I was. I'm not nearly as nice a guy as Mr. Roberts was. I don't know that they've done anything to me or changed me. I know I have an image, because people talk about it. And I am cast sometimes for the image of Henry Fonda, like when Joe Mankiewicz cast me in *There Was a Crooked Man* because there's a kind of an O. Henry ending that you're not prepared for. Because Henry Fonda would never take that gold and swim his horse across the Rio Grande River in New Mexico to get away with it. But he does at the end of that film.

I

Your image is what created the twist.

HENRY FONDA

Of course. He chose me for that reason. Sergio Leone cast the image of Henry Fonda so that audiences would be astonished at the moment I massacre a farm family, and they don't know who it is. I'd just shot the father and the daughter and the son, and then a nine-year-old son comes out, and he's standing there when we come up, the five of us. I'm the leader with my henchmen, and they all have handguns and rifles. The camera's on this terrified boy, and it comes very slowly around to me. And Sergio cast me because he could hear the audience say, "Jesus Christ, it's Henry Fonda! He wouldn't massacre a farm family!" After that, bang! I shoot this nine-year-old boy point-blank and kill him right then. That was a kick because it threw people. It threw the audiences; it threw my friends. My daughter, Jane, who saw it in Paris, wrote me a fan letter. It was one of the best parts I've had because it was against the image. I had a ball playing him. I don't see the Fonda image. I just hear about it. I mean, I can remember quotes that say I'm the most typical American face and voice, and in every way a typical American. A man of integrity, honest—that kind of business.

I

Does having that much integrity ever get a little dull—as an actor, that is?

HENRY FONDA

Sure. And that's why it's fun to rock 'em. But I don't get that opportunity too often. That many good parts aren't written like that. But in *Lady Eve* with Barbara Stanwyck, he was not an against-type part as far as I was concerned, but it was to Groucho and to Jack Benny, and to many others. It was a different part from what they expected of me. They said, "That son of a bitch is funny!" and here I wasn't even trying to be funny.

I

That's what they thought was funny, that you weren't trying. The minute it shows that someone is trying to be funny, it's not funny anymore. I remember one night Groucho said to you, "You're a funny man."

HENRY FONDA

Well, he was telling me, and I loved hearing it.

I'll show you my paintings now. I didn't show them until recently. I'd just give them to friends. When I paint, I do it to

please myself. Then I hope it pleases someone else. I do everything as if I'm just going to keep it.

I

Has Andrew Wyeth ever seen your work?

HENRY FONDA

He saw an oil that's upstairs that I'll show you. General Electric
bought the reproduction rights. It was a barn lantern hanging
on a rusty nail, and I guess a barn door. They'd seen it in New
York, celebrity Sunday painters, and they offered me $1,500
reproduction rights, and I said, "Why not?" So they took it and
reproduced it, and gave me the original back. And when I was
going up to Maine, I thought, "I'm gonna show it to Andy." So
I had them send me a reproduction, up to the hotel where I was
staying. Then I went to Andy's, and I took this with me.

"What am I doing taking this up to show Andrew Wyeth?"
And I wouldn't have taken it out of the back of the car except
that Andy came out of the house and walked to the car to greet
me. So I pulled it out, and I laid it on the ground, leaning
against the car. "I just wanted you to see this."

He got down like this and looked at it for five minutes,
shaking his head like this. He said, "It's Harnett." And I knew
then what he meant, 'cause William Harnett, an American artist about 1860, '70 and '80, painted that *very* sharp-focus *trompe
l'oeil* kind of painting. And it was like that.

Henry Fonda had painted his own life—that which was familiar
in his world. The pictures were understated and restrained, but
their simplicity was deceptive, for they were achieved through
talent and technique. He rarely drew anything that moved, yet his
still-life paintings evoked a sense of people, even though none
was in evidence. It seemed as if the human occupants of each
scene had either just left or were just about to return.

HENRY FONDA

[We walk through the house looking at his paintings] This is an oil. I've
only done five or six oils. And these are all watercolors. *[Most of
the pictures are of ordinary household objects]* These are my work
shoes. That persimmon is from my persimmon tree. It's a

wonderful feeling growing things. I like to plant things on my land and watch them grow. Then, I use them as models for my paintings. After that I eat them. That's an advantage of still life. You can eat your models.

I

And no problem finding models!

HENRY FONDA

Sometimes I get something that's spoiling from the refrigerator, and I paint it. Then, even if we don't get to eat it, it doesn't get wasted, like that loaf of bread. I never liked waste. If you've been poor enough to be hungry, you can't ever understand waste. This is the house where we lived in London when I did Darrow. And this was the set of the Sergio Leone western. I'll show you what I use for a studio. It's the billiard room, but it's the only place I've got to work. *[We enter the billiard room]* It's all cluttered up 'cause I put my easel and my drawing board in here.

I have recently been doing things from graphite. I picked this up because Jane asked me to do this thing for her, to reproduce for a charity. It was a page of *Grapes of Wrath* with a paragraph magnified so you could read it. Making the printing look like printing from a book was a laborious thing. Anyway, it was so successful that I've been working almost exclusively with graphite ever since.

I

Harnett did a painting called *Ease,* a still life which is really a *tour de force* of the *trompe l'oeil* genre. He reproduced among the numerous objects on a table a page of a newspaper that was a stunning accomplishment.

HENRY FONDA

Yeah, I know that one. Harnett was great. *[Indicating one of his own paintings]* There's no color there, so it's almost like a photograph of three Mason jars.

I

I can't think of anything more difficult to draw than an empty jar.

HENRY FONDA

I'm particularly proud. You can vaguely see the curve, and the raised letters are curved, too. And backwards, 'cause it's on the back of the Mason jar.

This one is of my own kitchen. I love all these little things of home. *[He indicates a picture of packaged and bottled foods]* A honey bear filled with honey, my protein drink, Vegit . . .

"Would you like to have some of my vegetables?" Henry Fonda asked. He held out some carrots. "They're organic," he added. I was persuaded, and he filled a brown bag with enough vegetables to make soup.

He was on his way to visit his old friend Joshua Logan, who was recovering after a bad accident, and I rode with him to the Beverly Hills Hotel. As we walked into the Polo Lounge, which was crowded at the height of the cocktail hour, the only competition Henry Fonda had for attention was my large, crumpled brown grocery bag, overflowing with his vegetables, scallions peeping over the top. It was just about to break.

We stood there waiting to use the phone so he could call Joshua Logan's room. Amid the din of voices and ice cubes clinking in glasses, a memory out of context came floating back to him, and he shared it with me:

"One of the things I remember best was when I was a little boy and my mother woke me up to see Halley's comet. She didn't wake up my sisters. My mother said, 'It's only once in a lifetime.' "

"It appears every seventy-six years," I said. "It's coming again soon, in 1986."

Henry Fonda smiled. "Maybe I'll see it again."

"I didn't realize then that King Kong and I were going to live together for the rest of our lives, and longer"

FAY WRAY

THE LEGEND IS A special category of celebrity. Legends are not subject to the pressures of competition anymore. They do not have to worry about their position in the pecking order of success. Usually, though not always, they do not have to worry about money either. There is, in fact, a pressure on legends *not* to accept work of lower quality or for less money than befits their exalted status.

"I don't work cheap," Groucho said. "Free maybe, but cheap never." In his middle eighties, whenever there was any commercial bargaining, he drove the hardest deal imaginable, and then often gave the money to charity.

One of the characteristics shared by the legendary figures I met was their enthusiasm for the present and the future. Even in their seventies, eighties, and nineties they did not like to dwell upon their past accomplishments. They were proud of their achievements, but if they talked about their work it was usually about their most recent work. It was with current projects that they were most concerned, and they were all deeply involved in the planning of their future work. The most terrible loss is that of looking forward. These people still had hopes and dreams.

Those who created the legend were actually working in the present at the time they did their legendary work. They were not thinking about creating legends. Few directors or film stars of the past could have foreseen that their work had any purpose beyond the immediate entertainment of the contemporary audience for which it was intended. Director John Ford told me, "We didn't think then that we were making pictures for our children and grandchildren."

"I would never have believed that one of the most enduring relationships of my life was going to be with King Kong," Fay Wray said. "Do you remember, 'And lo, the beast looked upon the face of Beauty and stayed his hand from killing, and from that day forward was as one dead'? That was supposed to be 'an old Arabian proverb,' but it was really written by director Merian C. Cooper. It was his idea, the great basic theme, that King Kong represents all men in their total vulnerability to the charms of a woman. King Kong is vulnerable to these charms, and this vulnerability takes him from the jungle, where he is dominant, into civilization, which is represented by woman. Woman is civilization, which deprives him of his strength and ultimately destroys him. I didn't realize then that King Kong and I were going to live together for the rest of our lives, and longer."

When a person becomes a legend, he relinquishes certain personal rights. The public expects him to assume his place in the pantheon and not to risk his reputation by continuing to take the professional gambles that won him legendary status in the first place. He is expected to recognize the exact moment at which his powers cease and to desist from trying to reach high C or running for an election he could lose or making the film that would bring disgrace upon his past body of work.

It is not easy to watch one's own wrinkles appear on a wide screen. Hubert Humphrey said it wasn't even easy to watch on a little screen. Laurence Olivier felt that being ill in public was highly embarrassing, while for John Gielgud, dying in public represented the ultimate embarrassment.

Bob Hope accepted that a celebrity legend had relinquished his right to the same kind of privacy that non-celebrities have. "After a while," he speculated, "people believe you belong to them, and they aren't entirely wrong. It's almost like creating a natural resource. If you create a natural resource, are you entitled to own it yourself?"

A career doesn't come to an end in one moment, just as a person doesn't suddenly grow a year older on a birthday. We usually don't know for a while when something has ended, partly because if it's something we don't want to end, we do our best to shut out any ominous forebodings. This may be a blessing, since it allows for easing into the new experience or, sometimes, lack of experiences. It would certainly not be cheerful to have one specific day on which middle age or old age begins, and to know about it in advance.

I remember Groucho telling Woody Allen, "I'm always being asked the question, 'One hundred years from now, what would you like people to say about you?' "

"I know what I'd like them to say about me," Woody responded. "I'd like them to say, 'He looks good for his age.' "

Being a legend is no substitute for working. René Clair believed that having the chance to do what you want to do and then having it taken away is worse than never having had it at all:

"It doesn't stop all at once, because you don't know that your last film is the last one until a long time afterwards. I think the moment I actually realized that everything was over and I was only a legend was when Henri Langlois [founder of the Cinémathèque Française] wanted a pair of my old socks for his museum."

Bette Davis thought there were better things in life than being a legend; practically anything, in fact.

"There's something rather terrible about hearing people call you a 'legend.' You don't feel like a legend, however a legend feels. Maybe that's the trouble with being called that. One doesn't think of a legend having real human feelings at all. I always thought of a legend as being dead. It's worse for a woman. Of course, *everything's* worse for a woman. But you live with it because you have no choice what people say about you."

I was standing with Luise Rainer at a party in the French consul general's residence in New York, and a man was looking at her. Aware of what he was doing, she fidgeted a little, then looked up and stared back.

"Excuse me," he said, "I was staring at your beautiful cap." Luise's face was framed by a white crocheted cap.

"Thank you," she said.

"No, that's not true," he said. "I was really staring at *you*. You remind me so much of my favorite actress. Has anyone ever told you that you look like Luise Rainer?"

She smiled and said warmly, "It's me."

The man was at first stunned, then thrilled. "I was in love with you years ago," he said.

"Don't say that," she rebuked him. "Don't say you *were* in love with me years ago. You must be in love with me *now*. Now is what counts. And you must not love just that person you saw on the screen. We all want to be loved for our real selves." She held out her hands to him. He took them and kissed them.

At the Motion Picture Academy's 1982 party honoring the foreign film Oscar nominees, Luise Rainer made her first appearance at an Academy event since the 1940s.

She was holding court in the center of the floor when composer Bronislau Kaper entered and saw her. Without a second's hesitation he came toward her, arms outstretched, saying, "Luise!"

Hearing her name, she looked up and smiled. "Broni," she said.

He reached her and they embraced. Then he stepped back and looked at her. It was the first time they had met since he scored *Escapade* in the late 1930s.

"Luise," he said, "you have a new dress."

Having attended the Academy Awards with Groucho and with King Vidor on the nights they received their Oscars for lifetime achievement, I was told by each that he missed not ever having received an Oscar for a specific film. They would have preferred being honored for a work in the present to being honored for long, distinguished careers in the past. Actually, both preferred working to being honored at all.

Billy Wilder told me that he recognized the honor accorded him by the Film Society of Lincoln Center in selecting him as its annual tribute honoree. He wondered, however, if longevity hadn't had something to do with it. "I'm the lion tamer who has lasted and not been eaten by the lions." I didn't ask whether he was referring to his most recent studio, M-G-M, or not.

King Vidor, who had been honored as much as any living legend, had a suggestion: "There are so many living legends these days and so many standing ovations at the Academy Awards, I was going to suggest that they, the Motion Picture Academy, just take out all the seats."

"I can't live in the past," Tennessee Williams told me. "Or *on* the past. In some ways it's like it happened to someone else. Being a legend isn't enough. That last work should be the greatest. Life is always now. People say to me, 'You should be happy because you wrote this or that.' Well, I think they are right. But it's not what I feel. I'm living now, not then."

The last time I had tea with Anita Loos in her apartment across from Carnegie Hall, Gladys, her friend and companion of many years, was gathering together paintings, photographs, and memorabilia for a tribute that was being planned.

"I never like to go to these things," Anita Loos confided. "People say all those wonderful things about you, and you feel like you're at your own funeral. I think I'll skip this one."

Sadly, she did. Anita Loos died the day before the opening of the exhibition.

That day in her bedroom, she expressed the feeling shared by the legendary figures: "The trouble with tributes is they make you feel old. Being old is bad enough without feeling old."

Once a celebrity has achieved legendary status, he becomes imbued with a mystique that often places him and his work beyond criticism. "I can never expect to receive an honest reaction to my work," Picasso told me. "It is not a matter of politeness. Any honest reaction is obscured by the fame. You are put in the position of the young artist and you go back to only pleasing yourself. The carrousel has come full circle. Thus, I become the only judge of my work, and even I am prejudiced by my own legendary nature."

When Groucho was to receive his special Oscar, he approached the occasion with extreme seriousness. Over the objections of his friends, he deliberately planned a speech that respectfully omitted any jokes. But when he began speaking that night, even though the words were sober, the audience began laughing because their anticipation and expectation of laughter was so great.

Afterward he told me that he was surprised by the reaction, although he shouldn't have been, because it was the usual response. He was disappointed rather than pleased. It meant that he could no longer count on public reaction to edit his material.

After her death, Marilyn Monroe achieved a legendary status

so great that even her possessions acquired celebrity status. The exhibition of some of her dresses in Paris and New York required extraordinary security measures and police protection. It became such an ordeal that Lee Strasberg, who had inherited them, retired them from public exhibition.

Late one evening, Lee and I were listening to a record in the study of his New York apartment when we heard different music coming from another room. Investigating, we found Lee's young son, David, dressed in his pajamas. He had wandered in from his bedroom and was seated at the white baby grand piano that dominated the Strasbergs' dining room.

"Why are you up and playing the piano?" Lee asked his son.

"Because I have a headache," David answered. "It makes my headache go away."

The piano had been Marilyn Monroe's most treasured possession. She had left it along with all of her personal effects to Paula and Lee Strasberg.

"Marilyn was very poor as a child," Lee explained. "Very little of her life was spent with her mother, and she was the only person Marilyn wanted to be with. During one of the best moments of Marilyn's childhood, her mother bought this white piano. I don't know if either one of them could play it, but it was their great treasure.

"Then, one day, her mother had to go back to the hospital, and Marilyn had to go to still another foster home. There was no one to keep up the payments on the white piano, and it was taken away. Years later, after Marilyn was a star, she got detectives to search for the piano. She could've bought a lot of pianos for what it cost just to locate this one. Then, when it was found, she paid an enormous amount of back storage cost to get it."

All about us were reminders of Marilyn—her makeup mirror, her white sofa, a whole series of drawings she had done for Lee, and favorite photographs of hers. "We didn't really have room for the piano," Lee continued, "but we *had* to keep it."

Anna Strasberg eventually assumed the responsibility for the disposition of the actress's possessions. Professional clothes were separated from personal clothes. The professional dresses were not just costumes, but her suits of glamour, designed to protect her vulnerable private self, to conceal her at the same time they were revealing her. All of the dresses intended to be seen by everyone, Anna kept in trust for the world. Undergarments, house dresses, and whatever Marilyn wore in the privacy of her home when she was alone or with those closest to her, Anna bundled up and delivered to a New York charity thrift shop where they were left anonymously. In this way, Marilyn Monroe's intimate wearing apparel served a good cause while keeping their secrets.

"I could never imagine Eva Perón growing old"

JUAN PERÓN

I DID NOT MEET the living Eva Perón. In her case, I met only the legend.

If Juan Perón is an historic figure, Eva has become a legend. Both remain subjects of intense controversy even years after their deaths. Eva's persona, especially, has assumed mythical proportions. Her Argentine followers apotheosize her, as if on death one could envision a beatified Eva being transported upward as was the character of the same name in *Uncle Tom's Cabin*. Her detractors share that vision, but they also see the wires and stage machinery.

I asked Perón if he himself might have been influenced by the legend during the many years that had passed. Could the legend influence even his memory of the real woman he knew so well? He thought for a moment and said, "Perhaps."

A leading European diplomat told me of his "affair" with Eva Perón. His friendly relationship with her had already been much reported to me by American diplomats who knew those involved. Of course, only two people could ever know if this is a true story: Eva Perón, long dead, and the man who told it to me many years afterward.

It was just after World War II and the diplomat was in Buenos Aires desperately pleading the cause of his country, which at that moment was extremely dependent on getting Argentine grain. Juan Perón, then President of Argentina, had the power, and Eva Perón had his ear. The diplomat had hers.

She had made clear her special preference for him, and he had been more than diplomatic. It was, however, a tightrope he was required to walk. He could ill afford to do anything that would offend General Perón, and he could perhaps even less afford to offend Evita, with whom his relationship was closer and who was more volatile.

He himself was confused as to what that relationship was. The aspect of it that afforded him special advantage and that he did not want to lose was his role as her "walker." Evita liked to sally forth on the arm of an appropriate and beyond-reproach escort to her pet charities or when she held her special kind of court for petitioners. There were only a few men around the Pink House deemed worthy by Evita to fulfill this mission, and the diplomat I knew was recognized by all as her favorite. Gossip was rampant and the speculation endless.

The diplomat would often have coffee with her early in the morning in her bedroom to plan the affairs of the day. He could not help but observe that she was sometimes so intent on planning her strategy that she did not notice that her peignoir had come open or that her nightgown had slipped. *He* always noticed, although covertly, averting his eyes or fixing his glance somewhere beyond, memorizing the pattern of the wallpaper.

He was not quite certain what was expected of him; he hoped nothing. Then, one day it was made all too clear. His reputation as a Don Juan had preceded him, and he was asked by the lady herself why he had not been more venturesome with her. Was it because she was not attractive to him, not desirable? He attempted to reassure her, but it became obvious that only one kind of reassurance would do. He could not afford to reject her and thus incur the wrath of which he knew she was capable.

A rendezvous was made for 6 A.M. the following morning. He was to come to her room for a conference, but the agenda would be private.

He couldn't sleep all night. First there was the dilemma of whether he should or shouldn't. With the fate of his country resting, at the very least, on his shoulders, he made the decision that while he could scarcely afford to say yes to *la Presidenta,* he definitely could not afford to say no to her. Then there was the question of whether he could or couldn't.

Even though he considered himself quite virile, he preferred to be the one to make the advances, and not only would Evita not have been his choice, but there was too much pressure on him to perform. He wondered if under the circumstances he could perform at all, not to mention up to whatever the expectation might be. He suffered the whole night, living through the event several times in every scenario his fertile imagination could construct.

It seemed that the actual moment would never arrive, and simultaneously that it would arrive all too soon. Arrive it did.

The diplomat kept his rendezvous, which he characterized for me decades later as even more than a command performance—as active duty in combat. He girded himself to be the consummate lover he hoped his experience had equipped him to be. The actuality, however, was different from any of the ways he had imagined.

He carried out his mission, doing his best, but found he was making little impression. Evita spent almost all of their time in bed discussing business—the business of politics. She was, as the story goes, particularly incensed over the behavior of a mayor in one of the provinces who had challenged her authority, as well as by a snub by an oligarch's wife. All of this, the diplomat said, interfered with his concentration and also sent him the message that he wasn't very distracting.

Wondering what he was going to say during the experience, he had tried to compose something in advance, but found no necessity to speak at all. Evita did all the talking, and none of it had anything to do with him. Just as his vanity was going down in total defeat, she suddenly gave a little cry and, right in the middle of a sentence, stopped speaking for a few seconds. Before he even knew what had happened, she started speaking nonstop again, picking up her sentence right in the middle of where she had left off.

His country got the grain.

Buenos Aires is one of the great gossip capitals of the world, a genuine rival in that respect of even Washington, D.C. In Buenos Aires, where the speed of sound travels faster than the speed of light, tongues were kept busy during the early 1940s with talk of the extremely unconventional nature of Perón's relationship with Eva Duarte.

Leopoldo Torre Nilsson, Argentina's most famous film director, told me, "Perón's attitude toward Eva was certainly not the prevailing one for a man in his position toward a woman in hers. It would have been exceedingly rare for an Argentine man to permit his wife so much public presence and peer group relationship as Eva enjoyed with Perón. But Eva was not only *not* his wife, she wasn't even a mistress of some social station. She was just a little actress, one of those girls the *macho* men of Buenos Aires kept in a 'nest'—a little apartment somewhere just off the Avenida Santa Fé, not right on Santa Fé where the flats were larger, more expensive, and where you paid for the fashionable address.

"According to the rules of the game, which were well understood by all, you would not take '*that* kind of girl' to one of those restaurants where a man took his wife. One would certainly *never* be seen at the fashionable Grill Room of the Plaza Hotel, or the elegant Alvear Palace Restaurant, or the favorite La Cabaña with a nobody like Eva Duarte. One wouldn't be seen having tea at one of the ranking *confiterías* like El Águila or the Confitería Gran Rex with that sort of woman. She would, however, be perfect to show off at a place where a man knew he would meet only his male friends with their 'back-street' girls; or better yet, a group of your men friends alone who could then envy your escapade and speculate on your pleasure, nudging each other with knowing snickers. That would be good for extra points. The Porteño male's concern was generally much greater for what other men *thought* he was doing with women than for what he actually was doing.

"My father was a very *macho* man who had to maintain his bravado even in old age. He [Leopoldo Torre Ríos] was the most famous pioneer director of Argentina's film industry. In his old age, every day, six days a week in the late afternoon, at the hour of vermouth, the traditional time which a Porteño man reserves to himself for his 'private' pleasure, my father left whatever he was doing and made his way to the little 'nest' he had kept for as long as I could remember, just off the Avenida Santa Fé. He would stay there the regularly allotted few hours, and then come home to dinner as he always had. On his way to or from his 'nest' he would pass his friends, who would smirkingly fathom just what he was up to. What they didn't know was that the little apartment he kept was empty, and had been for years. But he had to make his daily pilgrimage and sit there and read a magazine rather than face the 'disgrace' of having his male friends guess that he no longer kept a little bird in his nest.

"Perón, of course, knew the code, but he didn't choose to play by conventional rules; he made his own. Eva went where he went, and when visitors came to his apartment to talk about politics, military affairs, or labor problems, Eva was there. Quiet, perhaps, but there."

Norman Armour was the U.S. ambassador to Argentina during the period before Perón became President and before he married Eva Duarte. At that time, Perón and Eva were neighbors in the same apartment building, and were always linked as "very close friends."

Ambassador Armour had been invited to Perón's apartment to discuss informally their ideas about improving Argentine–U.S. relations. Just before I visited Perón, Norman Armour told me about what happened at their "private" meeting:

"The meeting had lasted quite a while, but as it was drawing to a close, I heard a rustling sound from behind the silk drapes. I watched in surprise and shock as the drapes moved and Eva came out from behind them, laughing and saying, 'I don't agree with that.' Obviously she had been there all the time."

When I mentioned the story to Perón, he smiled and seemed to savor the memory. "Eva Perón was a very serious woman, but she could also be playful. That was an example of her sense of humor." His obvious pleasure at the memory of the incident suggested that it was also an example of his own sense of humor.

I spoke with Juan Perón in Madrid just before his brief return to the presidency of Argentina. Perón was, at the time, preoccupied with the imminence of his return, something he had long awaited, *too* long, in his words. His energy and health were no longer up to the arduous schedule, and he recognized all of the difficulties facing him. He knew that his supporters were expecting him to have all of the answers, and he did not. He knew that they were not looking to him for uncertainty, but for a panacea.

Perón had been warned by his doctors that his life was certain to be shortened by a return to the pressures of Argentine politics. While ill health was the only acceptable reason Perón could have given for not returning, it was the one reason he could *not* bring himself to give. As he expressed it, "That would be like saying I am not a man." He believed that while the personal, private self of Perón could age, could grow tired and ill, the public self could not. To admit to age and illness was admitting to the loss of his manhood, and therefore worse than death. It would have been the disgrace of the kamikaze pilot who swerves at the last moment to avoid crashing.

Perón told me that he regretted going back to Argentina when he was no longer in condition for it. "I would like to be available for consultation but not to assume the full responsibility, because that requires a health and vigor which I no longer possess. I was always an athlete, but being the president of a country requires much greater energy than sports, as well as the ability to live with constant pressure.

"I always told them I was ready to return, and I wanted to do so. I wanted to return taking with me the benefit of my studies and thoughts during exile. But now it is late. Yet I cannot say I will not go back because my health does not permit. That is not what is expected from Perón."

Perón cared more, he always affirmed, about the survival of the movement that bore his name than about his personal survival. Without a child or political heir apparent, he knew that there were difficulties ahead for Peronism without Perón. The only other Perón was his third wife, Isabel, who dreamed of being Señora Perón, wife of the President, but whose dream was to turn into a nightmare when life forced her not to play the part of Evita but of Perón himself.

At Perón's handsome, well-guarded home in the Madrid suburb of Puerta de Hierro, Fuente la Reina, Isabelita Perón poured English tea from an ornate silver teapot. My cup was just a third full when she stopped abruptly. "Oh my fingernail," she cried

out, almost in pain. "I've chipped the polish." Pouting, she held
out her hand, contemplating the tiny chip in the dark red oval.

Perón comforted her in a patiently reassuring manner. "Why
don't you have it fixed while you're having your hair done? You
could go to the city now and do some shopping." He spoke in a
rather paternal tone.

Isabelita brightened and smiled at Perón. "Yes, I will pick up
my new dress at Loewe." She turned to me and said, "I have
problems finding my size, you know. I only wear a size six; maybe
sometimes a size eight." Turning back to Perón, she said, "Then
when I come home, you can take some pictures of us." There
were already dozens of snapshots as well as silver-framed por-
traits of Isabelita scattered about. "I love having my picture
taken," she confided. "I'll go into Madrid now, but first," she said
to Perón, "I want to show Carlota my new doll."

She left the room for a moment, followed by two poodles, the
Peróns' constant companions. Their parents had been given to
Eva by U.S. Ambassador Stanton Griffis. In a moment, Isabelita
returned carrying a Roldán boy doll. "He is for my doll collection," she explained. "Look—he has a navel!" She held him up
for my inspection. "There was a book here, you know, with the
title *All Navels Are Round.*"

As Isabelita departed, she called back to me, "Don't leave.
When I come back, I'll show you my new dress. Or maybe you
would like to come with me now and go shopping?"

I declined the invitation, staying on with Perón. It was not for
shopping that I was there. He waited until Isabelita disappeared
from view before speaking.

"She is so different from Eva Perón," he said. "Isabelita is like a
little doll herself—a bit delicate. She is young and needs to be
taken care of. You know, she is my third wife. Everyone thinks
that Eva Perón was my first wife because she was so visible. My
first wife, Aurelia Tizón, was a music teacher. She was quiet and
serious, and a good wife when I was a young army officer. I used
to enjoy listening to her play the piano in the evenings while I
worked. She died, poor thing, when she was very young."

During Juan Perón's last years in Spain, ever present at his home was José López Rega, who officially held the title of secretary to Perón. In effect, he was really more of a companion for Isabelita. He had come to his position in a most individual way, as perhaps the only person besides Perón to have known all three of Perón's wives.

He told me that when he was in music school, one of his fellow students was a young woman named Aurelia Tizón. After graduation, both played in a chamber ensemble. This was shortly after Aurelia Tizón had married a young army officer named Juan Perón.

In the years that followed, although López Rega knew her well, he knew Perón only slightly. He spent a great deal of time playing music with Perón's wife while Perón was occupied pursuing his military career. Aurelia Tizón died in her early thirties, at approximately the same age Eva Perón was to die years later.

Some years afterward, López Rega was walking along the Avenida Corrientes in Buenos Aires, looking at the movie theaters, trying to decide which film to see, when he happened to meet Perón, who was by then the Secretary of Labor. Perón introduced López Rega to the young woman with him, Eva Duarte, who would later become Evita Perón. She particularly liked López Rega. When Perón became President, López Rega became a "functionary" in the government through the intervention of Eva.

About a quarter of a century later, long after the death of Eva Perón, López Rega was in Madrid. Walking along the Avenida José Antonio, he was once again looking for a film to see, and once again he met Perón. This time Perón was with Isabelita, whom he had by then married. They were living in exile just outside Madrid.

As chance would have it, Perón had just lost a secretary and needed someone. What he *really* needed was a kind of "walker" for his young third wife. Isabelita had interests which were not Perón's. She loved to go shopping during the afternoons in Madrid, and afternoon in Madrid meant 5 P.M. to 8 P.M. Though Perón had a chauffeur who could drive Isabelita about in their blue Mercedes, Isabelita never liked to be alone. Perón did. He liked to spend his afternoons reading, or writing, or giving audiences to the endless parade of visiting Peronists who constantly passed through Madrid, ostensibly as tourists.

Perón had accepted Franco's condition not to engage in political activity or make political statements while he remained in Spain during his exile. The only "tourist" attraction for these Argentine visitors, however, was Perón's house, and the only souvenir they cared about was their photograph standing with Perón to take back and show off proudly to their constituents in Argentina.

Perón asked me to promise that I wouldn't write anything about him while he was living in Spain because he had agreed not to give any interviews. I kept the promise, though afterward I came to believe that it was not a promise he had wanted me to heed or expected me to keep.

During those later years of exile in Madrid, López Rega spent a great deal of time with an Isabelita who was largely left out and who wanted to be left out of Perón's numerous meetings with the visiting labor leaders and Peronists who came to pay homage to *el líder,* and to lobby for his support. A blessing from Perón carried great weight with a large number of Argentines during those years when Peronism was illegal in Argentina.

But all of that was for men, Isabelita told me, and it was not her place. Her place, she felt, was to preside as a gracious hostess. She had *her* interests; but while her clothes and hair occupied some of her waking hours, she was still left with time on her hands and few responsibilities. Morning diversions were no problem for Isabelita, who liked to sleep until noon, while Perón rose at six in the morning. In the afternoons López Rega was there to accompany her and thus free Perón.

Perón's public attitude toward Isabelita generally reflected the affection that would be appropriate toward a pretty little girl of whom he was proud. Toward López Rega, his attitude was what would be appropriate toward a piece of furniture one was accustomed to having around. The Argentine visitors always paid brief court to the Señora Perón as the wife of General Perón, but paid no attention at all to the same person as Isabelita.

Little did they realize that they were in the presence of the future, and not so distant future, first woman President of Argentina, and that the man they never even noticed was to be widely termed her "Rasputin."

One afternoon as Isabelita and I rode into Madrid, she opened her purse, revealing its tidy contents. Everything was separated in leather wallets and envelopes and tiny cosmetic bags. Meticulously she counted out in advance the tips for her hairdresser, the shampoo assistant, the girl who held the hairpins and handed them to the hairdresser, and the dressing-room attendant. "I like to be generous," Isabelita explained. "And of course they expect it because of General Perón."

Then she went on to talk about the high inflation rate in Argentina and some of the "mistakes" of the central bank. This led to a discussion of the Communist threat, terrorism, the problems faced by Catholicism in Latin America, those special problems faced by women in Argentina, the problem of dealing with opposing factions in the same union, both of which supported Perón, and the future of a Spain without Franco.

Her conversation was abruptly terminated by our arrival at the red doors of Elizabeth Arden. Picking up her copy of French *Vogue*, brought along for perusal under the drier, she said to me, "I do not talk about these things much with General Perón because he likes to feel that I am sheltered from the world."

When Perón talked with me about Evita, whom he always referred to as "Eva Perón," he spoke of her not as of his wife, but as of a personage who in death had become institutionalized:

PERÓN
Eva Perón had a hard life when she was very young, and I think this helped her. I think it made her very strong. She was illegitimate, you know. You cannot imagine what that meant in Argentina in those days. It is not a thing to be even now, but then it was an unimaginable burden few could surmount. She was born into extreme poverty and grew up without the advantage of education. Then, too, it was a difficult time for any woman who wished to pursue a career. It was not expected, and it was

barely allowed. You see, the Argentina of that time was a man's world.

I

I believe it still is. And not just Argentina.

PERÓN

[Laughing] Yes, but less so. At least now, women vote in Argentina. Before us, women could not even vote. We gave them the vote.

Eva Perón was a great woman. And she had not achieved her full greatness when she died. She was my protégée. Political leadership is an art and has a theory that can be passed on. I always thought of myself as a teacher, and she was my best student. I have never known anyone who learned faster. She could do anything she set her mind to. And *[Laughing]* she knew how to set her mind! I saw her go from being a girl who could not engage in a simple interchange of political ideas to one with whom one could discuss not only absolutely anything, but who could also contribute valuable ideas of her own.

Until that time women had always been held down and put down. But because it had always been that way was no reason why it should be so. Because something has always been done a certain way is the reason most people give for continuing to do things that way. It is, in fact, no reason at all.

Perhaps in the beginning my vanity was flattered by the way she absorbed my every word. But I quickly realized that there was nothing parrotlike in how she assimilated my ideas and directives. To them she added her intuitive capabilities and her experience. She gave them back to me with her own insights. From Eva Perón I learned a lot about how women feel. She did not accept the restrictions imposed by class. She knew these restrictions existed, but she was not resigned to being stopped by them. She was never a resigned person.

I also learned a lot about how the poor feel. Those were two plights I could sympathize with, but I never had those experiences. She had. And to face hard things in childhood, before we have had time to prepare ourselves in life, is particularly traumatic. Eva Perón was a person of courage, and what she had to endure only made her stronger.

She was wonderful at raising money for charity. Being a woman helped her in that. Men found it hard to say no to her. I, myself, have always had difficulty saying no to a woman. She did an interesting thing, too. Whatever they gave, she always wanted a little more for her charity. So, after a while, they realized that, and they did not give it all at once, but held a little in reserve for when she came back thanking them, saying that what they had done was wonderful, and then [Smiling wryly] telling them that she knew they could do a little better.

She was a model for the women of Argentina. They identified with her. The Argentine people called her their "Lady of Hope." When something catastrophic happened, when a flood washed away their homes, the people would say, "Eva Perón can help us." She represented access to the highest part of the government. She made it possible for them to reach her directly. That was very important. They knew she would never turn away from them. They felt she would save them. She gave them hope, and when people have this hope, then they can save themselves.

She was a truly exceptional woman with natural talents that qualified her perfectly for the role she was to fill. The natural talents must find a role in life to fulfill, or the person is frustrated. She would have been terribly unhappy if she had not, through me, found the outlet for her energy.

She had a great belief in herself. I helped her, but I did not give her this. She already had it when I met her. Without this belief in yourself, you cannot do anything. She was always learning. From everything she did, she learned something. Even while all eyes were on her, watching her, she was also observing, learning. That is a hard thing to do—to be observing and learning while everyone is watching you. She was watching everyone else and herself at the same time.

She was a tireless worker, a person of boundless energy. Energy is one of the most important gifts if you are to be successful. Sometimes I got tired just watching her, and I was myself always an athlete with great energy and stamina. Of course, there were moments when Eva Perón tired; but still she was, even if tired, always ready to go on. She just reached down a little deeper and drew on those extra resources.

Her only interest was in her work. She worked all the time, and would not even take care of her health. Even when she was near death, she only wanted to work, and she called her death-bed her "workbench." She would summon the people and the papers she needed to her workbench. I believe that her incredible bravery in facing a premature and painful death came from her already having put all of the private woman into the public person. It was beyond bravery. Her commitment to her unfinished work was so great that she did not feel the pain. Even at the end, she still tried to dress beautifully and look her best.

I

A great deal of the criticism leveled against her was because of the *haute couture* clothes and ornate jewelry which she wore even when speaking to the poor.

PERÓN

At first it did not seem right to me, either. But she was like a little girl dressing up. She took such a great delight in the pretty things she had never before been able to have, that I did not have the hard heart to suppress her enthusiasm. But I did not really approve. Then I changed my mind. I saw the looks on the faces of the poor of Argentina, especially the women. They wanted her to have beautiful things. They loved her. For them Eva Perón could do no wrong. But it was more than that. She wore the clothes for *them.* She personified their dreams. They thought that if she could have those things, perhaps one day they could. Every girl dreams of being Cinderella. As a girl Eva Perón dreamed the dreams of Hollywood, though she did not know she would live a life greater than any she could imagine.

Eva Perón always attracted a lot of attention wherever she went. There were those who did not understand it, who resented it, who were jealous. They complained because Eva Perón was always in the newspapers and on the magazine covers. Why was it so? We could not have achieved that even if we had wanted to compel it.

What happened was so clear. They noticed that where her

picture appeared, they sold more newspapers, and when she was on the cover, the circulation of a magazine went up. So they used more photographs of her, and then they sold even more copies. We could not have stopped them if we had wanted to, because we did not have that power. It is just like your Jacqueline Kennedy. When the President has a wife who is young and pretty and wears beautiful clothes, it is only natural that people should like to look at her.

I

How would you describe Eva Duarte, the girl you first met?

PERÓN

When I first met Eva Perón, she was a shy girl.

I

Is it possible that being an actress, she found that the costumes and props helped her to assume a character with which to face the world and be a public person?

PERÓN

Perhaps. She was the fairy-tale princess. I do not know if she realized it, but I think it was true that the clothes helped her to lose her self-consciousness. It was not an easy thing for her because she had to do it all very quickly. I exposed her to situations so that she could absorb and study without having any responsibility. I do not believe that you learn to swim best by being thrown into the water with no preparation. I wanted her to feel she did not have to do anything until she was ready. I am very proud that I helped her flower to blossom.

Her death was an extraordinary blow for the Argentine people. In Buenos Aires nearly everything stopped for fifteen days while homage was paid to Eva Perón. It is a terrible thing to have to die in public. I remember how it was for Eva Perón, poor brave girl. For myself, I would rather be like one of those animals who goes off alone. I would like that for myself—to disappear.

Perhaps she would not like my telling it even now, but she was a very vulnerable woman. She did not like to let that side of her show in public. She used her ability as an actress to hide that side of her nature, because she did not believe that it was appropriate to the role of public leadership she had assumed at my side. She believed that you cannot be a pillar of support and strength for others if you appear to need a shoulder to cry on. In the privacy of our time alone together, she had my shoulder to cry on, and did. But Eva Perón was also like a man in that she did not believe in revealing her emotions and most private feelings in public. A man does not cry. But her softer, more feeling side was what gave her insights into the often unexpressed but deepest feelings of the poor, and particularly of women. They had been unable to express it for themselves, but she articulated it for them. And they said, "Oh, yes; that is how I feel."

Eva Perón would say to me often, "I could never have done this alone. I can do it only through you. I could not have done it without your support and encouragement." But I think this is not only true for a woman, but for a man, too. Every one of us needs someone to whom we can turn who cares for us and who will never judge us harshly. I am a man who has been married most of his adult life, and I have always had that relationship in my marriages. I cannot imagine myself not being married.

Eva Perón would always say she was the little sparrow to my eagle. But the little sparrow is a great survivor. It does not need to follow the sun, but can survive the winter.

Although she respected many conventions, she liked to choose which ones. She did not understand the society ladies of Buenos Aires who frowned on her because she wore her hair down at a state occasion at one of the galas at the Colón Opera House. Once when one of those ladies mentioned to me that perhaps I would want to advise the Señora Perón about fashion protocol, which dictated that ladies wear their hair up, I thought it was funny, and I told Eva Perón, who did not laugh. The next time, she wore her hair down. The woman who said it was very old-fashioned.

I wish that you could have known Eva Perón. Isabelita always keeps that candle there lit for her. We are Catholic, you know.

I wanted her to be the Vice President of Argentina, but that was not possible. The Army found it too difficult to accept. Members of the oligarchy who lived on great estates, ate only beef steaks, and shopped in Paris found it easy to judge her harshly. But one day there will be a woman President in Argentina, and in the United States, too.

Eva Perón would never have left Argentina except as a corpse. If she had lived, she would not have accepted the overthrow of our government. I was elected by the people, and so she would have stayed to fight. There would have been a bloody revolution. But I did not believe as she did. It was a great difference between us. If I stayed I knew there would be fighting in the streets. All war is terrible, but civil war is the most terrible. I would have done anything to avoid Argentines killing Argentines. It was for that reason I chose to leave my country, even though I knew there were those who would say I was a coward.

Perón coughed and his poodles barked. "You see? They are imitating me. It is because they admire me. It is not difficult to be a hero to your dogs."

Perón's poodles were present during most of our conversations, and occasionally punctuated what was said with barks, like a Greek chorus with poor timing. Perón would merely laugh and say, "They think you have come to interview them, too. They don't want to be left out." Once he added, "They are extremely intelligent, but I never trained them. Tricks are for people."

Perón reached into a desk drawer and pulled out what looked exactly like a small automatic pistol. Pointing it at me, he pulled the trigger. A flame leaped up from the top of the gun, and he lit his cigarette with it. He laughed. Then he explained that the pistol-lighter was a gift from Stanton Griffis when he was the U.S. ambassador to Argentina. Stanton Griffis had already told me the story:

"As a gift for Perón's birthday, I bought a pistol-shaped cigarette lighter at New York's Hammacher Schlemmer. It looked just like a real gun. On his birthday, I went to the Pink House in Buenos Aires, and was shown into the presidential office. While we were talking, I suddenly whipped out the lighter and pointed it at him like a gun. Perón really jumped! I pulled the trigger. There was a popping sound, and a small flame shot up. Suddenly the soldiers on guard duty, who hadn't been paying any attention at all, came to life and were about to seize me when I showed Perón it was just a cigarette lighter. He was very amused and laughed for about ten minutes. After that, he played the same trick on people who came to see him. Later, at state affairs, Perón would occasionally catch my eye, and point his finger at me like it was a gun."

As we got up to go for a walk in the garden, I had the opportunity to take a closer look at a painting of which I had been subliminally aware throughout our meeting. The picture that had been vaguely intruding on my consciousness was an almost life-sized portrait of a woman which hung over the mantel and dominated the room. Her blond hair was severely coiffured and she was dressed in black. At first glance I assumed it was a poor likeness of Eva Perón.

Perón came and stood by me. "Ah, you've noticed our little picture. Who do you think it is?" Fortunately he did not wait for my answer. "You would have said Eva Perón, wouldn't you? Everyone does. You would have been wrong. It is really a portrait of Isabelita. The artist is very good, but he thought that I would like it if he caught the resemblance between the two. But he exaggerated it so much that it became a portrait of Eva Perón.

"Everyone says, 'What a wonderful picture of Eva!' to Isabelita. You did not do that, which was good. It is better not to mention the picture when Isabelita returns. It isn't that she says she doesn't like it. In fact, she says only that it is very nice. But she says it unconvincingly. To tell you the truth, I think she hates it."

"But you continue to keep the picture there," I said.

"Yes, but what can we do now that we have it? Besides," he added with a laugh, "maybe the artist will come to visit us."

Perón took great pride in his house in Spain. He had it built so that it would last five hundred years. Laughing, he added, "Maybe that's because in the back of my mind, I hoped that I could stay with it."

When we went outside, Perón said, "You see that wall around the house and that iron gate? They are there to keep those outside out. But they also keep those inside in. Walls are like that."

We were joined by a mongrel dog, a mixture of indeterminate breeds, although clearly somewhere in her background was a German shepherd. "It's better not to pet her," Perón cautioned me, "until she knows you well. And if you do pet her, don't reach out suddenly."

He explained that he had found her almost fully grown, after she had had a very hard life. "She was lying in the street in Madrid, and at first glance she seemed to be dead. When I realized that she was still alive, I rented a hotel room so that she would have a chance to recuperate before we brought her here. She had been beaten and almost starved to death. She is thus forever a victim of her early life which she cannot forget. The scars that do not show can be just as disfiguring. Understandably, she cannot bring herself to forget her past pain, and trust people. The sad thing is that even though the bad things are over for her, and she is now safe with us, she goes on torturing herself in her mind. Poor thing."

His tone was the same as when he had spoken of the life and death of Eva Perón. At his words, the dog burrowed herself against his trousers, seemingly trying to become part of him.

My last and shortest visit to Perón's home was the one that will live longest in my memory. On the phone Perón had prepared me, at least as much as one can be prepared for such a meeting. Few words were spoken during that "tea party." Time in one's mind is so relative to the experience one is having that this visit seemed both shorter and longer than it actually was. It was a striking momentary impression, and also a lasting one.

The Spanish maid opened the door, but the usual smile on her rosy-cheeked countenance had given way to a tight-lipped pallor that would not have been inappropriate if Count Dracula had been the preceding guest. I was shown into the living room, where I saw Perón, who was pacing about. Isabelita, wearing a dark gray suit, more sedately dressed than usual, was standing next to a small, deeply engrossed figure in a black suit. He was bent over and did not straighten up even to look at me as I entered. Isabelita nodded to me as Perón spoke:

"We have been waiting for you. This is Dr. Ara," he said,

indicating the man in the black suit, "the world's most famous embalmer."

Dr. Ara remained so involved in what he was doing that he still did not look up or offer his hand. It was just as well.

Isabelita came over to me and confided, "He did de Falla, too, you know." Then she led me over to the sofa.

Perón said it was important that I had come to pay my respects to Eva Perón. It was for this reason he had suggested that I come specifically on that day for an experience he said could otherwise never be recaptured.

Dr. Ara stepped aside, and I saw the body of Eva Perón. I don't know what I had expected to see; but whatever it was, as always, nothing is ever quite the way you imagine it will be. I don't know if I thought Eva Perón would look like a body, or a mannequin, or a wax doll, or something else. She looked like all of those and none of those. She was wearing a white dress which had acquired a shroudlike appearance. But her face was even whiter. Perón said to me, "She was fair, like you."

Eva looked so small, a tiny figure. Only the legend was larger than life; the person was smaller in death. From the photographs, I hadn't realized that she was so small. Conscious of her figure, she had always dieted rigorously, and during her last illness, she had lost a great deal of weight. Somehow, my being there seemed to me an invasion of her privacy. Perón responded to what I was thinking:

"Eva Perón would have wanted this, you know. It was her idea. When she learned that she had only months to live, she did not want to die. She had so much left to do, poor girl. So she had this idea. She had heard of Dr. Ara and of his miraculous work. Eva Perón felt that in this way she could go on inspiring her people."

For a few minutes, no one said anything, and then Perón continued: "Somehow I could never imagine Eva Perón growing old. You know, I don't think she would have liked getting old."

I was told that the body was being kept upstairs, but had been brought downstairs for the visit—not mine, but that of Dr. Ara. He had been summoned to repair any damage that had been done to the body during the years it had been hidden in Italy after Perón's mercurial departure from Argentina in 1955. Gossip persisted in Argentina that even as Eva Perón had stood in the open limousine at her last public appearance, she was actually propped up by wire supports under her fur coat, and was, in fact, already dead.

The maid served tea. Isabelita passed the toast and *dulce de leche,* a sweet spread that resembled melted caramels. When I didn't drink the tea, Perón asked me if I would prefer *maté* [Argentine herb tea], saying, "It's the best thing for your digestion, and it stimulates the appetite."

Dr. Ara was offered some tea, but he didn't even seem to hear the question, being so absorbed in his work. He just went on combing the hair of the bisque doll-looking Eva, as tufts of her blond hair kept falling onto the highly polished parquet floor.

"There was only one crack in her," Isabelita informed me. "But it was a shame about the hairpins. They rusted in her hair."

My last contact with José López Rega was a cordial greeting sent from Buenos Aires in December 1973 wishing me a happy new year. It was on the stationery of the Ministry of Social Welfare, and bore the crest of the Argentine Republic.

My last contact with Perón was not actually with Perón himself. It was a brief note dated August 14, 1974, from Carlos Alejandro Villona, private secretary to the President of the Nation, informing me of the death of Lieutenant General Juan Domingo Perón.

My last contact with Isabelita was a Christmas greeting from Buenos Aires in December 1975 from the President of the Nation, Isabel Martínez de Perón.

The body of Eva Perón finally returned to Argentina only after Perón himself had died. It was actually brought back to Argentina by Isabel Perón, who, on the death of her husband, had become President of Argentina.

Isabel Perón did not complete her term of office. She was arrested by the military junta that took over the government of Argentina, imprisoned, and then finally allowed to return to Madrid.

"What do you do when There *isn't there?"*

SIDNEY SHELDON

WHEN THEIR GOALS ARE reached, many people of great achievement find themselves dismayed by their own lack of elation. They discover that success is not nepenthe, that it does not represent the magical anodyne. *There* isn't there, and they are disturbed by guilt or at least the feeling that something is wrong with them because they are not experiencing the kind of happiness they assumed success would bring.

They know they are supposed to be happier than other people. Not only are they constantly being told how lucky they are, but they know it's true! Even if they wanted sympathy, they couldn't expect any.

Along the way they believed consciously or subconsciously that everything would be better once they reached the pinnacle, because success is widely assumed to be a panacea. Picasso told me that when he was very young he believed that even sex would be better when he became famous—not just that it would provide a greater choice of partners, but that it would actually feel better.

Success, however, did not bring everyone to that perfect state of happiness envisioned in their hopeful idealism and romantic dreams of youth. They found instead unexpected pressures and disillusionment. Personal happiness was not necessarily a concomitant of professional happiness, which is in itself elusive and illusory enough. Arriving *there,* many found *there* wasn't there for them.

Mervyn LeRoy put it quite succinctly when we talked about those celebrities who had not found Oz or who felt that Oz had not lived up to expectations and who had complained that fame and success had not brought them happiness in life:

"That's because they don't know what it would have been like without it."

I was sitting in the restaurant Méditerranée in Paris with Otto Preminger when we were joined by Ruth Gordon, Garson Kanin, and Arthur Rubinstein. The conversation proceeded from the subject of the freshness of the *oursin,* a sea urchin regarded by some as a great delicacy, to Otto Preminger's reference to the bad news in the headlines that day. Garson Kanin commented that this was always the nature of news. Otto Preminger added, "No intelligent person can be happy."

Arthur Rubinstein debated that statement, articulating a point of view in which I silently concurred:

"There are people who like to say that no intelligent person can be happy. I have always heard that, but I have never believed it. You can use your intelligence to make yourself less happy or more happy. I have always used mine to make myself happier, despite a tendency in the intellectual world to think it almost unfashionable to be happy."

Everyone has known the feeling of loneliness, which is more painful than and different from just being alone. Achieving fame and success surrounds you with more people, but it doesn't guarantee that you won't be lonely because part of being lonely comes from without and part from within.

For all people, famous or not, much of life is a search to avoid loneliness. Supposedly, not being lonely is one of the rewards of success. Being surrounded by large numbers of people, however, does not provide the warmth and intimacy which all of us crave. Hubert Humphrey was usually surrounded by people, but he told me, "The entourage isn't company."

A recurring disappointment for the celebrated is that becoming famous and successful does not solve for them the problem of loneliness. Sometimes, in fact, the successful career seems to lead them to even greater isolation. In the end, surprisingly often, their work becomes their best friend.

"I was a person who couldn't make divorce work," Bette Davis told me. "There's nothing lonelier than a turned-down toilet seat. My work is my company."

The time-consuming nature of their work, the discipline involved, the pressures that the rest of the world does not understand, all serve to cut them off. Like the rich who fear they will be
exploited if they know anyone poorer than they are, celebrities
are sometimes afraid of being "used." Fame and success are
hermetic.

When Picasso spoke with me, he was at the pinnacle of material
success and world acclaim. His comment on success was therefore all the more poignant:

"The success that is fun is the early success that you share with
your young friends. Nothing else is ever like that. Early friends
share experiences and feelings that can only happen once for the
first time. It is like young love.

"When you are young and without success, you have only a few
friends. Then, later, when you are rich and famous, you still have
a few—if you are lucky."

Chagall told me quite simply, "Fame sends you back to the
ghetto."

Woody Allen talked with me about the friends who cut themselves off:

"They decide you wouldn't really want to know them anymore,
so they stop calling you. If they call you and you're busy and don't
call them back, you've proven their thesis. If you call them, they
say, 'Oh, he's just doing that because he thinks he *has* to!' They
expect you to call them more than you used to, when you're so
pressed for time. So finally they say, 'He got too big to know me,'
and they've made it a self-fulfilling prophecy."

When Laurence Olivier was still an aspiring actor, someone
would pass him on Bond Street and call out, "Hi, Larry." Not
hearing or seeing the person, he would just go on his way. The
other person would assume he hadn't heard him, and would think
nothing of it. "After I made it, so to speak," he told me, "you
might say that every time there was a 'Hi, Larry' I didn't hear, that
was someone who didn't know me anymore. They would say, 'He
thinks he's a very big star,' or, 'It's really gone to his head,' and
that was that."

One of the supposed benefits of success is the access it provides to interesting people. The whole world was opened to

Hubert Humphrey, but just as *there* wasn't always there, *they* weren't always there, either. *They* could be a disappointment. Success could change perceptions, goals, and even people—and not always for the better.

Hubert Humphrey told me that it had been his experience that one discovers who and what a man is after he has success. Contrary to what is usually assumed, he had found that in war, natural disaster, or hardship, people were most likely to behave at their best.

"Having success reveals any basic weaknesses," he said. "You can't be a despot unless you get power."

The advantages of success are obvious, but there are some ensuing and concurrent disadvantages. The famous person is someone who is known by a multitude of people whom he or she cannot possibly know as individuals, while the individuals look upon the celebrity as a familiar figure, even as a friend. With fame, the right to privacy is different. Strangers suppose that they can ask questions even intimates wouldn't ask—about how much money the person has, about highly personal beliefs, about sexual preferences—as if the celebrity were a kind of public property.

LeRoy Neiman described what it was like when Frank Sinatra left the table in a restaurant to go to the men's room:

"Frank gets up and just starts in the direction of the men's room, and all of a sudden there's this wave through the room of men getting up and starting toward the men's room. That's real celebrity. You never piss alone."

Groucho was annoyed by the lack of discretion evinced by certain autograph hunters. More than once I can remember attending a public event with him when he would come out of the men's room grumbling, "They could at least wait until you're finished."

I was having lunch at New York City's Russian Tea Room with Woody Allen. We had gone there late in order to miss the crowd. Woody ordered the lunch, but he never ate one bite of it. The people who stopped at our table were all respectful. No one lingered unduly, but there were a great many. They didn't crowd around the table, but waited their turns discreetly, coming only one or two at a time to express their admiration for him and his work.

The soup arrived piping hot and remained on the table until it was room temperature, at which point the waitress returned carrying the entrée. She studied the bowl of evidently untasted soup. "Have you finished, Woody?" she asked. Although he had never seen her before, or if he had, he didn't remember, he was obviously a familiar part of her life.

"You can take it away," he said. She left giggling, as though he had said something uproariously funny.

Several times Woody lifted his fork and knife and even got as far as cutting some of the food, but never as far as eating it. He answered the questions he was asked politely, but as tersely as possible. He looked uncomfortable; no one noticed the difference.

The cold, uneaten entrée was removed. Woody looked at me and said, "I never eat dessert."

As we got up to leave, he commented, "I really like this place, but maybe next time we should go to Pearl's."

Back at his penthouse overlooking Fifth Avenue, we sat and ate a surrogate lunch of some cherry Jello his cook had left in the refrigerator.

Sydney Pollack told me that if you want to know what it's like to feel like nobody, go to a restaurant with Robert Redford. "It's like *you* didn't even exist. He always wants a back table, and then he takes the seat facing the wall so he won't see the people staring at him—but *you* do. On the plane, he buys two seats so no one can sit next to him and he won't *have* to talk."

Laurence Olivier and I had gone into a flower shop to buy some flowers for his wife. He was enticed into the shop by a handsome bouquet in the window. Inside, on closer examination, those particular flowers proved to be artificial. "I've been hoodwinked! I won't be able to trust any of those others," he said, indicating all of the other flowers. "You know how it is once you've been fooled. Once you've been hoodwinked, nothing is ever the same."

Before we went in, he said, "I'd prefer not spending more than fifty or sixty dollars." In the store, however, after being instantly recognized by everyone present and grandly received, he was unable to ask the price of anything. Whenever he showed interest in flowers that I sensed were going to exceed what he wanted to spend, I would ask the price because I knew he had been intimidated by his own celebrity from verbalizing such a mundane private consideration. His expenditure eventually reached over one hundred dollars. Celebrity can be expensive. It often costs more, especially in tips. Celebrities believe larger tips are expected from them. This is balanced somewhat because celebrities do sometimes get things free.

Laurence Olivier asked for a gift enclosure card and began writing his message. All of the eyes in the shop were riveted on him and on his hand as he wrote. He tried to appear oblivious to the excessive attention, but I noticed his hand was shaking. Finishing the brief message, he asked for an envelope. The clerk hesitated for a moment, and then said, "That was the envelope you just wrote on, Mr. Olivier."

Given another card, he started again. Once more all of the eyes fastened on his hand and what he was writing as he nervously made a mistake writing "Joan"—not easy to do, considering the number of times he had written his wife's name.

He tried once more, but wrote so downhill that he decided to try again. Finally, he completed one and tore up his mistakes, depositing them in the wastebasket.

We left amid exclamations of admiration for several of his performances, including lavish praise for his acting in some films in which he had never appeared. After all the fuss, it was really no surprise when the owner rushed out after Laurence Olivier with the change he had left behind.

As we departed, I noticed one of the well-dressed customers driven to shopping-bag-lady behavior by the occasion. She was rummaging through the wastebasket. Finding what she was searching for, she pocketed the scraps of Laurence Olivier's "autographs."

Sir John Gielgud told me what he considered the most terrible disadvantage of being famous:

"It's so dreadful to contemplate doing private and embarrassing things like growing old and dying in public view. I've never forgotten coming to America and seeing a picture in the newspaper of Fritz Kreisler lying on the street after he had been struck by a car. The indignity of taking a picture of a man like that at a moment like that. . . .

"It's also dreadful to have to give interviews. It's like writing your memoirs or going through an old address book. It forces you to live in the past, which, at my age, is too painful.

"I live in the country now because all of the streets in London have changed. All of those streets that meant so much to me, with the houses torn down where one had one's love affairs—it's like the death of old friends when these buildings are torn down.

"I was on my way into London one day, coming from Heathrow Airport, and I saw my aunt's ugly old house being bulldozed. It was the oddest coincidence to drive by at just that moment. All of the rooms in the house came back to me. I remembered every detail. I could see each piece of furniture, every object just as if I were back in each of those rooms I'd known so well. I didn't know I remembered all that. I thought of the biscuit box on the high shelf. I couldn't stop thinking of that biscuit box. Terrible. Terrible."

Martin Segal, chairman of New York's Lincoln Center, told me about Grace Kelly's appearance—or, rather, nonappearance—at the special dinner given by the Film Society of Lincoln Center preceding their gala tribute to Alfred Hitchcock. Everyone had been hoping she would be there for the dinner as well as for the tribute in the theater. She accepted, but the dinner began, and she had not appeared.

When Martin Segal left his table for a few minutes to take a phone call, he found Grace Kelly standing there waiting in one of the outer rooms. Surprised, he asked her why she hadn't come in and joined Alfred Hitchcock and the other guests. She said she couldn't. She was wearing an extremely clinging long white silk dress, and was not able to sit down because she couldn't afford to wrinkle the back of her dress before her appearance onstage.

"Of course. I understand," Martin Segal said. "Let me bring you some food out here, and we can eat it standing up."

"No," she said. "I can't afford to eat, either. My dress is so tightly fitted, I can't take the chance."

Maureen O'Sullivan described what she found especially jarring about her career on the stage:

"Seeing your understudy is always a big shock. It gives you an idea how people see you, and that's always a shock. Also, being in a Broadway play is like taking the veil because you really can't do anything else. The only thing worse than being in a Broadway hit show that runs forever is *not* being in one."

Fame makes those who achieve it visible targets. No one enjoys adverse criticism, nor does anyone ever truly adjust to it. William Holden told me, "You would think you would get more thick-skinned, but you only get more thin-skinned."

Of the people who paid the price of celebrity, none paid more dearly than Leslie Howard, who may have paid for fame with his life. British film director Thorold Dickinson was in Lisbon with Leslie Howard just before he was killed during World War II, and he told me this story:

"Howard was the archetypal Englishman, but he wasn't actually of English descent. His parents were Hungarian immigrants who had settled in England. He was terribly patriotic about England.

"During the war we were in Lisbon on a goodwill tour, about to return to England. Leslie had starred in some films that had particularly offended Goebbels and some of the other Nazis, and they'd said they were going to get Leslie. I felt one of the reasons they especially resented him was because he was *so* English.

"Now, Leslie had one weakness; he loved beautiful women. Well, that night I saw him with one. Lisbon was the world capital of espionage, and this was the most Mata Hari-looking woman I'd ever seen. She was ravishingly beautiful, but there was something slightly sinister about her. Leslie came to life in the presence of a beautiful girl, and this one had brought out the male peacock in him. I overheard him carrying on. Our departure early the next morning was top-secret because there would be German planes about. Leslie didn't come back to the hotel that night.

"The next morning before the flight, I confronted him. I asked him if he had told the girl anything about the take-off time of our flight, our route, anything. He didn't answer. I told him it was important because if he had, that flight shouldn't take off at all. He said he hadn't said anything. I asked him again to be certain. But *I* wasn't certain. I didn't take the flight.

"The plane was shot down."

Otto Preminger, referring to the loss of privacy that accompanies being a celebrity, observed that there are some residual benefits:

"Yes, it has advantages. A few weeks ago, I was crossing Fifth Avenue and I was hit by a taxi. While I was lying on the ground, some man came over and took off my tie. That was all he could think of to do.

"I didn't want to lie there and have an ambulance come and take me away, so I got up and walked home. When I got home, my wife called my doctor and the hospital, and we went there.

"Several days later, my tie arrived in the mail. The man who had taken off my tie had recognized me. And because I was famous, he was able to find out where I lived and to mail my tie back to me.

"So you see, there are advantages to being a celebrity. If I hadn't been famous, I wouldn't have gotten my tie back."

Maureen O'Sullivan, who as Tarzan's Jane brought the British drawing room to the African jungle, told how the world of the theater virtually saved her life:

"I was doing *Never Too Late* when John [her husband, film director John Farrow] died. My work saved me. I knew that somehow I had to go out and perform, and if I missed a single performance, it would have been even harder. I had to push to go on. Acting for me offered The Great Escape.

"When someone dies, you don't know how to behave. People don't know what to say or how to treat you in a moment of crisis, and you don't know just how to react. I didn't know exactly how I was supposed to be.

"But, every night for those few hours on stage, I didn't have to cope. I didn't have to think about how I was supposed to be. I knew. I had words that were familiar, moves that were familiar. The others never stepped out of their characters. In the midst of my personal trauma, my part in the play was such a secure world.

By the time the tour was finished, I'd had enough time to get hold, and my work saved my life."

The celebrity often receives gifts he doesn't need, especially when he doesn't need them. Marvin Hamlisch invited me to go to Carvel for some soft ice cream. He said that he first really knew he was a success when he went to Carvel and they gave him a free cone. "It's kind of fun," Marvin observed, "but you only get it when you don't need it. When you can really afford things, that's when you start getting them free." Getting things free is one of the perquisites of being a celebrity.

Elliott Gould was also the beneficiary of some celebrity advantages.

The very young, exceedingly buxom waitress at Rumpelmayer's approached us giggling. She stopped at our table and stood looking at Elliott. She was holding the menus but didn't offer them. She didn't ask what we wanted, and it was clear she didn't care what I wanted, or even know I was there. She just stood trembling and giggling. Elliott gave her the order for malteds and an egg-salad sandwich. "I'm Cathy," she volunteered. Then she backed away.

When she returned with his egg-salad sandwich, it was about one foot high. Between the two slices of bread was what must have been the restaurant's whole day's supply of egg salad. "I hope I didn't goof up," Cathy said. "The manager told me not to act silly."

Elliott looked not down but up at the "sandwich." Then he asked for two more slices of bread, divided the egg salad, and made me a sandwich.

Just as the ancient Greek and Roman gods were allowed to indulge their individual caprices in myth and metaphor, the modern media gods are encouraged, and even expected, to live their public lives in ways that might otherwise verge on the antisocial. The world grants celebrities something intangible yet quite real —*celebrity license*. They are permitted extreme self-indulgence, and if they choose to act like naughty children, their eccentricities are accepted as individuality. What they are not supposed to do is to disappoint by being ordinary.

They make up their own rules of decorum and are allowed to live by them. At formal social events they may come late and leave early. I remember Groucho accepting a party invitation while announcing, "I'll stay fifteen minutes." People thought he was joking. He wasn't. But I don't remember anyone being too disappointed as long as he made an appearance.

Celebrity perquisites include very special privileges. Billy Wilder told me that while he certainly would not expect his wife to condone his marital infidelity, under most circumstances, there was one instance where he felt she not only would have forgiven him but virtually would have notified the newspapers, like parents announcing the engagement of their daughter.

"My wife could forgive me if I had an affair with Marilyn Monroe—*more* than forgive me! She would go into her beauty salon and proclaim to all the women there that her husband was having an affair with Marilyn Monroe. It would enhance her status. It would mean she was not married to an ordinary male. Both our images would be improved. It would give me mythic proportions, and that would reflect on her—the man who could sleep with Marilyn Monroe had married *her.*"

One of the many rewards of celebrity is the opportunity it affords to put something back into life—a kind of *noblesse oblige* that isn't just an obligation of the most fortunate, but a privilege. The person of recognized achievement brings his or her celebrity with him, which equals more than just one person. Groucho, talking about his appearances for charity, said, "I count as more than one." I think of this force as *celebrity power.* The famous, depending on their current status, clearly have different amounts of CPs, units of celebrity power, an energy that not only can make people happy, but can effect constructive change.

There is also *celebrity burden*—a responsibility on the part of the celebrity to live up to the image projected by his extended self. People want their celebrities to be special, not just like everyone else. As a result, some of them choose to live in greater seclusion, with shrinking address books, closing their world to all but old friends who got there before success arrived and who will not expect them to perform. Others, however, enjoy a lifetime of pleasure from their celebrity. At best it can bring a lot of fun not only to the celebrity himself but to others as well.

I had gone alone to an event at New York's Lincoln Center and was standing by myself against one wall in the upstairs lobby during intermission. At the far end of the room, I saw Leopold Stokowski. He waved to someone in my direction. I looked around but didn't see anyone responding. He seemed to be waving to me, but that wasn't likely because we had never met.

He began to work his way through the crowd, not at all an easy task for someone who was then in his nineties. Everyone who had been in the theater, a full house, was now gathered in the lobby. Stokowski inched his way through, continuing to wave, smile, and make gestures indicating that someone near where I was standing should wait for him.

Finally he arrived and came straight toward me. The look on his face indicated that he had recognized me as a friend. He greeted me warmly with an embrace and kissed me, on the lips.

Then he stepped back, bowed rather formally, and, introducing himself, said, "Stokowski."

The next day I had tea with Stokowski at the Palm Court of the Plaza Hotel. Our conversation took place during the musicians' breaks because he would not speak while they were playing. When they had finished, he rose and lifted those famous hands above his head and applauded, leading the applause as he had led so many orchestras. Palm Court patrons, more accustomed to treating the music as background for talk, paused in their conversations and accorded the violinist and pianist an ovation worthy of Heifetz and Horowitz.

If someone else had done what Stokowski did, the person might either have been ignored or considered out of order. Stokowski, however, had celebrity license, though what he really exerted was celebrity power to express his public approval of a good performance which might otherwise have gone unnoticed. He knew that the musicians would love it and that the Palm Court patrons would, too. Everyone had a story they could go home and tell, including me.

Stokowski recognized the need of the artist for appreciation and encouragement. The person who has done something difficult himself has greater compassion and empathy for anyone else doing it on any level. Heart surgeon Denton Cooley told me that he had admonished his wife, "When I die, you must not cry in front of the doctor and make him feel badly. You can go home and cry."

Just hours before the Los Angeles Dodgers were to play the New York Yankees and win the deciding game of the 1981 World Series, I was invited to have lunch with the Dodgers at the Carnegie Delicatessen in New York City. I accepted and arrived in less time than it takes for a hot pastrami sandwich to get cold.

Manager Tommy Lasorda looked up from his frankfurter omelet. He had just heard Yankee manager Bob Lemon being verbally crucified at an adjoining table. The night before, Lemon had made some controversial decisions in the World Series game which was then lost by his Yankees, and the grandstand managers were saying that Lemon had "thrown away" the game.

"Remember, when you point the finger at someone else," Lasorda interjected, "three fingers is pointin' at you." To demonstrate, he pointed his forefinger with the three other fingers folded in and pointing toward himself. Then he turned to me and said, "If you use that, be sure and say '*is.*' "

Not all of celebrity time is glamorous. One night very late, Marvin Hamlisch called me. "I hope I'm not calling too late, but I've just thought of something—one of those basic concepts that we were talking about for your book, and I didn't want to forget it. It's 'the rest of the time.'

"I was out buying some oranges, and when I got back, I remembered that I needed to change the lock on my front door, and I saw a bag of laundry that hadn't been picked up. I called my mother. I looked for the name of someone I was supposed to call about some reservations, but I couldn't find the piece of paper with the phone number. And then, while I was brushing my teeth, the concept came to me: No matter how successful you are, most of the time is really the rest of the time. I mean, even Queen Elizabeth has to brush her teeth!

"It's something you don't think about before you have the success, when you're trying to get there. The celebrity's life isn't the way people imagine it—all parties. Oh, sure, some of it's all that glamour, like running up onstage at the Academy Awards to pick up your Oscar. But most of the time it's the rest of the time."

I enjoyed a "rest-of-the-time" relationship with Luciano Pavarotti. Actually, it was a "garbage-pail" relationship. Whenever he came to New York, he stayed at the hotel where I was living, and we shared a common wall between our apartments. Even if I hadn't heard his presence, singing or whistling, I would have seen it—and certainly smelled it. The telltale cans of tomato paste in the garbage pail we shared sang out, "Luciano has arrived!"

One day I met him in the back hall at the garbage pail where I noted the protruding contents of the brown bag he had just deposited. Observing the visible orange peelings, candy bar wrappers, and cans with a residue of tomato paste, I commented, "Oh, you only have *ordinary* garbage!" He caught my tone of mock disappointment and laughed. Then, putting a finger to his lips, he said, "Shhh! Don't tell anyone. We don't like that to get around."

He was always apologetic about his practicing, saying, "I hope my singing doesn't bother you," or about his whistling in the shower. Before performances, he frequently whistled in order to save his voice.

A part of happiness is finding the proper balance between the need for security and stability, and the opposing need for variety and excitement. Mae West's oft-repeated maxim "Too much of a good thing can be wonderful" is not necessarily true for everyone.

Marvin Hamlisch characterized success as "too much of a balancing act to ever just sit back and enjoy it the way you thought you would. You've got too many balls in the air at once, so if you sit back, you get hit on the head. You don't have time to enjoy things the way you thought you would.

"Kirk [Douglas] was talking with me about being very young in New York and dreaming about being in a Broadway show. He was walking along Central Park South past the Essex House, and he thought to himself, 'One day I'm going to have their penthouse.'

"Three years later, he was in New York in a big hit play, and he *had* the top of the Essex House. He took a look out the window at the park, but he couldn't take enough time to really enjoy it. Because he was on to his next project. You don't have the time to savor the moment because there are too many pulls."

One morning, I met Pavarotti in the hallway. It was much earlier than he was accustomed to appearing in public. He was wearing an ample double-breasted camel's-hair overcoat, which in his case was more than double-breasted, and he was in a great hurry.

He started toward the elevator, then rushed back to his door, saying, "I forgot something. It is always that way when I try to hurry. I have too much to do. I would enjoy everything more if I did a little less. But it is my own fault. I cannot say no to anything. I am always afraid I will miss something."

The private-line telephone in Woody Allen's apartment rang— about twenty times. He just let it ring. With a wave of his hand, as if he were shooing a small dog off the sofa, he said, "You have to tell your personal life to go away."

Picasso, who had his own view from the top, explained to me his concept of "The Big Success":

"When I speak of 'The Big Success' I mean the success that is too big to be felt. It has gone past where one person can comprehend it or appreciate or utilize it, or even be affected by it. 'The Big Success' thus becomes impersonal and really no longer belongs to you to whom it has been given. Perhaps it belongs to the work which bears your name, or perhaps only to the world that is bestowing its praise. After a certain point, it gets *so* big you cannot touch it—and it cannot touch you. You can only eat so many meals or go to bed with so many women. After all, each man has only one mouth with which to eat, and only one penis . . ."

When dreams do come true, they rarely happen as imagined beforehand. The strangest feeling is when something happens and you don't act or feel the way you thought you would. Laurence Olivier remembered how it was for him:

"I wanted appreciation, fame. I wanted everyone to love me. In my dreams I hoped that there would be hundreds of fans waiting out there for me at the stage door. First, I wanted to get parts, to have the chance. I knew when I got to act, I'd be happy. Then I was doing fine parts, and I had a certain success, but no one really knew who I was. I felt I wanted some recognition. I knew if I had that kind of success, I'd be so happy I'd go right out and embrace every person there. I'd be smiling, and I'd write elaborate autographs, putting everyone's name on the autograph, 'To Annabel,' and so on. I'd talk with every person and I wouldn't leave as long as anyone was still there. And then it happened.

"I had a great success, and they were waiting—for me. I saw them, and then without even a smile on my face, I rushed straight through. I never stopped to sign a single autograph. Why does one behave differently from the way you thought you would? I don't know. Perhaps something in the struggle along the way changes you."

There may be mitigating circumstances. The famous person is sometimes asked to sign autographs at difficult moments, a torrential downpour with no available shelter being no deterrent to the dedicated autograph seeker. Among these fans are a few suspiciously recurring individuals, each of whom wants a dozen signatures.

As I stepped into a limousine just ahead of Clint Eastwood, he hurried me into my seat with a rather unexpected push. After apologizing, he turned and spoke with obviously restrained irritation to a woman who was standing by the limousine blocking his entrance with her body.

"Not now," he said firmly. Then he got in and slammed the door shut as hard as a limousine door can be slammed.

"She has hundreds of my signatures," he explained to me. "Wherever I go, she's there. Sometimes I don't even know where I'm going myself, and then there she is with her autograph book and a pile of pictures for me to sign. She has more pictures of me and more copies of my signature than I have."

"What do you think she does with them?" I asked.

"I wouldn't want to know."

One of the advantages of being a celebrity is the profusion of invitations that you receive to film premieres, Broadway openings, parties, and gala events. Even those who spend energy moaning and complaining about all of the social events they "must" attend would probably admit that having such choices is preferable to not having them. A problem, however, is having to face people you know after seeing their work and not being able to say you liked it because you didn't like it and didn't like it to the extent that you aren't even able to tell the white lie that courtesy dictates.

Rouben Mamoulian's story summed it up for all who have "suffered" through two hours in the dark wondering what to say to the people responsible when the lights go on. A frequent guest at the home of Universal-MCA president Jules Stein, Rouben and his wife, Azadia, were among the celebrity guests at an after-dinner preview in their private screening room of Universal's just-completed *Gable and Lombard.*

Just before the film was about to begin, Jules Stein got up and said, "We hope you'll love the film, and go away and tell everyone how great it is. If you don't like it, please say you haven't seen the picture." Then they all went into the screening room.

Afterward, over drinks, everyone was saying how wonderful the film was. Rouben was very quiet. Doris Stein, Jules Stein's wife, came over and said, "Rouben, how did you like it?"

"Like what?"

"The picture."

"What picture?"

"Gable and Lombard," she said.

"I haven't seen it," he said.

Success, far from always being accompanied by automatic happiness, sometimes brings unhappiness when it is thrust upon someone unable to feel at ease with it. When King Vidor set out to make *The Crowd,* he was determined to cast an unknown for the lead, feeling that the ordinariness of the hero could not be conveyed by a known star. As soon as he saw James Murray walking by in a group of extras at M-G-M, he knew that he had the best person for the film. King later discovered that the film may not have been the best thing for the person.

The Crowd was an enormous success, and its new star acclaimed.

For Murray, however, overnight fame brought with it little happiness and a lot of unexpected pressures. He began to drink heavily. When King wanted to use him in another film, the drinking had become too great a problem. Murray disappeared from Hollywood. Only years later did King learn what happened to him:

"Murray was doing stunts for tourists in New York City. They would throw him coins which he would use to buy drinks. No one ever recognized him. He would do practically anything to get the laughs and approval. And the coins.

"One day he did one of his regular stunts, pretending he was drunk and falling into the East River. The tourists laughed. Then they stopped laughing. By the time they realized he'd been under too long, it was too late."

Getting *there*, reaching the goal, can be a letdown. Sidney Sheldon had returned from World War II a hero and had three hit shows on Broadway. "I had a contract with M-G-M and was dating the prettiest starlets, but I wasn't happy. I went to a psychiatrist and said, 'I have everything. I'm *there*. But I'm not happy. What do you do when *there* isn't there?'

"The psychiatrist couldn't help me, so I had to find the answer for myself. I found out that you can't ever afford to reach *there*. Once you've reached a goal, you always have to have new goals."

When I arrived in Key West to see Tennessee Williams, he expressed a similar feeling: "All arrivals are also departures. Once you have reached your destination, there has to be a new destination."

The drive that pushes the person to the heights does not go away just because he got there. That same drive remains and impels the person to keep reaching even higher. Then, too, the horizon is endlessly changing. A new goal, which can only be vaguely defined, may always seem just ahead; but it is an intangible Mount Everest, with the top already scaled and the descent well under way before the climber fully realizes that he may never again see the peak except from the valley.

Constantly rising expectations work against satisfaction and produce frustration, especially when the goal surpasses the ability of the person to attain it. Mervyn LeRoy told me a joke that embodied that concept:

"A man is complimented on the wonderful performance of his talking dog, and the man says, 'Yes, it's a great act. It was a brilliant performance. But he's not happy. He wants to direct.' "

A predisposition for happiness exists independently from what a person achieves in life. It may or may not be a factor in the success, but happiness isn't based so much on what happens to the person as on his own nature. Happiness is, perhaps, a way of viewing life—whether the cup is half full or half empty. Woody Allen talked seriously with me about this concept:

"The talent for being happy is a separate talent, different from other talents. It's appreciating what you have and liking what you have instead of what you don't have. It's liking what you get after you've got it as much as you thought you were going to like it before you got it. People are lucky who have this. But it you don't, you can't just talk yourself into having it. I'm the kind of person who worries about worrying too much."

I was sitting on the verandah of the Beverly Hills Hotel. It was the beginning of Oscars weekend, and the glitterati were arriving from all parts of the world. The New York contingent was already ensconced in rooms and bungalows with tennis clothes unpacked and the latest in rackets readied for action. As I sat there waiting, people in saris, kimonos, and the latest Paris originals, laden with Vuitton luggage, and carrying expensive cameras and bound scripts, began arriving from the airport.

At my feet was a man on his hands and knees. He was busily making final adjustments to the red carpet which was rolled out on such occasions to cushion the tread of the dozens of pairs of high heels that Oscar Monday brings. Every time someone would enter or leave, the man working there would look up at me and say, "That was Raquel Welch," "There's Olivia De Havilland." "That's David Merrick." He recognized everyone.

It was the end of the day, and the people entering were carrying shopping bags filled with purchases from Gucci, Hermes, and Bijan, the Rodeo Drive shop that sells the most expensive men's clothing in the world and opens only by appointment. Bijan sells a $1,500 bottle of perfume in a genuine Baccarat bottle insured against theft or damage by Lloyds of London, and the world's most complete line of high-fashion bulletproof clothing for men and women. The attendants at the front door were occupied parking the gleaming Rolls, Mercedes, and Jaguars. The people coming out were wearing navy blazers and white pants suits on their way to dinner at Chasen's, or formal attire for one of the black-tie studio premieres.

As they came and went, an amazing number of them wore tension frowns, and furrowed brows were commonplace. Bits of conversation that drifted my way were: "How could they . . . ?" "Why didn't they . . . ?" "They didn't even . . . ," "He has a lot of nerve to think . . . ," "I'll show them they can't do that to me," and so on. Disgruntled and sometimes quarreling, they took no notice of the red carpet.

The hotel employee gave the carpet a few final pats and looked up at me, saying, "It's really exciting here, isn't it?" He told me what films some of the directors and stars who had passed by were working on, and even what they might be working on in the immediate future. He knew everything *Variety* and *The Hollywood Reporter* knew—and more. He displayed greater enthusiasm and seemed to be getting more pleasure than many of those who were living those glamorous lives.

Putting together his tools, he said, "I'm the luckiest person in the world."

In life, no one is happy who doesn't think he is.

After age and illness had already taken happiness away from him, Jean-Paul Sartre talked with me about happiness:

"Not allowing oneself to be too happy, so that one will not be too sad when the source of happiness comes to an end, does not work. One can easily limit one's pleasure and diminish one's own enthusiasm, but one cannot prepare oneself for disappointment. It is like a woman with a man. She will spoil everything along the way because she is so afraid of losing what she has. She cannot enjoy it. Women think in terms of forever, and men in terms of the moment. Somewhere between those two perspectives, the two meet."

Anita Loos believed professional happiness is easier to pursue than personal happiness because it is more within one's own control. "Personal happiness needs more magic."

Through a lot of early successes, Marvin Hamlisch kept a clear perspective on personal and professional priorities. On the night he won three Oscars, he was a little late arriving at the Board of Governors' Ball at the Beverly Hills Hilton. The reason was he had stopped off with his sister and his parents at the hotel where they were staying for what Marvin said was the *real* party. His mother had baked his favorite chocolate cake and carried it with her from New York. They went first to the hotel and ate Mrs. Hamlisch's chocolate cake, and then they all went on to the Governors' Ball at the Hilton.

Being rich is one of the assumed rewards of success. There is a difference, however, between being rich and feeling rich. When I asked the question, "What makes you feel rich?" the answers were usually in terms of relatively small things rather than in terms of the accouterments of wealth one might have thought would be the measure.

Groucho used to sit in his sunny living room wearing his Mouseketeer cap while he played the piano and sang "Lydia, the Tattooed Lady" or other songs from his repertory. Sometimes he would finish a song, pat the top of the piano, and say, "You know you're rich when you can take the piano for granted. You come home and walk into the room and you don't even look to see if it's still there. You know it is.

"When you have rich garbage, you know you've made it. When I was a boy, all the neighbors had richer garbage than we did. You can tell a lot about people from their garbage."

Having been poor as a boy, and then making a great deal of money only to lose it all in 1929, Groucho was never able to stop worrying about money. Into his eighties, he still suffered from insomnia, and when he did fall asleep, he had nightmares in which he lost all his money.

Hubert Humphrey said using a new razor blade every time he shaved made him feel rich. Hotel room service made Charlie Chaplin feel rich, especially if he could order not just a whole dinner but something simple without minding the full room-service table charge for just a pot of tea. He told me, however, that he never truly achieved feeling rich. He said it was because he had been too poor for too long early in life—"like a swan who remains convinced he is still an ugly duckling."

For George Burns, successful work was happiness. The three of us were at lunch when he told Groucho, "Gracie and I were a hit on the sex scene when our show was a success. If we got a lot of laughs, our sex was great that night. If our act didn't do well, forget it. Our life was our work. We didn't think about our marriage. I guess that's why it worked."

The famous people with whom I spoke tended to resist and resent any control over them. Other people feel this way, too, but the success of celebrities permits them the luxury of being able to do something about it.

"I don't know how it is for a woman," LeRoy Neiman told me, "but for a man happiness is success, and success is ass and asshole. If you're successful as a man, you can get all the ass you want, and there are more people you can call asshole.

"It isn't that you want to call just anyone an asshole, but you want to be able to say it to anyone who deserves it. Power is how many people you can call asshole and how many people can call *you* asshole."

There is a great deal that money does not buy. Some of the most respected status symbols cannot be bought in stores. Film director Lewis Milestone could not show me his Oscar because it had been stolen. He said its loss was "one of the great sadnesses" in his life. It is not often that one can remedy a great sadness so easily. I told him that his Oscar could never really be taken from him and certainly could never belong to the thief. He called the Motion Picture Academy, and Oscar was restored to Lewis Milestone.

Bette Davis told me that the question most often asked her was, "Are you happy?"

"I always felt I was happier *before* they asked the question," she snapped.

Henry Fonda said, "What can you say when people ask you if you're happy? I just say, 'Yes.' "

Eubie Blake offered only qualified thanks for the doughnuts I had brought him, setting aside the bag without eating any.

"It was nice of you to bring me these doughnuts, but I'll tell you what old age is like: It gets harder and harder to really want anything. Young is carin'. At ninety-seven there isn't anything anybody can give you that's anything you really want.

"What makes you happy is different at different times in your life. I can remember when happiness was two cents for a bag of broken cakes and cookies. Unhappiness was having one cent because you could only buy half a bag. I was pretty young then.

"When I was a little older, I saw the clothes that the pimps were wearing, and I figured clothes like that would make me happy—Stetson hats, long pointed shoes with ten-dollar gold pieces set in the tips, and enormous yellow diamonds. I wanted those high-class clothes and the life that went with them. I'm not saying I wanted to be a pimp. Later I figured happiness was having a Paige automobile, and a wife and mistress who both love you, and who stay out of each other's way and don't tell you about it.

"I'll tell you what makes me happy now. Four sugar doughnuts and 7-Up at 3 A.M. I'm pretty old now, and things have come full circle.

"I can tell you my happiest moment. It was playing piano in the White House. If you wrote a book about me, I'd like you to call it 'From the Hookshops to the White House.' The White House was just fifty miles from where I'd been born, but it seemed a million miles away."

I told him I could imagine it as a scene in a film: *Eubie is sitting at a grand piano in the White House, his formal tails draped over the back of the piano bench, his incredibly long and distinctively expressive fingers caressing the keyboard. The President and Vice President and their families are seated in the middle of an audience of senators, cabinet members, presidential aides, and their wives, all reacting ecstatically.*

Dissolve to a *turn-of-the-century Baltimore hookshop. A young Eubie is playing the piano. Everything is different. Only the long, expressive fingers are the same. A crowd is gathered around the piano. The men are garishly overdressed and the women are visibly under-dressed. Their reaction, too, is ecstatic.*

Dolly in to a *head-and-shoulders shot of the youthful Eubie. As he looks up at the camera and smiles,* dissolve to *the aged Eubie, who is also smiling at the camera.*

Cut to a *full shot of the White House room. The elegantly attired dignitaries are still enraptured, but standing behind them in the shadows, they have been joined by the characters from the Baltimore hookshop.* . . .

Money does not necessarily buy happiness, but it does remove one reason for unhappiness—that caused by lack of money. As director Joseph Mankiewicz said to me, "Happiness doesn't buy money."

No one ever put it more strongly for me than Fritz Lang, for whom his work, directing films, was the essential element in his happiness: "When you can't work anymore, it's better to die. But I have to wait, because I don't believe in suicide." He still had the need and the drive, but no longer the physical capability, to do the thing that gave meaning to his life.

When I first met Fritz Lang, his thoughts and dreams were still occupied with plot ideas, scripts, and the hope that there was at least one more picture in his future. That film in his future meant more to him than any or all of the films in his past. In our conversations, he would always intersperse bits for films he was trying to work out in his mind, making up characters and stories about the people sitting around us in restaurants. I asked him what made him happy besides doing the work he loved.

'I like a real fire in the fireplace, with real coffee and a real woman," he answered.

"What do you mean by a 'real' woman?"

"Why do you want to know, my angel? Is your curiosity professional or personal? Ah, your blush, that is my answer."

Actually, my blush was occasioned by the situation. We were sitting at a table in the breakfast room of the Beverly Hills Hotel. Fritz, who had lost a lot of his hearing, was speaking so loudly that everyone in the room could hear every word he was saying to me. I was not unhappy to have the waitress interrupt our conversation by serving breakfast.

It was Fritz's favorite breakfast—scrambled eggs with martinis. Or rather, martinis with scrambled eggs. It was a breakfast he preferred not to eat *too* early in the morning. There were scrambled eggs for two, Fritz and me, and two martinis; one for Fritz and one for Peter, who was sitting in one of the chairs at the table with us. Peter was a German felt monkey doll who wore his sailor cap at a rakish angle, an apache sweater, a gold earring in one ear, and a roguish look on his face that indicated he knew Hamburg's St. Pauli district well. Fritz always ordered a martini for Peter, who was his mascot and alter ego, and then he helped Peter drink it.

Of Peter, Fritz wrote me, "Peter—who is he? I don't know myself exactly. My soul . . . ? My alter ego . . . ? My conscience . . . ? I don't know."

Fritz loved cheesecake. When I first met him, he was always in quest of a great cheesecake. I was often invited to join him in sampling various recommendations, but he never found that special one for which he was searching. The standard by which he judged them was based on New York's Lindy's, but Lindy's and their cheesecake had long ago ceased to exist and were only memories. No cheesecake in the present was ever as good as the venerated cheesecakes of the past.

As Fritz became more disconsolate about life, his peregrinations for cheesecake became shorter and less enthusiastic. He would say, "Hope is down the drain." The last time I visited him, I brought a special cheesecake with me that I hoped would cheer him up. He didn't even taste it.

Fritz wrote a sad letter to me one day. He said that on that day he had finally accepted that he would never be able to work again, and thus could never again be happy.

"Today is the end of my happiness," he wrote. "I realize that the film I have been waiting to direct will never be mine. Now, without my work, I am only a brontosaurus with a monocle. Or you might say, I'm 'The Last Coachman.' "

That was the one film Fritz Lang always wanted to make that none of us will ever see because it never happened. It was based on his own idea and would have been called "The Last Coachman."

After World War I, life changed in Vienna. With the advent of the automobile, no one wanted to ride in a horse-drawn coach. On the great avenue, the Hauptallee, the last coachman waited with his coach and horse, but no one came. He waited in vain until one day he died of a broken heart. Then his horse died of a broken heart, too.

The coachman rose up to enter heaven, driving his coach. But when he got there, St. Peter stopped him, saying, "It is fine for you to come in, but you cannot bring your horse. There is a separate heaven for horses, you understand. He will be quite happy there."

The coachman said, "You mean heaven is just like earth—a lot of rules. If my horse cannot stay, *I'm* not staying."

This caused quite a disturbance. God came to mediate. The rules were explained to the coachman, but he was adamant. Without his horse and coach, he would not stay.

Then God got into the coach and said, "You will be my coachman."

The coachman was very happy.

In the last scene, the coachman drove off with God, and they vanished into the night sky filled with the Big Dipper and stars.

One of the saddest aspects of *there* is arriving there and not being able to show your success to those who mattered to you in your life. For Henry Fonda it remained a tragic regret that his parents had not seen his success.

"They couldn't have been more supportive when I went to New York in 1928 to be an actor," he told me. "But I'm sure they didn't have any idea what was gonna happen with their boy. You know—that he'd ever make a living or be successful enough to be proud of him. And they didn't live long enough to know that I did well. That's one of the tragedies."

Henry Moore, however, did have the opportunity, if not the satisfaction, of showing a parent his success. "My mother didn't understand a lot of my work," he said. "I always remember she called it 'playing.' "

King Vidor found his success didn't impress everyone when he returned home to his Texas roots:

"I went back to Galveston to visit the house where I was born. I got out of my car, and as I did, I saw a very old man in a rocking chair on the front porch of the house next door. He looked up and said, 'Hello.' I said, 'Hello. I'm King Vidor.' He said, 'Hello, King. It's been a long time.' I guess I looked a little blank. He said, 'Don't you recognize me? Nealy. Nealy Campbell.'

"Nealy Campbell was a boy a little older than I was, and we used to play together when he was about nine and I was about seven. I hadn't seen him since I left Galveston. That was about 1915.

" 'It's been a while, King,' Nealy said.

" 'Yes, Nealy, it's been a while.'

" 'How are things, King?'

" 'Fine, Nealy.'

"I went in and visited the house my father built in the last century. It hadn't changed much. When I came out, Nealy Campbell was still rocking nonchalantly. He looked up.

" 'Good seeing you, King. Don't take so long to come back next time. So long.' "

Picasso touched on one of the most personal aspects of success:

"I tell you that while the work can only be done alone, the success cannot be enjoyed alone. Even Picasso needs sometimes to show his little drawing to someone in the next room, as I did when I was a boy showing it to my mother or father."

"It's really terrible," Marvin Hamlisch told me, "when, after all the great things happen for you out in the world, you come home, and suddenly you realize you're all alone. This awful wave comes over you, and nothing you do seems important, because you have no one to show it to. The whole world doesn't count. You've got to have someone you care about showing it to. If you don't, then you think, 'If I'm such a big success and I'm really someone— what am I doing here alone?' "

Everyone with whom I spoke wanted someone to do it with and someone to do it for. They wanted to show the product of their work and their success not just to an amorphic applauding mass.

Lee Strasberg told me it was essential to have someone you could tell anything and everything to so that by talking about it you could get it straight in your own head. That had to be a person who would not then think less of you.

Sartre said everyone has to have someone with whom he can be *before* breakfast. For Picasso it was important to have someone with whom you could be seen at your worst, with whom you could show weakness.

Laurence Olivier said, however, that the most difficult thing was not to find someone with whom you could talk, but someone with whom you could be silent. "The way you get along with a person when you're not saying anything is what really tells the story. When you can see the rapport between people without their even speaking together, that is what is special. It is rare, that kind of silence. What is common is the kind of silence that shuts people out."

Groucho summed it up when he told me, "There's no meal worth eating if you've gotta eat alone, and no breakfast that's any good unless you've got someone to complain to if the toast is burnt."

Not everyone who lives in the world of celebrity is famous. There are those who, through birth or marriage, live on the periphery of fame. For them, the glow of starlight brings disadvantages as well as the advantages of reflected glory.

Shortly after Anna and Lee Strasberg were married, she was offered a part in a play. It was a good part, and she was pleased because she wanted to continue her acting career. When the publicity announcements were made, however, it became clear that Lee Strasberg's wife had been given the part, not Anna Strasberg. "The publicity so emphasized Lee," she told me, "it seemed he was in the play, not me. I called Lee, who was in California, and you could have heard my screams of rage without a telephone. I said, 'Strasberg, they can't do this to me! It's so unfair. They only hired me because I'm your wife.'

"Well, Lee waited until I had run down, the way he always does, and then, in his quiet way, he said . . ." Anna paused in her story and turned to her husband, who was sitting next to us, saying, "Strasberg, tell Charlotte what you said."

Lee said, "I told her, 'If at 8:30 you get on the stage and everyone says, "That's Lee Strasberg's wife," it doesn't matter.

But if at 9:30 they're still saying, "That's Lee Strasberg's wife," then get the hell off the stage.' "

Many months after the death of Lee Strasberg, Anna remained inconsolable. "I knew he wouldn't have wanted me to break down and cry in public, and I didn't want my children to see me crying. So, somehow, I had to stay in control. Even at night when I would finally be alone, I was afraid that if I ever started crying, I might never be able to stop.

"Somehow I managed for about three months, but one night it happened. I started to cry and just kept crying. I cried until my eyes were so red and sore and swollen, I couldn't see through them and I couldn't breathe, but I couldn't stop crying. Then, suddenly, the telephone rang.

"It was 3:30 or 4:00 in the morning. You don't expect to get a phone call at that time. I picked up the phone and said hello in a voice that came out sounding like someone else's. It was Shelley calling, Shelley Winters, and she was crying, too, just sobbing.

" 'Anna,' she said, 'are you all right?' She was crying so hard I could hardly understand her.

" 'Yes,' I said, pulling myself together, because I wasn't about to let anyone know what condition I was in.

" 'Anna,' she went on, 'it's so awful. Lee's gone. It's the most terrible thing.'

"For a while I couldn't understand a word she said because of her weeping. Then I heard, 'Anna, it was the greatest marriage there ever was—the perfect marriage for thirty years.'

" 'No, Shelley,' I interrupted, 'fifteen years. Lee and I were married fifteen years.'

" 'I don't mean your marriage,' she said. 'I mean *mine* with Lee.' "

Anna smiled. "When I hung up, I started to laugh. It was the first time I'd laughed since Lee died, and after that I didn't have to cry anymore. I felt that Lee in heaven had made Shelley call.

"Of course, Shelley had never been married to Lee, but I realized right then what Lee had meant in the lives of so many people besides me. He had left a lot of widows."

Billy Marx, Harpo's son, said what always troubled him as a child was when, after his father was introduced onstage, he would be introduced and called upon in the audience to rise and take a bow. He hated it because he knew he didn't deserve it. "It was an unearned bow."

When Jean Renoir referred to his father, Auguste Renoir, he always called him Renoir, as did the world. Reminiscing in his Beverly Hills living room, he was surrounded by the works of Renoir *père*. "Sometimes when I was a young director," Renoir told me, "I would worry that what they respected was only my name." He laughed. "Then, sometimes I worried that they did not respect it enough."

Carlo Bergonzi told me that his wife had his headaches for him. On a day when he had a performance, she would have a headache which would grow progressively worse until he sang. When the successful performance had ended without a mistake, her headache would go away, not to return until his next performance.

Andy Marx summed it up for the wives, husbands, children, and, in his case, grandchildren of celebrities: "The most interesting thing about me for everyone is that my grandfather was Groucho Marx. That's difficult to accept."

Reflected glory, what I think of as reflected starlight, has its humorous moments. I was sitting in Rumpelmayer's in New York with Elliott Gould while a couple at the next table stared at him for almost the entire two hours we were there. As we left, we passed their table. They averted their eyes and looked at the floor. Elliott, well aware they had been watching him, stopped and said hello. They looked up surprised, but totally pleased and glowing. The man said, "We're from Iowa." The lady said, "We see all your pictures." Elliott shook hands with them. Not wanting to leave me out, the man looked at me and said, "You were very good, too."

Reflected starlight never shone more brightly than in New York with Laurence Olivier. As we sat eating lunch, a woman left the group at her table to come over and greet me warmly. No one in my entire life had ever before appeared so glad to see me. At first I thought she was coming to see someone at the neighboring banquette, because I didn't recognize her. After she had said a gushing hello to me, she paused, staring at Laurence Olivier, obviously waiting for an introduction.

I said I was sorry I didn't remember her name. Actually, I didn't remember *her*. She said her name, turned away from me, and began talking nonstop with Laurence Olivier. Fortunately he had ordered cold asparagus, because if it had not been that way, it would have been when she finished raving over his performances in two films he had never made.

She got his autograph and left without remembering I was there. When the same mini-drama was repeated a few more times during lunch with some other people I had never met who suddenly knew me, I realized that I had found a new popularity. I was like a door, representing convenient access to the irresistible.

Laurence Olivier's only advice to me was, "Try not to look up."

During lunch, I tipped over my glass, spilling the ice cubes and some water on the immaculate tablecloth. Gallantly, without missing a beat, he tipped his glass, too, deliberately spilling his drink over the puddle my accident had created. Then he gestured, calling to the captain and waiter, both of whom looked on past us without seeing us.

"On their tombstones will be inscribed, 'God caught his eye,'" Laurence Olivier quipped. Eventually he did succeed in attracting a busboy's attention. "Could you please clean it up," he said. "I had a little accident."

In the world of the famous and successful there are many pressures, chief among them being the pressure to hold on to whatever status has been achieved and the pressure to continue rising in status. Frequently, the pleasure of having reached a certain plateau of success is spoiled by these pressures.

"In a way, *A Chorus Line* spoiled everything," Marvin Hamlisch admitted to me. "After a success like that, it just isn't fun the way it used to be when it was only the doing of it that mattered. After that big a success, everybody expects you to have bigger successes. And each time, the success has to be bigger than the last one to be a success at all."

There are the more visible signs which indicate a rise or drop in status among the successful. The sign "House for Sale" usually means someone is moving up or someone is moving down. No places exist where the turnover has more ominous implications than in the insecurity capitals of America, Hollywood (actually Beverly Hills and Bel Air) and Washington, D.C.

Few existences are as tenuous and traumatic in the world of success as those of motion-picture executives and members of the House of Representatives. The motion-picture executive must constantly live with the reality that he should keep no more of his personal papers and possessions in his desk than he can carry away with him on any given Friday afternoon. The Representative barely has time for the ink to dry on the contract for the purchase of his house before he must begin the campaign for his re-election, almost immediately after his election. Whether 'tis better to have served and lost than never to have served at all remains a question each candidate has to answer for himself. There must be considerable unhappiness, though, at having to move out after one has developed a case of "Potomac fever."

The Hollywood measure of how one is doing is appearance. Thus, some live in houses so big that they are more of a burden than a pleasure; but a necessary burden, since any sign of shrinkage is instantly noted and taken as a signal of professional shrinkage. It is probably the Rolls-Royce capital of the world, especially the white Rolls-Royce capital. Finding that there is someone else in your reserved parking place at the studio is tantamount to the terror that strikes when your secretary, calling in your name, is informed that there is no room today at Ma Maison, a restaurant so exclusive that its telephone number is unlisted and unpublished.

No Hollywood director had greater success while still knowing what it was to face bleak times than Billy Wilder. "Slumps can't be figured," he told me. "You're the same person, same abilities. It's the secret element that you can't figure—when your timing, your luck goes off. It happens to ballplayers, film directors, even to vineyards. When you want a home run too badly, you press and strike out. The problem is that the lack of success changes you, and as you act more defensively or more desperately, you hurt your own chance of success. You look too hard for a script and then read into it the qualities you want so badly to find. But I'm still not ready to do the one about the scientist who has a secret formula tattooed on his penis that can only be read when it's erect."

Billy Wilder told me that the world is quick to let you know your standing in the celebrity pecking order:

"After a string of failures, you get a different 'hello' in the supermarket, a different reception from the maître d' in the restaurant, from your barber, and from the doorman at the studio gate, who looks at your car instead of you. You can hear it right away."

I mentioned that he must be in good standing at M-G-M, because when we went to lunch he got one of the choice corner tables in the Lion's Den. The Lion's Den is an area, about the size of a large walk-in closet, that juts out from one side of the M-G-M commissary. In it one might find important studio executives and prestigious directors currently working at the studio. One always knows that one is at the M-G-M commissary by the compulsory box of matzos on every table. Rumor has it that these matzos were a stipulation in the will of Louis B. Mayer. In a world of high-powered instability, the stale matzos lend an air of unchanging continuity. The Lion's Den charges 25 percent more for exactly the same food the extras are eating in the main section of the restaurant. I asked Billy Wilder if, after a string of failures, the most disheartening words one might hear would be, "There's no more room in the Lion's Den."

"Worse," he said. "You're not asked to be a pallbearer anymore. What's really terrible is when you start getting invited to be a judge at the Orinoco Film Festival somewhere in South America because they know you're not working. The last step before they bury you is you're a legend and everyone wants to honor you in your wheelchair.

"The festival circuit comes before you are a legend. It fills that time between working and admitting that you aren't going to work anymore. Now that there are so many festivals, the ranks have opened to those who would never have had enough celebrity. A faded starlet may find herself on the jury in Manila. I don't know if they are doing an Afghan Film Festival. The loss of

Tehran has been a big blow and has left those who follow this circuit with extra weeks on their hands—time they cannot fill.

"Being invited to attend film festivals, especially to serve on the jury, caresses one's ego and gives the illusion of working. Just all that packing. Those who have mastered the technique of being invited to film festivals can easily fill up seven months with the illusion that they are working when, in fact, they are only busy."

Nobody gets everything in life, not even Picasso. When I asked him if he had missed anything, he answered without hesitation:

"I would like to have been a hero. I missed having the experience of proving my manhood through physically testing myself. To be young and a warrior, to feel the exaltation of being a hero —to know I was one, to prove it to myself, to face fear and defy it. Proximity to death brings heightened life. But it must be a youthful confrontation when there is everything to lose.

"I didn't fight in wars. I didn't even fight the bull. It is with men as it is with bulls. There are the brave bulls and the others. This is a very important thing to a man—to know that you would measure up. More than measure up. You think you would. You tell yourself you would act with heroism, but you can never really know for certain. To have excelled in combat, to have been a brave gladiator—I will never know for certain. Not being a man, you could not understand what I mean. Every man knows."

I remember Laurence Olivier telling me that when he first comprehended all that was riding on his opening-night performance, some of the fun of doing it went away and never came back. He quickly added, however, that even if he could have turned back, he would not have done so.

Pitcher Jerry Reuss talked with me about his work and the emotion that went along with it which could be described but not explained:

"Standing on the pitcher's mound with almost 60,000 people watching, I looked up into the stands after the last out, and how can I tell anybody about a feeling like that? You can't convey that feeling to anyone who hasn't felt it.

"I did lose something along the way, though. It was a kind of innocent love of baseball. Now, I'm so involved in it, it's my whole life. But I don't have that innocent feeling toward it that I had when I was a boy. I don't know if you understand what I mean. . . ."

I told him I did understand. The realization of one's dream may not be without price, and that price may be a loss of innocence. As a little girl I loved to read. I read all the time, and there was nothing I would rather do than go to a bookstore. Then I grew up and wrote a book, and I went to the bookstores. But it was different. Suddenly it was a professional experience and something of the mystique disappeared. I would probably never again view a bookstore with the same wide-eyed innocence, but I didn't mind because I gained so much more than I lost.

"So did I," Jerry Reuss said.

"Is it chicken? Is it veal?" was the constant refrain. Tasting the entrée didn't bring anyone closer to the answer. The fund-raiser dinner was an experience Vice President Hubert Humphrey had lived through many times. His was a life measured in half-eaten baked Alaskas, he would say. "It hurts to gain weight eating food you don't really enjoy." Hubert Humphrey knew well that double unhappiness.

I asked him was it worth all those bad meals eaten on a dais with thousands of eyes watching you, all those rides in limousines to airports, all that time on airplanes in seemingly endless holding patterns? His yes could not have been delivered with greater certainty.

"Purpose in life is what it is all about," he explained. "You go to all the meetings, and sometimes it seems nothing is happening and, even worse, nothing is ever going to happen. You get so tired of all the sitting and all the waiting. You begin to wonder if anything is going to happen and why you're even there. Then, one day, there *is* something so important that all of the people in the world and history are going to be affected by what happens in that minute. Because you are there, in play, and because of what you say and do, everything can be different, better. Maybe what you change isn't the whole, maybe just a detail. But you have the chance to affect something. Power in itself is not an accomplishment. It's a privilege to know what you do can make a difference.

"That's what it's all about, maybe only sixty seconds, just that moment. That's what it's all for."

Success can be costly. Cynicism and loss of trust are part of the price that may be exacted from anyone who lives in the world of power or fame. Jack Valenti's love of movies took him from a boyhood job as an usher in a Houston movie house to being president of the Motion Picture Association of America. Between these jobs, he was, among other things, aide to President Lyndon Johnson. Experiences in such proximity to the White House take on a heightened drama.

"There is nothing else quite like it," he told me. "Being on the inside is very different from being on the outside. Once you've lived in the White House, you never quite get used to getting your news from the newspaper."

The story he went on to tell was an extreme example of finding out whether your friends are your friends or the friends of your success:

"When I first arrived from Texas as an aide to President Johnson, I didn't really know anyone in Washington. But almost as soon as I got there, I met this guy, and we seemed to have immediate rapport. He practically adopted me. He knew everyone and everything about Washington. He was a man of accomplishment. He introduced me to a lot of interesting people. He knew just where I ought to look for a house. It was nice to know you could call on somebody who was always glad to hear from you, who never made you feel like you were imposing. He was a very busy man, but he was never in a hurry when he was speaking with you.

"He was so genuinely interested in helping me and my wife, too, when she joined me from Houston. He gave this really big party and invited everyone. It seemed a kind and generous thing to do. He'd drop by my office at the White House sometimes just to say hello. If we went out to lunch, I had a real fight on my hands to ever get the check. He was a sophisticated and stimulating person to be with, and a thoughtful person. He was a dear friend.

"The morning I resigned as an aide to President Johnson in order to take the job as president of the Motion Picture Association, I happened to be meeting my friend for lunch that very day, at San Souci. We ordered and started eating. Then I told him. I said that after my wife and family and the President, I wanted him to be the first person to know that that morning I had just resigned as aide to the President. I'd been thinking about it and talking with President Johnson about it for quite a while. Finally, I'd given him all my reasons and persuaded the President to accept my resignation.

"Well, he stopped eating and just about finished chewing the bite he was on. He looked at his watch and said he'd just remembered an appointment he had. He got up and left. This time I was able to get the check.

"I was surprised when I didn't hear from him. I called but couldn't seem to find him in. His secretary always said he was away from his desk.

"I heard that he was having a really big party for someone who had just arrived in Washington to take a post in the White House, but I wasn't invited.

"At Christmastime he didn't send a gift. Before that, he'd always remembered every holiday, even my daughter's birthday. It was almost embarrassing, he'd been so considerate. I was stricken from his Christmas-card list, which must have numbered in the thousands. After that, from time to time we'd be at the same cocktail party, but he'd never seem to see me. He'd look right past me and he never said hello.

"For him, I was my job. He was my job's friend, not mine, and when I didn't have the job, I didn't exist anymore. Of course, he wasn't the only one, just the most dramatic example. Before that, I always thought I could tell when a person was sincere. After that, I knew I couldn't.

"You have to try not to let it make you bitter, but once you've been badly fooled, you're always just a little more suspicious, never quite as trusting. You learn you have to be careful—if you can figure out what careful is. A position of any power is a terrible place to make new friends."

I suggested that perhaps the best lesson that could be learned from the experience was—none at all. The important thing is *not* to learn too much from past experience. Perhaps it's better not to know how something will end, so the experience can be enjoyed while it's happening.

I told the story of Jack Valenti's disillusioning experience to Otto Preminger. I said that Jack told me the experience had made him feel like a perfect fool, and that even though none of us is perfect, I had had at least one occasion to feel that way myself when I wasn't able to tell sincerity from insincerity. It's hard to admit to oneself that one cannot recognize the sycophants and the opportunists, the gaspers and the graspers.

To that, Otto Preminger added his own insight, saying that it isn't possible to tell the difference, because there is no one more sincere than the person who is there to get something from you. "He is perfectly sincere. It's just that what he is sincere about is his desire to use you. Because it's not false sincerity but real insincerity—sincere self-aggrandizement—it's not possible to tell the difference."

In Key West, Tennessee Williams was bemoaning the number of times he had been disappointed in people he felt had only "used" him. He admitted he had made a lot of mistakes in judging people, perhaps because he wanted to believe in them and so, rather than having been fooled by them, he fooled himself. He asked me, perhaps rhetorically, "How do you know if you can trust a person?" And I answered for myself, the only way I know, "You trust him."

"Nobody who knew my day-to-day life would envy me"

TENNESSEE WILLIAMS

ONE ALWAYS HOPES to meet someone interesting at a cocktail party, or to have someone you like sit next to you on an airplane. It always seems to happen to someone else. The night I met Tennessee Williams, it happened to me.

It was at a cocktail party at the New York City apartment of Milton Goldman. As I entered, a volley of names was exchanged. In the confusion, I heard peripherally, "Miss Chandler, Mr. Williams." Among so many, two such plain names did not register. What I did notice was the man. He was certainly distinctive-looking, but it was the way he was rather than the way he looked that attracted my attention.

We stood talking in the hallway of the apartment for a while, but as more people arrived, we moved farther into the living room. He got a glass of Perrier for me, looking only slightly askance at it, and a glass of white wine for himself.

Contrary to what is considered proper cocktail-party protocol, I made no move to circulate among the other guests, nor did I ask him if he would like to do so. If he left me, he was going to have to do it on his own. I hoped that wouldn't be for a long time.

"Do you like sunsets?" he asked, after a while.

"Of course," I answered. "Doesn't everyone?"

"Have you ever seen a Key West sunset?"

I had never been to Key West. He went on to describe the sunset in Key West as the most beautiful in the world, and told me that Key West was his home. He was flying back the following day, and he invited me to go along with him to see that sunset for myself.

I remember wishing I knew his name. I thought I ought to know before answering yes.

I noticed that we were the object of discreet glances, though no one came over to join us. It was as if there were some kind of inhibition barrier around him. At any celebrity gathering, and this was certainly one of those, you can look through the room and see who is the most powerful, most famous, most respected, or most rarely seen great name. There is a pattern the guests make which points like an arrow to that person. At this party, the focus of attention was on the sofa where we were now sitting. I knew I wasn't the one at whom they were looking. Obviously, the other person was too well known for me to feel comfortable asking his name, and I didn't want to get up to ask anyone else and risk my place.

At that moment, Douglas Fairbanks, Jr., came over and joined us. With me between them, the two of them began an animated conversation of shared anecdotal recollections and sparring repartee. In the midst of the reminiscences, Douglas said, "Do you remember the last time we were at the White House together, Tennessee?"

Then I knew.

When Douglas Fairbanks, Jr., left us, I said, "Yes."

Tennessee Williams understood the question I was answering. "Which flight do you prefer?" he asked. "I haven't decided yet what time I can leave tomorrow, but I can call you in the morning."

I thought he ought to have a day or two alone at home after his travels, so I said I would call him in Key West and come a few days later.

I declined the invitation to stay at his house. I appreciated the offer and though I said no quickly, it was with regret. I knew I was relinquishing a unique experience—to be a house guest at Tennessee Williams' home. It meant a much greater sharing experience, as well as more of his time. What I also understood was that Tennessee Williams was an emotional and generous spirit—and an impulsive one. I did not want him to repent at leisure his momentary gallantry. Telling him that I would prefer to stay at a hotel, whichever one he recommended, I added that if he invited me to come back a second time and to stay at his house, then I would accept.

When I bought my ticket to Key West, I was told by the ticket seller, "That's where Tennessee Williams lives." In the Miami airport, when I asked about the flight connection to Key West, the gate attendant prefaced his directions with, "That's where Tennessee Williams lives." During the flight to Key West, the man sitting next to me volunteered the information that, "Tennessee Williams lives here."

I was totally ensconced in Key West with two local sunsets behind me, when Tennessee Williams proclaimed that he had something to ask. He paused for dramatic effect. Usually he revealed all without waiting for the questions I would have been too reserved to ask. I knew he never asked personal questions in a way that required a direct answer because that would have been in violation of the elaborate chivalric code that was innately a part of him. "Even if it wasn't worth coming here to see me"—he began, with a gesture of his hand waving off my first syllable of denial—"was it not worth coming here to see the most beautiful sunset in the whole world?"

Though not an authority on sunsets, I had to admit that I had never seen a more beautiful one—but in truth it was not for the sunset I had journeyed to Key West.

Having failed to recognize Tennessee Williams, I enjoyed the idea that I was so positively impressed by him before any influence of the celebrity myth could have conditioned my response. He later told me he liked that, too.

Happiness was not exactly what Tennessee Williams sought, and it was not exactly what he found. "Happiness is insensitivity," he said. Though Tennessee Williams called himself a pessimist, it seemed to me he was an optimist. Only an optimist could have been so disappointed.

He met me one evening at the restaurant of the hotel where I was staying. Outside, there was a sudden violent storm, unique to the Keys. It was that special kind of rain that while it was happening made it seem as if it had always been raining and always would be.

TENNESSEE

How are you, Miss Charlotte? You look as if you think something wonderful is about to happen.

I

It *is* happening.

TENNESSEE

Enthusiasm is the most important thing in life. *Élan vital.*

I

Are you happy to be back in Key West?

TENNESSEE

Nobody who knew my day-to-day life would envy me. I'm a leper. Oh, not physically; but I might just as well be. It's like having a physical illness, a contagious one. Did you notice the other night when we were speaking at the party, and all the others stood apart? It's the opposite of when you are a great success and people hover about you to bask in the glow of your limelight.

Failure is the other side of that. People move out of the aura of your failure. They shun you because they don't want to catch your failure. The most terrible thing that can happen to a man is to outlast his pride.

I

I thought the people didn't approach you the other night because of your celebrity. Those who didn't already know you were hesitant.

TENNESSEE

I'm glad you're here. If you weren't here, I'd be eating at home, and this man who was cooking for me cooked this terrible thing for me tonight. I believe it's called a *picadillo.* You don't know what that is . . .

I

Oh, but I do. It's a Spanish dish made from ground meat.

TENNESSEE

This man took some meat out of the fridge that had been there for about two months, and he cooked it with a lot of spices. It didn't smell good when he first took it out, and it didn't smell any better when he'd cooked it. He tried to give it to my dog.

I

That sounds more like a peccadillo—a sin. Did your dog reject it?

TENNESSEE

Of course. He has better judgment than to eat that. I wouldn't have a dog without taste.

I

I'm grateful to your cook for sending you out of the house, out to dine with me.

TENNESSEE

He's not the reason I'm here. It's just that he didn't entice me to stay at home.

I

Then I'm very glad that he didn't entice you.

TENNESSEE

I enjoyed the party the other night. And it's gone well here, too, hasn't it? But we must begin building down so we won't be disappointed.

I

I don't subscribe to that philosophy, perhaps because I don't know how to "build down."

TENNESSEE

I don't know how to either.

It's nice that you came here without waiting. I thought you would do it, but I wasn't certain because very few people are impulsive.

I

I don't consider myself impulsive, but I think it's good if one can manage it—not to have to wait *too* long for things. Waiting too long does rather take the edge off.

TENNESSEE

They might change, or you might change. Or your desire for them might change while you're waiting.

I

Actually I didn't want you to change your mind about my coming here. The last time I saw you, you quoted Byron's line in *Camino Real:* "Make voyages, attempt them. There's nothing else."

TENNESSEE
It's one of my favorite lines and my philosophy of life. An exciting, adventurous life is not easy to find. You have to work at it all the time. Even for the most ingenious and privileged, it frequently takes tremendous effort. But that's my life—an *intense* life, for my intense life is my work.

Everything a writer of fiction creates has to come out of himself. What we write may develop in a heightened or exaggerated form, but it's usually something we experience or observe. Sometimes I think I only live so I'll have something to write about. People think that an exciting life just *happens* to someone, but it's not so.

I
I suppose risk-taking is a big part of it.

TENNESSEE
Yes, you always have to pay the price.

I
I don't believe there's always a price.

TENNESSEE
Always a price.

I hope you won't regret your trip here. You know, you'll never like me as much as the first night we met. Nobody does. I wear quickly.

I
I don't believe that. Why do you feel that way?

TENNESSEE
Experience. I have often disappointed. To know me is not to love me. At best it's to tolerate me. You know, my dog is the only one of my animals who likes me. I have two male parrots who don't like anyone, especially each other. They use terrible language. I came back the other day and one was lying on the bottom of the cage. One of them had almost killed the other. I thought he was dead. They are both male parrots, and that's the way males act. My cat likes some people. They say animals love the person who feeds them. Even when I feed my animals, they don't love me.

I
You spend so little time in Key West. Maybe your animals don't know you.

TENNESSEE

Perhaps. Sometimes I think about selling my house here, but I have to keep it for the animals. They have nowhere else to go. I never met an animal I didn't like.

I had an English bulldog named Madame Sophia who traveled everywhere with me. She liked Paris best because there I could take her with me to all of the great restaurants. But she preferred the bistros and patisserie places because her favorite thing in life was croissants. She would go from table to table pitifully begging croissants at every table, as though I never fed her. She was wonderful, and I've always blamed myself, because I think so much traveling isn't good for a dog and I shortened her life.

I've been asked to do a reading for an animal shelter here. I'll have to do that.

Did you get very wet coming here?

I

I only had to come a few steps, but it's a really impressive storm. I'd been listening to the high tide reports. When you're on an island, the weather report is so different. The temperature is merely a detail, but the tide is everything.

TENNESSEE

I hope you are enjoying the Pier House. Sometimes when I have guests, I leave them in my house, and I check in here.

I

You didn't tell me that when you invited me to stay at your house. Now I'm glad I didn't accept your invitation. I wouldn't have wanted to force you out of your own home. It would have been strange to come in with my suitcase and pass you leaving with yours.

TENNESSEE

I meant what I said sincerely, or I would not have offered.

I

I know that. But sometimes one offers a great deal in a moment of generosity and spontaneity, and wonders later about one's own rashness.

TENNESSEE

Done is done. Next time we shall have this very discussion.

I

I hope so because that means there will be a next time. But, for the moment, I'm very happy with this time.

TENNESSEE

I like this restaurant because it's comfortable and it's not piss-elegant. Key West was even lovelier when I first came here. It has wonderful mornings, and morning is so important to me. I like to be up with the sun, and I prefer an early sunrise. One can be completely alone at that time.

Did you get the room I suggested? It's not a frugal room, but one shouldn't stint. I don't believe in being frugal with money, time, or energy, because there are no guarantees in life. I never know where I'll be tomorrow, or even *if* I'll be. Once you have had a close brush with death, you never think the same way as before.

I

I got exactly the room you suggested.

TENNESSEE

I wanted you to have the feeling that the water was coming right into your room.

I

I had the feeling! The water actually did come right into the room, with the high tide, and it totally soaked the rug.

TENNESSEE

I'm sorry.

I

I didn't mind. At least I knew I was somewhere different. It's the exciting thing about traveling. I don't want the world to become homogenized. I don't like places to be too much alike.

TENNESSEE

The world *is* getting more alike. You must go to Tangier. That is something different. I could show you Tangier. Maybe I will go there soon myself.

Do you have a good view? You said you appreciated a view.

I

I left the drapes wide open so I would wake up with the sun, looking at the ocean. I got up at six because I didn't want to waste any of the time here, and it is a beautiful time of day. I thought while you were writing, I would go for a walk and see Key West. When I came back, I looked out at my view, but it had changed. You didn't tell me about the rest of the view besides the ocean and the sunrise and the sunset! Through the floor-to-ceiling picture window, I saw a row of naked people in beach chairs. You didn't tell me about that.

TENNESSEE

Life must be full of little surprises.

I

But they weren't just lying there getting *complete* tans—they appeared to be striking poses. They were doing things like applying suntan oil, but in a very exaggerated, conspicuous way, and they would keep applying it over and over again, beyond any possibility of absorbing all that suntan oil. Then they would wave at the hotel windows. I thought I was in a Tennessee Williams play.

TENNESSEE

Were they male or female?

I

There seemed to be both.

TENNESSEE

Seemed to be? Couldn't you tell for certain?

I

Yes, I was able to tell.

TENNESSEE

What else did you see?

I

I love the architecture. I walked along Duvall Street, and I particularly enjoyed looking at the wonderful early-1800 houses, with their widows' walks and ironwork and the tropical art deco. I bought all of the books I could find about the architecture of Key West. I suppose it's like trying to take the place away with me when I leave.

TENNESSEE

Do you know what the widows' walks are for?

I

I was told they are the platforms on the tops of the roofs where the wives watched for their husbands' ships to return home.

Sometimes what they saw was a shipwreck, and then their husbands never came home. After that, they watched the ships of the others from their widows' walks.

TENNESSEE

That's the more romantic version, but it's not correct. Key West was the home of the wreckers, those who lived like vultures on the remains of the unfortunate. They used the walks to spot ships in trouble on the dangerous reefs that surround the island because the first ones there could claim the rights of salvage. I hope I haven't ruined it for you, my dear.

I have a shell for you. Do you have room in your baggage for that?

I

There's always room for one more shell. Can you hear the ocean in it?

TENNESSEE

This one has voices, but don't pay any attention to them. They are all crazy.

I

Maybe I won't hear the same voices.

TENNESSEE

That's entirely possible.

I would like to have taken that walk with you this morning, but at my age, I have to save all my energy for work. When you are young, there is enough of you to go around. Now I must write in the mornings and as much as I can. The only thing I do besides write is swim, and I swim better than I write these days, if one is to believe the critics.

Dr. Mudd was imprisoned here in Key West. He treated John Wilkes Booth after Lincoln's assassination. It was said that Booth shot Lincoln because of sibling rivalry with his brother, Edwin Booth. That's hard for me to understand. I love my sister and brother. Don't you love your brothers and sisters?

I

I don't have any.

TENNESSEE

One shares so much with them. I can't imagine feeling negatively toward them, being in competition. I wanted my sister to come and live with me here in Key West, but she didn't want to. They know her at the sanitarium, you see. She has her friends there. Everyone knows and loves Miss Rose.

What are you going to have? Order anything on the menu, anything you want.

I

Since it's your favorite restaurant, and you come here all the time, I'd like your recommendations. I assume it should be fish here in Key West. I'd thought about a grilled fish. There's one called "Yellowback" on the menu.

TENNESSEE

[He begins coughing] Don't get the yellowback fish unless they bone it for you. In fact, you can't trust their boning. Don't order a fish with bones, especially since we will be talking. It's too dangerous. Once I had an accountant who choked to death on a bone at a wedding. *[He coughs some more at the memory]* I saw a program on TV about what you can do if someone chokes on a bone, but I wasn't watching carefully, so you'd better not take any chances. I don't want to lose you. And it's a mistake to depend on me. I let people down, especially my friends. Why don't you play it safe and get the *fritto misto?* Then you get to taste everything.

I

Good. I wouldn't want to miss anything.

TENNESSEE

That's the way I always felt about life, but now I'm coming to think that one doesn't need to experience everything, that some things are better skipped. Perhaps I'm just getting lazy. Would you like to experience everything, Miss Charlotte?

I

No, only the good things.

TENNESSEE

[Touching my arm with a certain urgency and speaking in a rather intimate tone] There is something which you must experience here—the key lime pie. You've never tasted anything like it. We're famous for that. Do you know our enticing limes?

I

I went out to buy some this morning. I went to Fausto's Food

Palace, your local supermarket. But I was disappointed. They come in prepacked cartons covered with plastic. That wasn't so enticing.

TENNESSEE

We'll make it up to you. But first you must begin with the conch chowder. Have you ever had conch chowder?

I

I don't think so.

TENNESSEE

Then you never had it, because if you had, you would remember. There are certain things in life one never forgets. It is like saying, "Have you ever had sex?" Could anyone respond, "I don't think so"?

There was something I wanted to ask you the other night: I'm fascinated by the character of Evita. I think she was one of the great characters in history. Douglas [Fairbanks, Jr.] said you had done some interviews with Perón. That's a wonderful scene when he has her embalmed body there in his house while it was being prepared for its return to Argentina, and all of you are sitting there sipping tea and eating cake.

I

I didn't eat any cake.

TENNESSEE

What an extraordinary moment! I would like to use that scene in a play. Would you object to being a character in one of my plays?

I

I probably wouldn't recognize myself. Several writers have told me their friends mind most when they don't find themselves as characters in their books. I suppose they're insulted because they weren't judged to be interesting enough. But in your case, maybe it's better *not* to find oneself in a Tennessee Williams play.

TENNESSEE

My characters *do* suffer.

I

Sidney Sheldon told me that when he gave the world's largest male organ to a character in one of his novels, he was worried that men he knew might think the character was based on them. Then it turned out that so many of the men he knew were pleased and said, "Sidney, I know you based that character on me."

TENNESSEE

Size seems to be a subject of greater fascination for men than for women. I once knew a man whose whole life was ruined by embarrassment because he thought he was inadequately endowed. Actually, he was perfectly normal.

The other evening there was a question I wanted to ask you. I saw the play, *Evita,* and there was one thing I kept thinking about: Was Evita really sincere? Do you think she really cared about the "shirtless" poor?

I

I never met her, but I find it difficult to believe that anyone could pretend that much or that anyone could play a part all of the time without it being real or becoming real. Her followers gave her such adulation, it would seem she had to feel that wave of love. I spoke with many people who knew her, and even those who hated her said they believed she was sincere.

TENNESSEE

Good. I have always believed that, too. I have to think she was sincere. It would be terribly disillusioning not to believe that.

I

Of course, belief in her sincerity doesn't necessarily mean I agree with her ideas.

TENNESSEE

Nor do I. But I would like to have met her.

Douglas is quite witty, isn't he?

I

Yes.

TENNESSEE

Do you find Douglas attractive?

I

Of course.

TENNESSEE

Men are never good at understanding why other men are attractive to women. Why do you think women like Douglas?

I

I'm sure there are a lot of reasons, and each woman finds her own. But one of them is that he likes them. I read something Mary Pickford once said about his father: She wrote that when he left a room, no matter how many people remained in the room, it seemed somehow a little empty. I believe that applies to Douglas, too.

The waiter came to take our order. He spoke with Tennessee Williams in a tone of restrained reverence, obviously well aware of his celebrity and just as obviously trying to appear oblivious to it.

Tennessee Williams ordered everything we had discussed, and everything else on the menu, too. The waiter pointed out that it was a lot of food to order for two people. It soon became clear, however, that it was only for one—me. For himself, he ordered a *fritto misto* with a bottle of white wine to accompany it. As it turned out, the *fritto misto* accompanied the bottle of white wine.

TENNESSEE

I went to a poetry festival in England. It was a very serious event. Of course I'd just gotten out of an asylum. Can you imagine, they had me in the violent ward! You cannot imagine what that's like, and I wasn't even violent. You'd be violent if they did that to you. If you aren't violent to get out, it means you *are* insane. But when I was committed, I knew I had to survive. You have to be a survivor to come out. I'm a survivor. I didn't realize I even wanted to survive until I was in there. Then I knew I had to, because I could not let *them* win.

Sometimes if you're tired or have been shut up somewhere, you start to laugh, and things seem funnier than they might at another time. Anyway, at the poetry festival, I got up and started telling jokes instead of the sort of stuff they were expecting. They said I was the fifth Marx Brother. I got a lot of laughs. Then, I got the headlines for it. I was stunned. A lot of people criticized me for being funny at a serious occasion.

I

That's what happened to Groucho when he went to London to

appear at T. S. Eliot's memorial tribute. He was criticized for telling a joke, but Groucho felt it was what T. S. Eliot would have liked.

TENNESSEE

I enjoyed speaking at the festival. I've always rather fancied myself as being a bit funny and wondered why other people don't see me that way.

I met Groucho once. We were both coming out of the Plaza Hotel at the same moment, and the light changed and we couldn't cross. We looked at each other and laughed. It wasn't really very funny, but people sometimes do that when they feel a spiritual rapport. I recognized him, but I'm certain he didn't recognize me.

Was Groucho so funny in real life?

I

Sometimes even funnier. It was his perspective—the way he saw life. Groucho said he didn't tell jokes, only the truth, and the truth is often funny.

TENNESSEE

For me, the truth is shocking. I tell the truth, and people are shocked. I do publicly what other people do privately. Extravagance is everything in life for me. I don't like middle things. I like excesses. I'd do just about anything not to bore people. I hope I won't bore you. I shall try to refrain from telling you too much trivia, but it is amazing how much of one's life is trivia.

I

Maybe then it's the trivia that counts.

TENNESSEE

I've always wanted to be considered funny and to make people laugh, but my jokes grow worse with age. I suppose I'm trying harder. Perhaps it's desperation, which is never funny. Perhaps it's just that since one can't remain the same, one either grows sweeter or more sour. I hope to be sweeter. The ideal thing would be to find a way to remain the same. No one you've talked with has revealed any tricks for not growing old, have they?

I

I never talked with him, but Oscar Wilde's portrait in the closet

is intriguing, though it didn't seem to work out very well for
Dorian Gray. For one thing, every decade or so, he had to find
new friends.

TENNESSEE

That's what I do anyway. In fact, I go through friends faster
than that. What about Picasso? Did you ask him his secret of
prolonged youth?

I

I didn't even have to ask; he volunteered it. Sex.

TENNESSEE

But was it the cause or the effect?

I

I think he meant it was both.

TENNESSEE

Sex is no longer the governing force in my life. Work and
human intimacy are the most important. Even when love did
come, work was the primary concern. Writing is my life, failure
my death. A desperate writer—that is what I am. When I can't
write, that's the most terrible thing. When I can't write, I'm
filled with self-loathing.

How does one cope? This is what is important in life—how
you cope. You never get used to a critical world that turns
thumbs down. When they don't like your work, it is worse than
if they said your child is homely. So, you must despise them.
You must despise them first, before they despise you. You must believe
yourself better than they are or you can't go on. I don't think
anyone has ever known, with the exception of Elia Kazan, how
desperately much my work meant to me, and treated it with the
necessary sympathy of feeling. There are moments when that
sympathy of feeling from someone else is very important and
precious.

I like to work on several things at one time, like people who
are reading several books at a time. But I want *you* to talk! You
must tell me about *your* writing. Do you like to work in the
morning? How many hours are you able to write? Do you type?

I

Talking about writing my book with you is rather like discussing how I boil water with Escoffier.

TENNESSEE

[Laughing] My own working habits are more private than my daily and nightly existence. One has certain secrets, dear Miss Charlotte. You know, I would prefer discussing with you the most intimate details of my sex life, because my work is more personal. Can you understand that?

I

I might not feel the same way, but I can accept that you feel that way.

TENNESSEE

I've always been leary of talking about my professional life. I suppose I'm afraid it will be startled away. Writing is the continuous pursuit of an always evasive, ultimately illusive quarry which will always be just beyond one's grasp. I am a compulsive writer. Or perhaps a compulsive typist.

Do you *like* to write?

I

A psychiatrist in Switzerland, whom I met socially, not professionally, said I was a graphomaniac because I was always writing something. But writing a lot doesn't have any qualitative implications. He went on to explain that he had been treating a man with a serious case of graphomania. The man had been writing a novel for many years, and had completed thousands of pages when his wife, overwhelmed by curiosity, secretly looked at his manuscript. It turned out he had been writing the same sentence over and over and over again, just that one sentence repeated for years.

TENNESSEE

What was the sentence?

I

That was my question. But the psychiatrist wouldn't tell me. He said it was a violation of professional confidence. But maybe it's just as well. It might not have been an interesting sentence.

TENNESSEE

Sometimes it's better to know less rather than more—in fact, *most* times. Too much knowledge brings disappointment. But you will not be disappointed in the key lime pie. Do you know the intimate secret of key lime pie?

I
No, I've never met one.

TENNESSEE
I'm glad you saved the experience to share with me. Otherwise
you might have encountered a green one and not even known
the truth. The truth is, a veritable key lime pie is never green.
They do *that* with artificial coloring. *[The waiter serves us]*
    In 1943 I was an usher at the Strand in New York. I got
seventeen dollars a week. I loved it. It covered my room at the
"Y" and left me seven dollars for meals. I've made a lot more
money than that in my life, but it never made me feel rich.

I
Rich, I suppose, is in the mind, not just in the bank.

TENNESSEE
That is so true. Responsibilities and sickness make you feel
poor. Whenever I'm in New York, I'm always reminded of how
happy I was as an usher at the Strand Theatre. I can remember
the feeling, but I can't recapture it.

I
It's too bad some happiness can't be put in the bank and saved
for a rainy day.

TENNESSEE
Before that, in 1939, I was a feather picker on a squab farm
near Los Angeles. The squabs had their throats cut and then
were held over a bucket while they bled to death. I couldn't do
that work; I wouldn't kill anything. But after the bird was dead,
I plucked its feathers.
    I lived in a little cabin, and I ate beans and stolen avocados,
but I was happy. Those were care-less times. Care-less is the
best time in a person's life, and once you lose that, you can
never be as happy again no matter what success comes. My
favorite painting is one by Gauguin called *The Careless Days*.

I
I would assume the Broadway opening of *Glass Menagerie*
brought you happiness.

TENNESSEE
For the Broadway opening of *Menagerie*, I don't remember feeling a great sense of triumph. In fact, I don't remember it very

well at all. It should have been one of the happiest nights of my life. I'd like to have that night now, and perhaps enjoy it more.

I did make someone happy. My mother was pleased by my delayed success. Not by the delay, but that it came at all.

After the success of *Menagerie* I felt a great depression, probably because I never believed that anything good would continue. I'd spent so much of my energy on the climb to success that when I'd made it and my play was the hottest ticket in town, I felt almost no satisfaction.

Sudden success is startling, and you have to adjust to it. Success makes you feel self-conscious. It would seem there would be no need to adjust up, but you get used to whatever way things are, and change can be depressing. It is easier to be poor and unsuccessful when you are young and don't know any better and have compensations. Of course, once you have had success, it is even more difficult to adjust to the loss of it. And fame is ephemeral.

I

There are some lines I like by Emily Dickinson: "Fame is a bee. It has a song; it has a sting. Alas, it has a wing."

TENNESSEE

One never understands what makes it come and go. If success comes at all, you've been lucky.

I

Did you think you were ever going to be so famous when you were living on those beans and avocados?

TENNESSEE

I never had any expectations of being anything. I wrote because I had to. I couldn't stop. There wasn't anything else I *could* do. If no one had ever bought anything I ever did, I'd still be writing. It's beyond a compulsion.

But while money was never my prime motivation, it's never really good to be without money. Those who tell you that poverty is good for the soul weren't ever poor or they would know better. Poverty for too long is deforming. It's humiliating. I had to write. I also had to escape from extreme poverty— jobs that paid me so little I could hardly live and that I hated so much I could hardly hold them. I could not even afford insecticide to kill the bugs who shared my domicile. I lived on black coffee in a state of caffeine.

It seems natural to be inspired and encouraged by success, but I believe that I have always been pushed by the negative. I found success becalming. The apparent failure of a play sends me back to my typewriter that very night before the reviews are out. I am more compelled to get back to work than if I had a success. The morning after *Summer and Smoke,* I wanted to get back to work, alone and right away. Once when I thought I was dying, I wrote most frantically and furiously. I felt I had to hurry. I wrote with a particular passion, perhaps because I was so angry at the idea of having to die before I was ready. I have this anger without its being specifically directed. Writing is my punching bag. My character is anger and endurance.

I

I've noticed a kind of pervasive male rage among many of the successful men I've met.

TENNESSEE

Perhaps it's one of the differences between men and women. In *Camino Real,* Casanova says to Camille, "My dear, you must learn how to carry the banner of Bohemia into the enemy camp." Camille replies, "Bohemia has no banner; it survives by discretion." Women are more diplomatic.

I like women, and understand women better than men. I think women are more complicated and they suffer more. Life is harder for them, and they are more feeling.

I

What do you look for in people, men *or* women?

TENNESSEE

I like people who are "different."

I

The people you create could certainly be called that. I think some of your characters are more a part of people's lives than real people they have known.

TENNESSEE

Blanche says it for me: "I don't want realism. I want magic." I don't tell the truth. I tell what ought to be the truth. Magic is precious in life. I spent my life waiting for something wonderful to happen.

I

I remember reading that Clarence Darrow felt that way, too. In his autobiography, he wrote that he'd been waiting all his life for something wonderful to happen. Then, one day, after he had passed seventy, he realized that whatever it was, it wasn't going to happen. I always remembered that because the loss of the dream seemed so terrible to me—to face the future without that hope.

TENNESSEE

I have a dream which has been very much a part of my life. I'm in a grandstand, and I'm waiting for something wonderful to happen. I hear the music of the calliope. I'm very happy, and I think, "And now the parade."

The parade is just about to begin. Then all of a sudden, I sense someone standing there next to me, a dark figure of authority. I look up, and I'm told to move. It's started to rain, and the parade has been canceled. I look around the stands, and I see that I'm all alone. But I remain there waiting obstinately. It seems more real than reality, more a part of my life than what has really happened. What I have learned in life is that only dreams are true.

It's terrible when nothing is new anymore. I suppose that is what getting old is about. One of the things that youth has, which is now so difficult for me to find, is astonishment. Variety, surprise—these are what life is about. One needs elements of stimulation. When you get to be as old as I am, you know, you don't look forward anymore.

I

It would seem that what's really diminished are expectations rather than the actuality.

TENNESSEE

As it gets harder to believe that there is something wonderful that is going to happen to you, it gets harder to be happy.

If I survive, I'm leaving America. Once I thought of going to Italy. I could see Fellini. I could buy a little farm in Sicily. But now I have decided to live in Bohemia. Bohemia is everywhere

and anywhere the counter-culture resides—proud to despise
hypocrisy. You can't live with hypocrisy. You can exist, but you
can't live, because hypocrisy stifles. We are suffocated by the
big lie.

I

What is "the big lie"?

TENNESSEE

The big lie is that we are governed by truth. The only way we
can have a free press is to *buy* a press. And put out what you
want, what you *know* is true. Otherwise there is no free press in
America. You know it's true. We're *not* governed by truth, we're
governed by continual lies which will eventually create nuclear
warfare which will destroy most of the planet. That's why I'm
leaving America if I survive my operation. *[He looks closely at my
plate]* Don't eat too much. You have to save room for that key
lime pie I told you about. Once you've tasted it, you'll never
forget it.

I

It's already an unforgettable part of my life.

TENNESSEE

And you must call me Tom. That's what my friends call me. It's
my real name, you know.

   Do you like this world we live in?

I

It's the only one we have. Do you have any advice for living?

TENNESSEE

Yes. Fucking is healthy. *[Looking around the restaurant]* Look at
those people over there. Do you see how bored she looks? He's
deeply involved in his own thoughts, and they certainly aren't
about her. You see how preoccupied he is? If I were writing a
play about those people, the voice you would hear would be the
one that is speaking to him, and only he is hearing it.

   They aren't bored in the way people who are married are
bored. You see, there's no resignation there. Their mistake was
coming away together like this to a place where they are thrown
together on their own, and they don't have the resources for it.
There isn't enough between them, and this shows it up. Once
they know this, though, they don't admit it even to themselves.

When they go back to their natural habitat and to the crutch *the others,* their friends, provide, it will never be the same. The joining of spirits, even momentarily, is rare. The joining of bodies is so much easier and so much less intimate, though it can be very nice.

I have had enough one-night stands in my life to tell you that they are meaningless. Promiscuity is a distortion of the love impulse. Of course, one must have a few little adventures. That is because of the animal that is in each of us. And man is closer to the animal than woman.

I don't like to be alone at night. I remember many times when I took someone home to bed with me, not especially for sex, but because I didn't want to be alone. Sex is easier to find than love. Sex has been very important in my life. Love has been precious when I could get it. But work, my work, is everything.

Sex is now so minimal; it is so lacking. I mean, in my seventies I have no sex. Many people continue sex until ninety. I wouldn't like to see it. What did Groucho have to say about it?

I

Groucho was in his middle eighties when I knew him, and he said it was a good time to read a book.

TENNESSEE

Or to *write* a good book.

I

Even better!

TENNESSEE

I'm writing a book called *The Banner of Bohemia.* It's my last work.

I

A novel?

TENNESSEE

No. I'm writing it about the difficulties, about the *supreme* difficulties of remaining *honestly* bohemian in the critical world which is totally against me. Or is it? I think so. But things against me are of no importance now. Whatever I've done that is of some value has survived, if anything survives in the theater. I used to write well, but life's changed, my style's changed. I am continually informed that what I do now is terrible. I have in mind that what I do now in effect belongs to those who come after me.

I

Do you think you would have gone on writing if the critics had been . . .

TENNESSEE

Favorable?

I

No, had been unfavorable in the beginning. If it had been hard in the beginning, would you have gone on writing?

TENNESSEE

Oh, yes. There was no other outlet. I tried everything. One must learn to cope, especially on Broadway. You understand it. You despise it. You go on. Your theater is the studio in which you work.

The critics don't hate you. Many of them love you. But they're controlled by the people who hire them—newspapers, magazines. We have no free press. *[Emphatically] We have no free press.* Did the instrument hear me? *[He indicates the tape recorder beside his plate]*

I

I think so. *[He had spoken so loudly that the people at every table turned to look] They* did.

TENNESSEE

Everything is for the record now! I am not afraid. My life is nearly complete.

I

What about the longevity in your family? You might go on a long, long time.

TENNESSEE

Only my grandfather remains miserably competent. My mother, who died at ninety-four last June, thought she had "haunts" in the room with her. But she was a beautiful woman.

Don't eat too much of the salad. I want you to save room for the key lime pie.

I

I would *always* have room for the key lime pie!

The man and the woman whom Tennessee Williams had observed earlier were no longer bored and preoccupied. As their meal had progressed, apathy had been replaced by whispered intensity and an aura of tension. We did not hear the conversation, but we couldn't help being at least subliminally aware of what was transpiring. The mood grew more strained, and they left most of the food on their plates. The solicitous waiter asked them if anything was wrong. He meant with the food, of course, and they answered, "No."

As their voices rose in anger, I couldn't help hearing their reconstructions of ancient grievances nurtured against each other and suddenly recalled. In vain I tried to appear engrossed in the remnants on my own plate.

"Look, look," Tennessee Williams said. "You're missing it all."

The people got up and made a hasty exit, dropping their napkins on the floor, the woman preceding the man by about six feet. The waiter rushed after the man to give him his credit card.

"They're leaving!" Tennessee said.

"Without having any key lime pie," I contributed.

Tennessee laughed either at my joke or at his. "The murder," he said, "is going to take place elsewhere."

TENNESSEE
The arguments people have are not usually about what they seem to be arguing about.

I
I understand that Gilbert and Sullivan apparently broke up because they couldn't agree on the choice of a new carpet for the Savoy Theatre, but I'm sure it was much deeper than that.

TENNESSEE
Arguments are really about the buildup of friction that usually occurs when two people are together in intimate contact. In relationships I have had, I think what was often wrong was that I wasn't in love with the other person, but impressed by myself

and my effect on that person. Finding someone to share your bed is easier than finding someone you want to wake up with.

There is an irritation factor in living together. It's always over what seem to be little things in the beginning, and then one day they are the big things. In the beginning they don't seem apparent. Why do you think this is?

I

I suppose life is really made up mostly of small things, so there are more of them to get in the way. Then, in the beginning, there is courtship. Both people, though usually one more than the other, are concerned with impressing the other person, so they do a lot of things to please that don't really come naturally, and they can't keep it up. After a while they may even resent what they feel was having to try too hard. Then, too, while the irritation seems to be over little things—who gets the best part of the Sunday paper first and crumples it—I think it's often really about more important things that are difficult to verbalize.

TENNESSEE

Predictability is the greatest destroyer of relationships between people. Perfect predictability equals boredom. No relationship can be very good once the boredom of predictability sets in.

I

Perfect inconsistency can also be disconcerting.

TENNESSEE

But the worst is inconsistency for the sake of inconsistency, to keep the other person off balance. It's like conforming noncon-formity—the nonconformist who grows a beard because all of the other nonconformists have them.

What I have always liked best in a woman is the special tenderness that only a few women have. Only a woman has that tenderness. The reason I like young men is for their male energy—their libido and sex drive. There is a male energy and enthusiasm that is found in the young man that I have never found in a woman. The young homosexual is also like the young woman who wants to be seduced. They don't want to take responsibility for their actions. Women don't reassure you. Courtship is more a part of the relationship between a man and a woman. In the homosexual relationship, courtship does not play that important a role. An advantage of being homosexual is that I saved alimony. I couldn't have afforded to marry my lovers.

Do you know what a *tequila dansant* is?

I

I assume that it's a *thé dansant* with tequila instead of tea.

TENNESSEE

The one I went to was in Mexico, and there were all boys. We danced and drank tequila. That was a long time ago. *[Wistfully]* Perhaps I will go to Mexico . . .

I

Do you think whether a writer is homosexual or not has any effect on his writing?

TENNESSEE

No. Homosexuality has no effect on your writing. But there is more sensibility, more talent than among straights.

Perhaps the major theme of my writings is loneliness—my greatest affliction. All the days and nights of my life I think I've been lonely. There are so few times in one's life when one has that closeness with another person, man or woman. The bedroom is either the loveliest room or the most abhorrent. I judge a person more by his or her bedroom than any other room. I'd like to see your bedroom.

I

I work a lot in my bedroom, so it's filled with books and papers.

TENNESSEE

I wrote in the most terrible conditions, and I thought how much better I'd write in good conditions. Then, when I had the good conditions, I couldn't write better and sometimes I couldn't write at all.

Did you see *Clothes for a Summer Hotel?*

I

I did. At the Cort on the second night.

TENNESSEE

Yes, one had to be swift. *[Putting a finger to his lips]* Don't tell me what you thought of it. You would feel you had to be kind. But do tell me what the person you went with thought of it.

I
Nothing.
TENNESSEE
Nothing?
I
I went alone.
TENNESSEE
Do you like to be alone? You seem like someone who would like
to be alone.
I
Sometimes, yes. But I don't always get to choose the moment.
TENNESSEE
It has always been an immense problem for me to be alone
some of the time. Not just when I write or when the ideas are
not coming well, but even when I am in euphoria. It is difficult
to find people who understand my deep need to be alone some
of the time and who don't resent it. They usually take it as some
kind of insult directed personally against them.

I used to write with Carson McCullers. She would sit at the
other end of the table from me, writing her book. Her physical
presence was comforting because writing is such a lonely occu-
pation.

I liked the way you touched my hand when we met. It was
tender. Touch is very important in life. It is all we have in trying
to reach out to another person. We do not often succeed, but
we have to try for the warmth of life. We have to. I have always
been sensitive to touch.

When I was young, I suffered from a terrible shyness. I am
still shy, though perhaps not as painfully, and I've learned to
hide it better. I was always shy with women. One who should
have intimidated me rather than drawing me out was Garbo.
But she inspired me with a greatness of charm that transported
me right out of my timidity, because I so wanted to impress her.
I think that a great part of her magic was that she made the man
feel immensely worthy and totally at ease. I could see my own
reflection in her eyes.

It was George Cukor who arranged it for me. Cukor was a
dear friend of Garbo's. She just loved him. He was the one

director I think she would have returned to the screen for. I'd told Cukor I'd written a screenplay. It was called, I believe, *The Pink Bedroom,* and I thought it would be perfect for Garbo for her return to the screen.

Garbo received me at the Ritz in New York, and she read through my script as we sat there. She smiled from time to time. She was deeply engrossed and seemed pleased. She finished, looked up, and said, "Wonderful!" I thought I could hear my own heart beating. She looked straight into my eyes and said:

"Wonderful. Give it to Joan Crawford."

None of us likes to hear the word no. I personally have always particularly hated it. But Greta Garbo's no was more exciting than another woman's yes.

Garbo was like a boy. She had an androgenous quality.

The thing I could never understand about Garbo was how she could retire. How can anyone retire? How can you stop doing what you do? How could Garbo leave her career? I cannot leave mine, even when it has left me. I think an artist abandoning his art or losing it is much sadder than death. Whenever I can't write, it seems like the bottom has dropped out of the whole world.

I don't care about meeting famous people anymore. Most of them are disappointing. But I can tell you one that was not disappointing, even though I didn't get what I wanted from the meeting. I'll always remember the day I met Garbo.

What surprised me was that I was at my best with Garbo, or at least I thought I was. Usually, my extreme shyness makes me a difficult person to know. To protect myself, I attack before I can be hurt myself. Some of the bluster when I get angry at a person is because I am angry at the person who has made me feel shy. Can you understand that?

I

Perhaps it's rather like when men get angry at an attractive woman before she's rejected them because they're certain she would if they gave her the chance. She's become the victim of the scenario in their heads.

TENNESSEE

Yes, and that's why I'm most likely to be most terrible to a person I most admire. But knowing the reason doesn't mean I can do anything about it. It's amazing how strong people are, what they can survive, especially what they can inflict on themselves.

Will you have some more wine?

I

No, thank you.

TENNESSEE

I don't drink anymore. Only white wine. That doesn't count. They tell me to be sober, but who can improve on *Streetcar?*

I would like to give you a rose. *[He looks at the vase on the table, but there are no roses]* I'm sorry I don't have one with me. My grandmother was named Rose. My sister was named for her.

What has pleased me most in my life is being able to make someone I care about happy. It's very hard to make anyone happy, even yourself. Especially yourself! The best thing my success and money has given me, the best moment in my life, was being able to rescue Miss Rose from this horrible asylum where they were punishing her, claiming she attacked some woman. She never did a deliberately unkind thing in her life.

My sister is a survivor. She survived those years before I could rescue her.

Besides keeping her out of a public institution, I was able to buy her the pretty dresses she always loved. I used to look with her in shop windows when we were very young, before that great harm befell her. She couldn't afford the dresses we admired, but she loved to look in the windows. Now I buy her the dresses, and she wears them in her mind.

She can't keep all of her clothes with her and she has no place to wear them at all. Maybe she wears them in her dream life. That would be just as good as long as she has the pleasure from it.

I received an invitation to Buckingham Palace, and I thought of taking my sister with me. It would be an opportunity for her to wear her beautiful dresses. I asked Miss Rose if she would go with me to meet the Queen of England, to have tea with her at

Buckingham Palace. But she just looked at me and said, "I *am* the Queen of England."

I've wanted her to come and live with me, but she doesn't want to. She has her own life in which *she* is important. If she came to live with me, she would only be a part of my life. She has her friends. It is impossible not to like her. She lives a life in her own mind, but she lives it no less intensely. In her world, no one ever dies. Everyone just goes on living, even if she doesn't see them anymore.

I gave her a canary once, and she loved it. She always had a lot of love to give. It is a terrible thing to have a lot of love to give and nowhere to put it. The canary lived to be quite old, but one day when I went to visit Miss Rose, the nurses said to me, "Her canary died several days ago and she won't let us take it away." I went into her room, and the little bird was dead on the floor of its cage. She let me take it away, but she wouldn't admit to the idea that it had died. As long as I didn't bring in another canary, hers lived on. She is very faithful. In some ways her world is superior to ours.

Miss Rose has lived her life with elegance and gallantry. She is truly a lady because she always does what she believes is the right thing to do. Although my mother often did the wrong thing, she was a lady. She did what she *believed* was the right thing to do.

Our lives are somewhat predetermined by others. Life is a struggle of our own individuality against our conditioning. We don't know ourselves how much of us is other people living out their lives through us.

My sister has a great capacity for loving. We were always close, but at just the moment she needed me, I was groping for my own way and was not there. There was a young man who would call on Miss Rose, and she was deeply in love with him. She nearly expired every time the phone rang. And then, he stopped coming. Cruel. How could anyone be so cruel? It was the start of her decline. There is nothing more terrible than deliberate cruelty. I have never understood those who perpetuate it. My sister was too fragile for the disappointment. She was only looking for love. Now she is sheltered in her mind from disappointment when those to whom she gives her love prove themselves unworthy. I, myself, find life a series of disappointments, great and small.

I

It's important to be able to find people who *can* disappoint you.

TENNESSEE

I find no shortage in that regard. To have loved and lost is better, even if you pay for it the rest of your life with an empty feeling. I have always preferred experience—to live intensely, even with the accompanying pain that this always carries with it —to absence of sensation.

Harsh words hurt me more than sticks and stones. But I would rather have the words said to me than for me to say them to someone I care about. For some reason, the harshest things we ever say are often said to those about whom we most care. I suppose it is the very caring that makes that so. The terrible thing is that the words, once spoken, can never be truly taken back.

When they locked me up, there was one woman in the asylum who was always very kind to me. She was one of the "guests," an inmate we shall call "Sugar." She was a big black woman, and whenever she saw me, her face glowed with a warmth that was welcome indeed in that coldhearted place. It was a tender look, little gestures that in some ways reminded me of the black lady who took care of Rose and me, and who was our childhood confidante and playmate. Perhaps I saw this resemblance only because I wanted to. Later I couldn't understand why I had seen it.

Loneliness and desperation have a will of their own and create their own fantasy life. I felt a need, and I had made up a character to fill that need. I was glad to have a friend in that vile place. I identified with her. I decided she must be sane, too. We were the only sane people in the place, including the doctors and nurses.

There is no way to convey the horror of a place like that to anyone who has not had the experience. And, Miss Charlotte, I can see in your innocent eyes that you have not had that experience. Eyes mirror what they have seen and reveal it to those

who know what to look for. You have seen only beauty. How
have you managed that?

I

I'm careful, I suppose.

TENNESSEE

I can tell that you have never been to a psychiatrist or even
entertained the thought of going to one. Is that true?

I

True.

TENNESSEE

When you are in such a place, you feel invaded. You are
stripped of all personal privacy. They endeavor to leave you
exposed and naked not only physically, but psychologically and
emotionally. They said I was violent when I am only verbally
violent. It would be foolhardy for a man of my physical stature
to be overly belligerent, though certainly I will not hesitate to
physically defend myself or those I love. In such a situation,
held by force, not knowing when or if you will leave, one is so
desperate for any show of affinity or human kindness amidst
the suffering and interminable boredom.

The others warned me about "Sugar." They said she was not
sweet. But I felt they only wanted to deprive me, that they
wanted to take away what little I had. Then, one day she looked
warmly at me, smiling slightly. I passed close to her, and as I
did, she hit me—really hard, and I reeled, not so much from the
physical blow—what really hurt was the betrayal. She was much
bigger than I, and really strong. She had hit me for absolutely
no reason at all. Oh, I suppose there was a reason, but one
which existed only in her head, nothing I could fathom.

In that situation, there is a pervasive distortion of perspective. It doesn't seem that something like that happening to you
in the insane asylum would matter that much; but when you are
there it becomes your world. The asylum comes to seem to you
like it is the whole world because it *is* your whole world.

Health. You have to have that. If you don't, you needn't
worry about anything else. Until I was eight, I was happy. I had
my health and just took it for granted. Then sickness changed
my life and my personality. I went inward instead of outward. I

learned to be alone, and perhaps I learned the lesson too well. I learned to live in my imagination and create the world there. And I became aware of my own vulnerability. Being ill changed me—not only during the years I was sick, but afterwards. I always knew it could happen again.

My mother was put away, too. She had fantasies. But I didn't let them keep her there. She wasn't going to harm anyone. She'd done the harm already. Rose's operation was her idea. She meant well, but some of the worst things that have ever been done have been done by people who meant well but were exceedingly foolish. Poor Rose—she said some shocking thing to my mother, who was puritanical and hated sex. She screamed when my father had sex with her, and we children were terrified. My father was such an unhappy man. Perhaps that is one of the things I learned from him—how to be unhappy. It is terrible to be so unhappy and not to be able to do anything about it. I did not understand that at the time, but I can look back now and pity him. He cared more what the world outside his family thought of him than for what his family thought. And after achieving what he considered success, it was all thrown away in a terrible gambling brawl in which a man bit off his ear. He was marked.

I hope that no one ever pities me. The thing I never want is pity. I hate self-pity. I try not to be bitter. Everyone has his own problems you don't know about, their own reasons for being unhappy.

I will always find a reason to be unhappy. Unfortunately, my reasons now are not fictions but reality; however, if they were not such good reasons for unhappiness, I might be just as unhappy. But I do have a good disposition. Don't you think I have a good disposition? *[He does an exaggerated smile for me]*

I

That's Lillian Gish's *Broken Blossoms* smile.

TENNESSEE

Perhaps she could be in one of my plays.

I

I liked what she said at Milton's party the other night when you asked her if she was trying out.

TENNESSEE
I was only joking, of course.

I
But I thought it was interesting when she said, "You have to try out every time—it's what you're doing *now* that counts."

TENNESSEE
The box of chocolates you brought is for Miss Rose. She'll love it. I had to tell her today she couldn't come to Key West. It was terrible. She so looks forward to our visits. But I want to make a trip to Houston and see my great friend Mrs. Muldauer. Unless I go to Taos instead. I don't know if it isn't a mistake to leave at all though. I have to keep the house here for the animals.

I
I hope you'll come to New York again soon.

TENNESSEE
[Thinking] Yes, I *could* go to New York. But big cities are so cruel. Why are they so cruel? Why do big cities say no? There must be a kinder way.

I
Perhaps there is no kind way to say no.

TENNESSEE
I'm afraid of being rejected. I can't bring myself to ask anything of anyone. The thought of being in the position of having to ask is mortifying even when you know the answer will be yes. A no crushes me.

I
I find that true of everyone. Everyone hates to ask favors, but this seems to be even more true for men. Men especially seem to hate asking other men for things. Women can ask, but men can't, at least not without great difficulty. I don't know which is more difficult, though—asking or rejecting.

TENNESSEE
When you are successful, you have to endure the terrible people who all suddenly want something from you.

I
How do *you* say no to people?

TENNESSEE
I stay in Key West. By the way, I saw in the *TV Guide* that you're

on television tomorrow night here—a program called "Over Easy." Just like Gore Vidal.

I

Not *exactly* like Gore Vidal.

TENNESSEE

He likes being on television to talk about his books. Well, I don't know if he likes it, but he does it. When I appear on the talk shows, I often wonder if I don't sell fewer books—if seeing me doesn't unsell my work. I don't know if I'm good for my work. I think when people see me, they like it less.

Being interviewed, however, does have the advantage of self-revelation. I must articulate my feelings, and I may learn something about myself. It makes me more self-aware, more aware of my own unhappiness, or lack of happiness.

I

I wish you could have been at a performance I saw of *Something Cloudy, Something Clear* at a small Bowery theater recently. You would have been pleased by the audience, especially at their reaction to the funny lines.

TENNESSEE

Did they laugh?

I

They certainly did.

TENNESSEE

But were they laughing in the right places?

I

If by the right places you mean where you intended they laugh, I think the answer is yes. I remember what got the biggest laugh. It was when the manuscript is dropped and someone says, "Were the pages numbered?" That got a tremendous laugh. I assume there were a lot of students in the audience. Or former students.

TENNESSEE

Be sure and save this for my death. Have it all ready. That's the moment when it will be most valuable.

Knowing your decease will give you a moment of prominence in the media gives one a strange feeling. My obituary is shrinking all the time in the New York *Times*, but perhaps I will have another hit first, and then it will be more valuable and they will restore some paragraphs.

I

Groucho was at the New York *Times,* and someone showed him his obituary. He told me he didn't like it, and he wasn't referring to its literary style.

TENNESSEE

I'm told, if one outlives one's moment of greatest fame, one's obituary starts shrinking. It makes people feel superior, perhaps even immortal, to read about the death of someone else, especially someone famous. When we're young, we don't think about these things—old age, death. Those are things that happen to other people. But when we read of the death of somebody, especially someone prominent whom we have outlasted, it is with a certain satisfaction. It is then that we know we have also lost our greatest luxury—the feeling of limitless future that is youth.

Any artist dies two deaths—that of his physical self and that of his creative power. Thus, the important part of me is really already dead. A man competes with the others—and with himself. And they take your measure. You are always being measured. I'm a fighter, and I've come a long way from St. Louis. I have never been the passive person. I do have violence in me, but it is verbal.

Do you know why I look forward to death? Death is the release from competition. Death is the one thing no one competes for. And there is probably no competition after you get there.

I'm not afraid of dying. You get used to death. It doesn't worry me. I've been told I was going to die so many times and have come so near to death so many times that I've grown rather accustomed to it. I believe it's like the sleepy person being ready to sleep. If you have insomnia, it's because you are not really ready to sleep, even though you think you are. When you are ready to sleep, you do. It is the same with death.

I don't like planes much, but not because I'm afraid. I just don't like being confined that way, powerless. It's not that I'm a hero. I'm afraid of many things. The things of which I am afraid are not physical, but psychological and emotional.

Close shaves with death are fascinating. I've had many. You think you will be overwhelmed by fear, but it isn't like that at all. The fear is eclipsed by the violence of one's struggle to hang on. Gladiators had that thrill. There is a kind of exhilaration about it.

I

Especially when you survive!

TENNESSEE

Who is happy? Is anyone happy?

I

You've made me happy. I've loved spending the time here with you in Key West.

TENNESSEE

I love your saying it, and I thank you for telling me. It's a wonderful feeling to make someone happy, but it's not easy to do. And people never let you know if you've pleased them. Why is that? You try hard to do so, and they leave you suspended, not knowing. Why do they begrudge you your little bit of satisfaction?

I'm always looking for a place to be happy. It always seems to be some place I might go to, never the place I'm in. I've been thinking now it might be New Mexico. Or Tangier. I used to think it was New Orleans, except when I was there.

When I'm in New York, I can't wait to get back to Key West. In Key West, I think about a trip to New York. Last week in New York, I told you I was looking forward to being in Key West. Now we're here, and I'm planning a trip to New Orleans I'm rather excited about—until I get there.

I

Perhaps it's too much to ask of the place—that it provide the happiness. A place can't give happiness all by itself.

TENNESSEE

Perhaps. Now death seems to be the trip I most look forward to. It doesn't offer achievement and excitement, but it does offer peace. Or I think so. Maybe even death won't live up to my expectations.

If I could choose my spot to die, I would like it to be in a Broadway theater on opening night, listening to the wild ovation at the end of my newest play.

I

That would be an unusual ending for a Tennessee Williams play—a happy one.

TENNESSEE

Yes, but only fiction can offer happy endings. Life offers no happy endings, because life can end only one way—with death.

When we leave, don't forget your little machine. I remember when Walter Kerr left one of his cassettes behind. It reassured me. It meant he was nervous, too.

I hope I'll see you in New York soon. I've decided to make my next trip to New York. New York has so much to offer. It is stimulating. Much of my work is there. I have an apartment in New York, but I stay in a hotel. I've stayed away from New York too long. I'll be there next week, or the week after, unless . . . unless I decide to go to . . . Tangier. . . .

[Summoning the waiter in grand style] We're ready now. Would you please bring one slice of the key lime pie.

WAITER

I'm sorry, Mr. Williams. The key lime pie is all gone.

TENNESSEE

[Shrugging] It doesn't matter. *[The waiter leaves and Tennessee Williams lifts his glass in a toast]* To postponed pleasure! All of life is an attempt to escape loneliness—the search for another warm body.

I

And a warm mind?

TENNESSEE

That's the ultimate sex, if it can ever be achieved. That's when the nightingale sings.

Index